PEOPLE, MARKETS
ECONOMIES AND SOCIET
Volume 1

C000156617

Shoplifting in
Eighteenth-Century England

PEOPLE, MARKETS, GOODS:
ECONOMIES AND SOCIETIES IN HISTORY

ISSN: 2051-7467

Series editors
Barry Doyle – University of Huddersfield
Steve Hindle – The Huntington Library
Jane Humphries – University of Oxford
Willem M. Jongman – University of Groningen
Catherine Schenk – University of Oxford

The interactions of economy and society, people and goods, transactions and actions are at the root of most human behaviours. Economic and social historians are participants in the same conversation about how markets have developed historically and how they have been constituted by economic actors and agencies in various social, institutional and geographical contexts. New debates now underpin much research in economic and social, cultural, demographic, urban and political history. Their themes have enduring resonance – financial stability and instability, the costs of health and welfare, the implications of poverty and riches, flows of trade and the centrality of communications. This paperback series aims to attract historians interested in economics and economists with an interest in history by publishing high quality, cutting edge academic research in the broad field of economic and social history from the late medieval/ early modern period to the present day. It encourages the interaction of qualitative and quantitative methods through both excellent monographs and collections offering path-breaking overviews of key research concerns. Taking as its benchmark international relevance and excellence it is open to scholars and subjects of any geographical areas from the case study to the multi-nation comparison.

PREVIOUSLY PUBLISHED TITLES IN THE SERIES ARE
LISTED AT THE BACK OF THIS VOLUME

Shoplifting in Eighteenth-Century England

Shelley Tickell

THE BOYDELL PRESS

First published 2018
The Boydell Press, Woodbridge

ISBN 978-1-78327-328-7

The Boydell Press is an imprint of Boydell & Brewer Ltd
PO Box 9, Woodbridge, Suffolk IP12 3DF, UK
and of Boydell & Brewer Inc.
668 Mt Hope Avenue, Rochester, NY 14620–2731, USA
website: www.boydellandbrewer.com

A catalogue record for this book is available
from the British Library

The publisher has no responsibility for the continued existence or accuracy of URLs for
external or third-party internet websites referred to in this book, and does not guarantee
that any content on such websites is, or will remain, accurate or appropriate

This publication is printed on acid-free paper

Typeset by BBR Design, Sheffield

Printed and bound in Great Britain by
TJ International Ltd, Padstow, Cornwall

Contents

Illustrations

Plates

Charts

Map

Tables

Acknowledgements

I am particularly indebted to John Styles and Sarah Lloyd for their inspiration and wise guidance in this research, and grateful to Helen Berry, Tim Hitchcock and Anne Murphy for further encouragement and advice. I should also like to thank the many friends and fellow historians who have provided me with practical assistance and moral support in bringing this book to fruition, including Jeanne Clegg, Alice Dolan, Jennifer Evans, Bridget Long, Katrina Navickas, Deirdre Palk and Cate Robinson. I greatly appreciate the help I have received during this process from a number of libraries and archives, and from the editors and readers of the Economic History Society and publishers, Boydell & Brewer. And finally and always, thanks to my family, my mainstay throughout.

Abbreviations

HC	House of Commons
HL	House of Lords
JHC	*Journal of the House of Commons*
LMA	London Metropolitan Archives
OBP	*Old Bailey Proceedings Online*
TNA	The National Archives

Note on Text

Where excerpts from contemporary documents are reproduced in the text, eighteenth-century abbreviations, grammar and spelling have been retained, but italicisation and capitalisation of nouns removed for ease of reading.

Pre-decimal currency is denoted in pounds, shillings and pence (£ s d), in which £1 (one pound sterling) = 20s (twenty shillings), 1s (one shilling) = 12d (twelve pence) and one guinea = £1.1s.

Introduction

In the summer of 1719 William Marvell entered a shop in the City of London and 'cheapened' the price of some silk handkerchiefs with the owner. Cheapening or bargaining for goods was standard practice in an age before fixed pricing. He then took the handkerchiefs to the door to show a female companion. Again, this desire to see goods in daylight was not unusual: early-eighteenth-century shop interiors were invariably dim or poorly candle-lit. Marvell declined to purchase at the offered price of 12 shillings, but no sooner had he left than the handkerchiefs were found to be missing. Only then, too late, did the shopkeeper realise that his customer was a shoplifter. Sending his daughter fruitlessly after the thief, she returned shortly with the information that he had been seen by a neighbour who had recognised him as London's former hangman. There was to be no escape from justice for such an infamous figure. Six weeks later Marvell was captured in farmland on London's outskirts and taken to a local alehouse where he was identified by the shopkeeper's wife and daughter. His initial offer of recompense and claim he had been drunk at the time rejected, Marvell was swiftly charged with shoplifting and committed to appear at the next session of the Old Bailey. Within a fortnight he was found guilty and facing a sentence of death. Only witnesses to his character as 'an honest and industrious man' narrowly earned him the reprieve of transportation.[1]

Marvell's celebrity appearance in the dock focused public attention on this newly capital crime, but it also highlighted many of its paradoxes. Was his theft driven by need? It was common knowledge that he had lost his executioner post two years earlier through debt. Or could it be the compulsion of greed? This period was witnessing a relaxing of older moral constraints on consumption, and social commentators were swift to predict the criminal implications of the poor coveting luxury. The silk handkerchief, worn as a neck adornment, had become the quintessential fashion accessory for working Londoners. But even so, what madness would cause a hangman to risk his neck? Marvell had stated he was drunk, and in court denied all guilt

---

1 *Old Bailey Proceedings Online* (hereafter OBP) (www.oldbaileyonline.org, version 7.2, March 2015), October 1719, William Marvell (t17191014-2).

and accused the shopkeeper of malicious prosecution. His plea of diminished responsibility carried limited weight: judges were hesitant to admit alcohol as an excuse for crime. More pertinent was the uncertainty of prosecution and conviction. Not all retailers chose to prosecute, perhaps explaining Marvell's accusation, and even when they did the eighteenth-century justice system might not deliver the outcome they hoped. This book explores each of these strands: the impact of deprivation, the force of consumer desire, the nature of contemporary understandings of the crime and the uneasy congruence of commercial reaction and judicial response. Weaving them into a coherent narrative, it reveals how these factors interacted to make shoplifting the most emblematic of eighteenth-century crimes.

Shoplifting was not new to eighteenth-century England. As early as 1673, *The Canting Academy, or, The Devils Cabinet Opened* had offered a dictionary definition of the 'shoplift' as 'one that filcheth commodities out of a shop, under the pretence of cheapning or buying them of the shop-keeper'.[2] However, it was becoming an increasingly intractable problem. As shops multiplied to meet a new consumer demand their displays fostered the unwelcome attention of ever more proficient shop thieves. The anxiety of shopkeepers at their inability to protect their stock from pillage was resonant of a wider public discontent in the final years of the seventeenth century. The Glorious Revolution of 1688 had heralded a decade of warfare, marked by rising prices, currency failure and financial crisis.[3] These conditions encouraged a wave of property crime which communities were struggling to control. But the fiscal requirements of the new political regime had also ensured regular parliamentary sessions, allowing politicians to respond with a hardening of legislation, an increasing of the number of crimes subject to the death penalty which became known as the 'Bloody Code'.[4] In 1699 active lobbying by retailers in the City of London for harsher penalties for shoplifting bore fruit. Tory members representing City interests found common cause with wider Whig commercial and public order concerns in Parliament and passed the Shoplifting Act.[5] Stealing goods from a shop, a minor non-violent crime, acquired a conspicuous new legal standing as a capital offence.

Yet for retailers this was no magic solution. Within twenty years we find a hangman, one of the Bloody Code's most visible symbols, on trial for stealing ten silk handkerchiefs. Eighteenth-century England offered a peculiarly fertile

---

2   Richard Head, *The Canting Academy, or, The Devils Cabinet Opened* (London, 1673), p. 44.
3   Brodie Waddell, 'The Politics of Economic Distress in the Aftermath of the Glorious Revolution, 1689–1702', *English Historical Review* 130/543 (2015), 318–51 (pp. 322–5).
4   Tim Hitchcock and Robert Shoemaker, *London Lives: Poverty, Crime and the Making of the Modern City, 1690–1800* (Cambridge, 2015), pp. 60–1.
5   J. M. Beattie, *Policing and Punishment in London, 1660–1750: Urban Crime and the Limits of Terror* (Oxford, 2001), p. 327, n. 28; Steve Pincus, *1688: The First Modern Revolution* (Yale, 2009), pp. 369–72; 10 & 11 Wm III, c. 23 (1699).

climate for shoplifting to flourish. The number of shops and the range of
goods they stocked were expanding at an unprecedented rate. Overseas
trade, a developing manufacturing capability and improving transport links
were bringing a greater supply of goods to market, stimulating new demand.
In fact historians have contended that this period witnessed a consumer
revolution. Neil McKendrick initiated the debate in proposing that a boom
in consumption, fuelled by social aspiration and active marketing, permeated
every stratum of society.[6] This concept has been subjected to sustained
questioning and modification in succeeding years.[7] Nevertheless, there is
broad agreement that the period did see a greater consumption and marketing
of certain newer commodities including tobacco, tea, sugar, household goods
and, in particular, cotton textiles.[8] Demand for these accelerated what was
already an irreversible movement towards fixed shop retailing, displacing
older forms of selling through markets and fairs.[9] Retail expansion was most
rapid in urban centres, where it was accompanied by increasing specialisation, but even smaller settlements could sustain a number of shops, serving
their hinterland. By 1759, excise records reveal that England had over 137,000
shops, almost treble that of the late seventeenth century, while the population
had increased by less than a fifth. In London the 21,600 shops at mid-century
was equivalent to one shop for every thirty customers.[10] The historian John
Beattie has observed that, to these retailers, 'shoplifting was an ever-growing
scourge that threatened the livelihood of men and women like themselves, and
more generally the commerce and prosperity of the City'.[11] Yet, as this book
will show, concerns that the crime would undermine a nascent commercial
sector were premature. Marketing development served in time to overcome
the sense of helplessness that had initially prompted such an authoritarian statutory response. Such was the acquired expertise and subsequent
experience of retailers in managing the risk of customer theft that, by the
time the Shoplifting Act was eventually repealed and replaced in 1820, its
significance had radically declined.

6 Neil McKendrick, 'The Consumer Revolution of Eighteenth-century England', in *The Birth of a Consumer Society: The Commercialization of Eighteenth-Century England*, ed. N. McKendrick, J. Brewer and J. H. Plumb (London, 1982), pp. 9–33.
7 Those that have questioned McKendrick's premise include John Styles, 'Manufacturing, Consumption and Design in Eighteenth-Century England', in *Consumption and the World of Goods*, ed. J. Brewer and R. Porter (London, 1993), pp. 527–54, and Jan de Vries, *The Industrious Revolution: Consumer Behaviour and the Household Economy, 1650 to the Present* (Cambridge, 2008), ch. 2.
8 P. D. Glennie and N. J. Thrift, 'Consumers, Identities, and Consumption Spaces in Early-Modern England', *Environment and Planning A* 28/1 (1996), 25–45 (p. 31).
9 de Vries, *Industrious Revolution*, p. 169.
10 Hoh-cheung Mui and Lorna H. Mui, *Shops and Shopkeeping in Eighteenth-Century England* (London, 1989), pp. 40, 44.
11 Beattie, *Policing and Punishment*, p. 36.

This book investigates the experience of shoplifting in England in the 120 years between the passing of the Shoplifting Act and its repeal, presenting for the first time a comprehensive account of the crime and its contexts. But this is not simply the history of a single law. Although draconian, the impact of the Act was muted by two circumstances. First, it had a restricted definition of shoplifting, designed to target the more serious offender: thefts had to be of a value of 5 shillings and conducted privately, that is, without being observed. As a consequence the accidental glance of a shop assistant, or a few pence difference in the cost of a remnant within reach on a counter, could result in the crime being tried as non-capital larceny. Secondly, it was within the power of juries to bring in 'partial verdicts', likewise reducing the charge. Irrespective of the evidence, juries could declare that the value of the goods stolen was only 4s.9d or that the theft was not done privately. Thus, in practice, shoplifting offences were brought to trial under a number of felony laws, and even some as petty larceny, a misdemeanour. This was particularly apparent in London, where between 1699 and 1820 several thousand shoplifting cases were heard by the criminal court at the Old Bailey. And while the scale of the problem in the rest of England did not match that of the metropolis, assize court records testify that provincial shops still bore regular loss. The material revealed by these many cases significantly enhances our understanding of crime, marketing and consumption in this period, but in falling at the juncture of these three histories, shoplifting has previously escaped the specific attention it warrants.

Shoplifting has seldom attracted crime historians' interest and then only as a composite with other crimes, not as a discrete offence. John Beattie's seminal work on the eighteenth-century criminal justice system, *Crime and the Courts in England*, set a pattern for later scholarship of treating property crime generically.[12] The work of Beattie, Peter King, Heather Shore and Drew Gray, among others, has substantially advanced our knowledge of the operation of the judiciary, development of policing and the handling and disposal of defendants by the courts. But their emphasis has been on broader trends and patterns in judicial administration and sentencing. This is also true of the one study that more explicitly identifies the crime. Although Deirdre Palk scrutinises shoplifting together with pickpocketing and uttering forged banknotes, her focus is on gender, exploring differences in treatment and outcome for men and women as they negotiated the judicial process between 1780 and 1830.[13] By

---

12   J. M. Beattie, *Crime and the Courts in England, 1660–1800* (Princeton, 1986); Clive Emsley, *Crime and Society in England 1750–1900* (London, 1987); Beattie, *Policing and Punishment*; Peter King, *Crime, Justice and Judicial Discretion in England, 1740–1820* (Oxford, 2000); J. M. Beattie, *The First English Detectives: The Bow Street Runners and the Policing of London, 1750–1840* (Oxford, 2014); Drew Gray, *Crime, Policing and Punishment in England, 1660–1914* (London 2016).
13   Deirdre Palk, 'Private Crime in Public and Private Places: Pickpockets and Shoplifters in London, 1780–1823', in *The Streets of London: From the Great Fire to the Great Stink*, ed.

contrast, this book departs from the established historiography of crime and punishment. Taking an individual property offence, and one newly prominent at a time of rapid retail expansion, it approaches eighteenth-century crime from a fresh perspective. It explores the extent and practice of shoplifting, the impact on its commercial victims, its place in urban survival strategies, and its role in the spread of new consumer goods, capital law reform and changing perceptions of crime.

As part of this undertaking, the book necessarily engages with existing studies of the social context of offending. King and Shore have both included shoplifting among forms of thieving pursued as a type of makeshift in times of economic hardship.[14] Building on earlier gender analysis by Beattie, King has proposed that women were particularly susceptible to such contingency, with the demographic of those prosecuted for property offences at the Old Bailey later in the century demonstrating a correlation with life-cycle patterns of deprivation.[15] This book draws on a wider chronological and geographical context than previous scholarship, examining both London and the provinces over a century, to present a fuller and more nuanced portrayal of offenders. It argues from an analysis of those indicted in this period that shoplifting was overwhelmingly an amateur, occasional crime and one primarily driven by need. While a proportion of offenders were professional, making a living from theft, the majority of those who came before the courts are revealed to be from the most vulnerable sections of society, their stealing concurrent with part-time or irregular work. And although it was a property crime with one of the highest proportion of women charged, shoplifting is shown to be strongly attractive to both sexes. The study also addresses the contentious issue of middling shoplifting, reflecting on the difficulty of assessing its currency given retailers' demonstrable reluctance to prosecute higher-class customers.

The book traces the evolution of the criminal law on shoplifting and the response of its intended beneficiaries: the English retail sector. The crime's significance has been registered by both those historians charting the development of the Bloody Code and those concerned with the later movement for capital law reform. Beattie has outlined the genesis of the Shoplifting Act in the context of rising public alarm at crime in late-seventeenth-century London, and Randall McGowen, Vic Gatrell, and Richard Follett have

T. Hitchcock and H. Shore (London, 2003), pp. 135–50, 233–5; Deirdre Palk, *Gender, Crime and Judicial Discretion, 1780–1830* (Woodbridge, 2006).

14   King, *Crime, Justice and Judicial Discretion*, pp. 193, 196; Heather Shore, 'Crime, Criminal Networks and the Survival Strategies of the Poor in Early Eighteenth-Century London', in *The Poor in England 1700–1850: An Economy of Makeshifts*, ed. S. King and A. Tomkins (Manchester, 2003), pp. 137–65 (pp. 149–50).

15   J. M. Beattie, 'The Criminality of Women in Eighteenth-Century England', *Journal of Social History* 8/4 (1975), 80–116; Peter King, 'Female Offenders, Work and Life-Cycle Change in Late-Eighteenth-Century London', *Continuity and Change* 11/1 (1996), 61–90.

acknowledged Samuel Romilly's singling out of the Act to spearhead his parliamentary campaign for reform.[16] This book maps retailers' relationship with the law over the course of the eighteenth century, from their formative role in bringing the Shoplifting Act to fruition and their continuing interaction with a judiciary attempting to implement crime control measures, to their equivocal reaction to criminal law reform. It reveals that during this period retailers became increasingly less reliant on the Act as they turned to lesser laws, and more significantly their own resources, in managing the crime.

Looking to the history of marketing, we find surprisingly little attention has been afforded to shoplifting in a literature which examines shops and shopping extensively. Although long undervalued as an enterprise, early shopkeeping was a substantial sector, playing a significant role in the economy; by 1798 shopkeepers were estimated to comprise up to 14% of London's population.[17] Approaching the subject from a largely cultural perspective, retail historians have made extensive use of a range of sources, including plans, prints, advertising and shopkeeper memoirs, to chart the development of shop design and selling practices.[18] But while acknowledging shoplifting as a routine business risk to traders, they have made no attempt systematically to either examine or analyse the phenomenon. The works of Nancy Cox, Claire Walsh and Jon Stobart nonetheless alert us to the fact that customer theft was a constant and material concern to retailers in their daily trading.[19] This book fills a lacuna in the historiography by exploring the practice of shoplifting, the range of preventative measures taken by retailers and, for the first time, its effect on shopkeepers' economic viability. Shoplifting losses were insidious and marginal in relation to the financial risk posed by mismanaging credit,

---

16   Beattie, *Policing and Punishment*, pp. 328–31; Randall McGowen, 'A Powerful Sympathy: Terror, the Prison and Humanitarian Reform in Early Nineteenth-Century Britain', *Journal of British Studies* 25/3 (1986), 312–34; V. A. C. Gatrell, *The Hanging Tree: Execution and the English People, 1770–1868* (Oxford, 1994); Richard R. Follett, *Evangelicalism, Penal Theory and the Politics of Criminal Law Reform, 1808–30* (Basingstoke, 2001).

17   Nancy Cox, '"Beggary of the Nation": Moral, Economic and Political Attitudes to the Retail Sector in the Early Modern Period', in *A Nation of Shopkeepers: Five Centuries of British Retailing, 1550–2000*, ed. J. Benson and L. Ugolini (London, 2003), pp. 26–51; Leonard D. Schwarz, *London in the Age of Industrialisation: Entrepreneurs, Labour Force and Living Conditions 1700–1850* (Cambridge, 1992), p. 60.

18   Nancy Cox, *The Complete Tradesman: A Study of Retailing, 1550–1820* (Aldershot, 2000); Jon Stobart, Andrew Hann and Victoria Morgan, *Spaces of Consumption: Leisure and Shopping in the English Town, c. 1680–1830* (London, 2007), pp. 86–139; Claire Walsh, 'Shop Design and the Display of Goods in Eighteenth-Century London', *Journal of Design History* 8/3 (1995), 157–76.

19   Nancy Cox and Claire Walsh, '"Their Shops are Dens, the Buyer is their Prey": Shop Design and Sales Techniques', in N. Cox, *The Complete Tradesman: A Study of Retailing, 1550–1820* (Aldershot, 2000), pp. 76–115 (pp. 101–2); Stobart, Hann and Morgan, *Spaces of Consumption*, pp. 135–6; Jon Stobart, *Spend, Spend, Spend: A History of Shopping* (Stroud, 2008), pp. 93–4.

but nevertheless onerous for smaller enterprises and those experimenting with cash-only selling. Yet through examining shopkeepers' trading practice and the business and social value to retailers of trade protection and prosecution societies, the book argues that business temperament was a stronger determinant of a retailer's response to shoplifting than the crime's financial impact.

Perhaps most pertinent to the crime are the shopping studies which have developed as an increasingly important adjunct to the field of marketing.[20] These directly address how the period's consumer revolution was reflected in retail practice, examining the cultural processes by which goods changed hands. However, even here the picture that emerges of shoplifting is patchy. Studies of middling and elite purchasing, mainly by women, dominate the literature, overshadowing earlier scholarship that examined a more diverse range of customers.[21] The later treatments have implied that eighteenth-century shoplifting was a problem predominantly for elite stores selling fashionable merchandise to leisured women.[22] This is a proposition the book rejects. Court records confirm that both elite and petty stores prosecuted, but a plotting of their type, size and location indicates that the stores most commonly targeted were smaller specialist retailers operating in local working neighbourhoods. This is particularly observable in London's expanding metropolitan outskirts, but also in the north as specialisation increased. The book reveals the degree to which the variables of trade, class and location determined an individual shopkeeper's risk of being exposed to this crime.

20   Jon Stobart, 'Shopping Streets as Social Space: Leisure, Consumerism and Improvement in an Eighteenth-Century County Town', *Urban History* 25/1 (1998), 3–21; Jon Stobart, 'Leisure and Shopping in the Small Towns of Georgian England', *Journal of Urban History* 31/4 (2005), 479–503; Stobart, Hann and Morgan, *Spaces of Consumption*, pp. 142–60; Stobart, *Spend, Spend, Spend*, pp. 73–96; Claire Walsh, 'Shops, Shopping, and the Art of Decision Making in Eighteenth-Century England', in *Gender, Taste, and Material Culture in Britain and North America, 1700–1830*, ed. J. Styles and A. Vickery (New Haven, 2006), pp. 151–77; Claire Walsh, 'Shopping at First Hand? Mistresses, Servants and Shopping for the Household in Early-Modern England' in *Buying for the Home: Shopping for the Domestic from the Seventeenth Century to the Present*, ed. D. E. Hussey and M. Ponsonby (Aldershot, 2008), pp. 13–26.
21   John Styles, 'Clothing the North: The Supply of Non-Elite Clothing in the Eighteenth-Century North of England', *Textile History* 25/2 (1994), 139–66 (pp. 149–50); Glennie and Thrift, 'Consumers, Identities, and Consumption Spaces', pp. 35–6.
22   Elizabeth Kowaleski-Wallace, *Consuming Subjects: Women, Shopping and Business in the Eighteenth Century* (New York, 1997), pp. 74–98; Helen Berry, 'Polite Consumption: Shopping in Eighteenth-Century England', *Transactions of the Royal Historical Society*, 6th series, 12 (2002), 375–94 (pp. 382, 384–5); Deidre Shauna Lynch, 'Counter Publics: Shopping and Women's Sociability', in *Romantic Sociability: Social Networks and Literary Culture in Britain, 1770–1840*, ed. G. Russell and C. Tuite (Cambridge, 2002), pp. 211–36; Claire Walsh, 'Social Meaning and Social Space in the Shopping Galleries of Early Modern London', in *A Nation of Shopkeepers: Five Centuries of British Retailing, 1550–2000*, ed. J. Benson and L. Ugolini (London, 2003), pp. 52–79 (pp. 62–5).

Arguing from the evidence of court, excise and elite shopping records, it contends that shoplifters seldom sought out the newest and most fashionable goods in elite shops, but routinely operated in more mundane neighbour-hoods. Constrained by the conventions and exigencies of the working communities to which most belonged, they sought items they judged to be most easily and profitably exchanged for subsistence.

The finding that plebeian shoplifters generally eschewed elite stores naturally leads us to consider how responsive the lower ranks were to the sirens of eighteenth-century consumer culture and the role of theft in trans-mitting novel and stylish goods. It bears on a long-standing historical debate on the degree to which new consumer goods were accessible to the lower, plebeian ranks of society.[23] Whether working families could afford more than the basics of daily survival remains in dispute. The concrete evidence that might have been supplied by probate inventories is largely limited to the period before 1725, and particularly sparse for labouring families, who rarely left wills.[24] In the absence of this, the most commonly pursued alternative strategy has been to estimate plebeian purchasing power through the detailed extraction of wage and price data, and analysis of contemporary tax revenues and household budgets, extrapolating from them any potential surplus in household income that could be expended on consumer goods.

While economic historians continue this debate, the nature of the data renders most findings speculative and generates conflicting conclusions. Research by Robert Allen has emphasised the high level of English wages at the beginning of the eighteenth century, and there is evidence from this time of working families starting to consume tobacco and foodstuffs such as tea and sugar, previously held to be luxuries.[25] Allen and Weisdorf have also suggested that during the second half of the century urban workers had the potential to increase their income beyond that required for subsistence, giving them considerable scope to partake in the consumer revolution.[26] Nevertheless there remains a sizeable consensus that there was little improvement in plebeian standards of living between the middle and end of the eighteenth

23 John Styles, *The Dress of the People: Everyday Fashion in Eighteenth-Century England* (New Haven, 2007), ch. 7.
24 Lorna Weatherill, *Consumer Behaviour and Material Culture in Britain, 1660–1760* (London, 1996), pp. 2–3.
25 Robert C. Allen, 'Why the Industrial Revolution was British: Commerce, Induced Invention and the Scientific Revolution', *Economic History Review* 64/2 (2011), 357–84 (pp. 358–60); Carole Shammas, *The Pre-Industrial Consumer in England and America* (Oxford, 1990), pp. 77–86.
26 R. C. Allen and J. L. Weisdorf, 'Was there an "Industrious Revolution" before the Industrial Revolution? An Empirical Exercise for England, c. 1300–1830', *Economic History Review* 64/3 (2011), 715–29 (p. 723).

century.[27] Real wages only increased slowly over this period, and fell towards the end, while food prices rose sharply as production failed to keep pace with population growth. In spite of Jan de Vries's contention that the eighteenth century witnessed an 'industrious revolution' as family members increasingly contributed to the household's income, evidence indicates that it was only in the succeeding century that poorer families began to experience any significant financial benefit from industrialisation.[28] As an ever-increasing range of novel textiles and household goods were manufactured and imported, there is little doubt that many of the poor would have struggled to afford their purchase.

This book enters the debate from a new angle. As an alternative, if aberrant, form of consumer acquisition, shoplifting potentially enabled the working poor consciously to select from the same range of new manufactured and imported goods available to wealthier shoppers. It is therefore telling to find whether they chose to do so. This book's detailed analysis of what items were stolen in practice, and their subsequent disposal, allows historians of consumption to assess the direct extent to which the poor sought to participate in the period's famed 'consumer revolution'. It finds that while there is scarce evidence that thieves targeted elite fashions, shoplifting did contribute to the makeshift economy which facilitated the introduction and transmission of new textiles and styles within plebeian communities, a practice extensively explored by Beverly Lemire.[29] However, it argues that the workaday nature of many of the goods shoplifters chose to steal points towards a predominant desire to capitalise on the demands of an eclectic marketplace where many consumers retained more modest tastes. It concludes that the crime reflected, rather than propelled, the pace of acquisition of new consumables by the poor.

While shoplifting may have operated as a form of makeshift, its increasing prevalence did not grant it legitimacy, even in working communities. Surveying contemporary attitudes to the crime, the book reveals that the offence was viewed with at best a guarded tolerance and, more frequently, moral outrage by those conforming to newly acquired conventions of consumer purchasing.

---

27   Stephen King and Geoffrey Timmins, *Making Sense of the Industrial Revolution: English Economy and Society 1700–1850* (Manchester, 2001), pp. 150–9. See also the chapters by Jane Humphries ('Household Economy'), Hans-Joachim Voth ('Living Standards and the Urban Environment') and Maxine Berg ('Consumption in Eighteenth- and Early Nineteenth-Century Britain'), in *The Cambridge Economic History of Modern Britain*, vol. 1: *Industrialisation, 1700–1860*, ed. R. Floud and P. Johnson (Cambridge, 2004), pp. 238–67, 268–94 and 357–87 respectively.

28   de Vries, *Industrious Revolution*; King and Timmins, *Making Sense*, pp. 299–307.

29   Beverly Lemire, 'The Theft of Clothes and Popular Consumerism in Early Modern England', *Journal of Social History* 24/2 (1990), 255–76; Beverly Lemire, 'Peddling Fashion: Salesmen, Pawnbrokers, Taylors, Thieves and the Second-hand Clothes Trade in England, c. 1700–1800', *Textile History* 22/1 (1991), 67–82.

Court testimony advertises the remarkable level of interest and engagement shoplifting occasioned among the man and woman in the street. Their extensive collaboration with retailers in combating the crime is conspicuous and diverges from prevailing evidence that community policing declined as the century progressed.[30] In a climate of alarm at rising property crime, attitudes to criminals became more polarised. Simon Devereaux has proposed that an older understanding of crime as resulting from a moral lapse, to which any class could succumb, was overtaken during the course of the eighteenth century by a new concept of the criminal as a congenital class of offender, invariably originating from the lower orders.[31] Such thinking only reinforced and sustained retailer attitudes that served to shield higher-class shoplifters from identification and indictment. And it goes some way to explain the shock with which the shoplifting charge against Jane Austen's aunt, the wealthy Jane Leigh-Perrot, was received at the close of the century. More than simply exposing and recording the transition in retailer confidence in crime protection over the course of the century, the book reveals the mentalities that surrounded this change.

By synthesising approaches from the three histories of crime, marketing and consumption, this book presents the first fully comprehensive study of shoplifting as a commercial crime, determining its impact and significance within eighteenth-century society. At its core is a systematic analysis of the characteristics of eighteenth-century shoplifting: its participants, prevalence, spatiality and practice; the provision of the law; the working of the judicial system; the items that were stolen and the consequent economic impact on its victims. But overlaying this, the book also approaches the crime from three, more subjective viewpoints: those of the offender, the retailer and the general public. In doing so it endeavours to add depth to the conclusions drawn, to tease out or suggest the 'why' which may further elucidate and explain the 'what' and 'how'. It represents shoplifters and retailers not as archetypes, but as notionally similar collections of individuals whose activities reflected a range of disparate life choices, attitude and outlook which distinctively characterise the practice and reception of this crime.

The chief sources for this study of shoplifting are transcripts of London trials, as recorded in the *Proceedings* of the Old Bailey, and deposition evidence from Northern Circuit assize courts. The *Proceedings* are the most comprehensive record of London shoplifting trials in this period. Although a commercially produced and edited account of courtroom proceedings, its public reputation and demonstrated correspondence with other manuscript

---

30   Robert Shoemaker, *The London Mob: Violence and Disorder in the Eighteenth Century* (London, 2004), pp. 46–7.
31   Simon Devereaux, 'From Sessions to Newspaper? Criminal Trial Reporting, the Nature of Crime, and the London Press, 1770–1800', *London Journal* 32/1 (2007), 1–27 (pp. 12–18).

and published accounts of its trials, speak to its authenticity.[32] There are some gaps in the published series between 1699 and 1714, but even the early editions of the *Proceedings* appear to have reported most trials, and during the course of the eighteenth century came to be treated as a legal record of Old Bailey trials by the City authorities.[33] The Northern Circuit depositions cover the eight assize sittings for York, Yorkshire, Kingston upon Hull, Newcastle, Northumberland, Cumberland, Westmorland and Lancashire.[34]

Eighteenth-century indictments rarely clarify under which statute the charge is brought and shoplifting was in any case, as noted earlier, prosecuted under a range of laws. Shoplifting incidents have therefore been identified by internal evidence from the text of the transcripts and depositions. Although the Shoplifting Act contained its own specific legal definition of the crime, the term shoplifting was used in common parlance, much as it is today, to refer to any 'theft of merchandise during store hours, by someone who is shopping or pretending to shop', irrespective of value or oversight.[35] Consequently, the scope of this study is the theft of retail merchandise by customers or feigned customers, from shops or stalls. It includes those engaging with shop staff and those merely 'window-shopping', but excludes any theft by force, or by shop employees.

Given this practical definition, the *Proceedings* contain over four thousand shoplifting cases for the period. From these, a sample has been selected for detailed examination, comprised of all shoplifting trials heard at the Old Bailey during four periods of years at roughly twenty-year intervals. Where it is not obvious from the context, this is referred to in the text as the 'London sample'. For comparative purposes, each of the four period subsamples is of similar size, approximating 200 to 250 cases. As the frequency of cases increased throughout the eighteenth century, the earlier subsamples are drawn from a longer period of years than the latter. The earliest of these subsamples covers the years 1743–54.

---

32 John H. Langbein, *The Origins of Adversary Criminal Trial* (Oxford, 2003), p. 185. However, Robert Shoemaker argues that the editing prior to 1778 favoured prosecution testimony (Robert Shoemaker, 'The Old Bailey Proceedings and the Representation of Crime and Criminal Justice in Eighteenth-Century London', *Journal of British Studies* 47/3 (2008), 559–80 (pp. 566–74)). See note 37 below.

33 Clive Emsley, Tim Hitchcock and Robert Shoemaker, 'The Proceedings – The Value of the Proceedings as a Historical Source', OBP (https://www.oldbaileyonline.org/static/Value.jsp, accessed 19 April 2018). The *Proceedings* of the Old Bailey were first published in 1674, and regularly from 1678 until April 1913.

34 Durham, the remaining county on the Northern Circuit, was excluded from the study, as depositions only survive for the period after 1773.

35 See p. 2 above. The definition of shoplifting is taken from Terry L. Baumer and Dennis P. Rosenbaum, *Combating Retail Theft: Programs and Strategies* (Stoneham, 1984), as cited in Dena Cox, Anthony D. Cox and George P. Moschis, 'When Consumer Behaviour Goes Bad: An Investigation of Adolescent Shoplifting', *Journal of Consumer Research* 17/2 (1990), 149–59 (p. 149).

Although a continuous series of the *Proceedings* exists from 1714, many cases reported prior to 1742 are so summarily recorded that it is impossible to be certain that the offence described is shoplifting. For this reason, and the briefer reporting generally of shoplifting cases prior to this date, 1743 has been chosen as the earliest date for sampling. The remaining subsamples include all cases tried between 1765 to 1774, 1785 to 1789 and 1805 to 1807. Although not selected for that purpose, the sample years include periods of both peace and war, of relative economic prosperity and of financial stress. They contain in total 922 trials, at which were heard 934 indictable cases.[36] Some reference has also been made to individual cases from outside the period of the core London sample where these contribute qualitatively to the study.

Shoplifting cases heard at the Northern assizes have been drawn from the substantial archive of eighteenth-century court depositions from this circuit, held at The National Archives. Although none survives for the period 1700–24, it has been possible to identify conclusively 147 shoplifting cases, comprising 167 different shoplifting incidents, or indictable crimes, spanning the century from 1726 to 1829. These are referred to as the 'Northern sample' where not clear from context, and 'Combined sample' when aggregated with the London sample. Due to the nature of the source and rate of survival, there cannot be the same assurance as with the *Proceedings* that this smaller Northern sample is comprehensive. A best estimate would be that the 147 trials represent around 80% of all shoplifting trials heard at the eight Northern assizes during this period. The character of the depositions from the Northern source inevitably differs from that of Old Bailey trial transcripts, the former usually supplying a fresher account of the crime and often from a wider range of voices, while the latter records are often enhanced by judicial questioning and cross-examination. However, the content of the two sources is sufficiently similar to apply an analogous methodology, interrogating them quantitatively and qualitatively to answer questions on the profile of shoplifters, their modus operandi, the goods they stole and the impact of their crime on retailers.[37] Both quantitative and qualitative analyses fully exploit the wealth of information – material, relational and chronological – contained in the transcripts and depositions.

---

36   At two points in the study, when discussing the demographic profile of shoplifters in the 1790s, and the level of threat posed by shoplifters in the 1690s, additional samples have been drawn from the *Proceedings*. These are clearly identified as such in the text.

37   Prosecution evidence was routinely privileged over that of the defence in the trial reporting of the period, resulting in little or no qualitative difference between transcripts where the defendants were ultimately found guilty or acquitted. Further, where a reason for acquittal was given, this was frequently on technical grounds, or determined by character evidence, both of which might be considered uncertain indicators of guilt or innocence. Consequently, in interrogating the 1101 sample shoplifting cases in the study, a decision was made to treat all prosecutions as shoplifting incidents irrespective of the trial verdict.

In addition to court records, the study employs a wide range of other primary sources to build a rich and multifaceted representation of the crime. Parliamentary Journals, papers and reports furnish a basis for explaining the development of shoplifting law. Prosecution Society Minute Books, tax records, bankruptcy papers, retailer's diaries, memoranda and business records support accounts of how retailers managed the risk of the crime. And, throughout the book, contemporary newspapers, guides, manuals, maps, prints, novels, plays and poetry serve to illustrate and enhance our understanding of how the crime was both perpetrated and perceived by participants, victims and the general public.

A final mention must be made of the debt the book owes to modern criminology. There is an extensive and steadily accumulating corpus of research on present-day shoplifting which has applied a forensic thoroughness to determining its causes and controls. This has developed hand in hand with new methodologies for examining and interpreting crime. While neither can, nor should, be transplanted wholesale to an earlier age, they offer concepts and approaches for a better understanding of the phenomenon of eighteenth-century shoplifting. So where appropriate, and particularly in chapter 3, theoretical concepts from modern criminology have been used as a framework to clarify the relationship between criminal, victim and social environment.

The book now proceeds by introducing the eighteenth-century shoplifter, asking what we can know of those who perpetrated the crime. Constructing a demographic profile of indicted offenders, chapter 1 explores whether they were professional or amateur, and what this might reveal of their motivations. The succeeding chapter discloses the extent of their activities. It calculates the prevalence of shoplifting by collating prosecution figures, retailer and offender estimates, providing a more accurate context for assessing the crime's scale and impact on retailers. Chapter 2 also addresses the spatial dimensions of the crime, plotting the geographical distribution of prosecuted incidents over time to highlight the specific areas and neighbourhoods at greatest risk. This finding is reinforced by an investigation of the type, size and class of shop most commonly targeted, and the rationale for shoplifters' choice in this respect.

In chapter 3 we enter the shop itself to examine closely how shoplifters stole and the countermeasures taken by retailers to protect their stock. It uses the framework of 'routine activity', an influential criminological theory, to assist in explaining the concerns of the thief and the dynamic between the parties. The chapter explores the art of eighteenth-century shoplifting, drawing on the wealth of tactical detail given in court testimony, and describes how shoplifters honed their performance skills to match the class of shop targeted. It reveals that shopkeepers increasingly employed situational prevention techniques, designed to hamper and discourage thieving, and regularly co-operated to contend with their mutual threat. The chapter also highlights the role played by customers and bystanders, who spiritedly participated in combating theft, even as regular police patrols were introduced late in the period.

The following chapter examines what was stolen, recognising that shoplifting was a direct, albeit illicit form of consumption. It questions whether thieves craved the novel and stylish goods that so appealed to middling shoppers and examines the degree to which shoplifting enabled the poor to participate in the century's fabled consumer boom, and particularly to indulge in fashion. Chapter 4 discusses the implications not merely of what was taken and by whom, but also of its quality and value, and compares goods stolen through shoplifting with those taken in other forms of property theft. It reveals that such illicit dealings served multiple ends, sustaining a complex web of economic exchanges in working communities.

The study next addresses the commercial implications of shoplifting. Returning in chapter 5 to the retailers' struggle to combat shoplifting, it explores the economic impact of such theft on their livelihood. The book considers the significance of business size, credit relations and the growing popularity of cash-only selling, and weighs the contribution of trade protection societies. It proposes that sociological factors, in particular retailers' business temperament, might be a more dependable indicator than financial considerations in predicting traders' response to the crime. Chapter 6 examines retailers' agency with regard to the law on shoplifting as this was variously enacted, interpreted and applied over the course of a hundred and thirty years from the 1690s to 1820s. An exacting account of the development of the law, this chapter is nevertheless presented from the perspective of the trader rather than given a more conventional juridical treatment.

The book concludes in chapter 7 with a broader look at how the eighteenth-century public viewed the crime. Using a range of print sources, and in particular contemporary literature, it studies attitudes to shoplifting among different strata of society and the mentalities that influenced their understanding and behaviours. This final chapter reflects on the transformation in perception which saw a society that exclusively associated the crime with the immorality of the poor in 1699, start to come to terms with the realisation that shoplifting was also a crime that the middle ranks might commit.

Taken together, these chapters show how retail expansion, retailers' temperament, the attitudes of wider society in particular to morality and consumption, and the working of the market economy were all determinant in encouraging and enabling this form of crime to thrive. They demonstrate how these separate factors interacted to make shoplifting the concern it was to eighteenth-century commerce. The book examines the effectiveness of retailers and the judicial system in containing this threat of customer theft, revealing how commercial responses to the crime first forged, and eventually tempered, its prominent status in the judicial canon.

1

Customer Thieves

The prisoners came into our shop, in Chandois Street, Covent Garden, and looked upon some striped thread sattins and at last bought 14 yards. I heard a piece fall, and one of them took it up and laid it on the counter. I observed that they were shuffling something under their riding-hoods, and I told Mr Young, that I suspected they had stole a piece, upon which he presently follow'd them, and found this piece of satin upon Ward ... They were both carried to Covent-Garden Round-house: and the same day examined before Justice Hilder, who granted a warrant for committing them to the Gatehouse, but in their way thither, with two constables with them in a coach and the Beadle behind, they were rescued, by several men.[1]

This account of the trial of Ann Ward and Sarah Bream in 1735 only served to fuel contemporary suspicion that shoplifting was a form of organised crime. Pleading some years earlier for harsher laws, London retailers had complained bitterly that shoplifters 'personate all degrees of buyers, in all their respective qualifications, having their several societies and walks, their cabals, receivers, solicitors and even their bullies to rescue them if taken'.[2] While we may question the sincerity of their conviction, shopkeepers sought to convey a message that professional thieves, masquerading as customers, were plundering their businesses. By design or through ignorance they promoted a false understanding of a crime that, from the evidence of this study, was principally an intermittent form of makeshift for the poor. As this chapter discloses, those brought to court were more often amateur than professional, occasional than full-time, and opportunist than conspiring. This book begins by examining who within society became a shoplifter and why they stole. While offending behaviour formed a spectrum that stretched from recurrent through intermittent offending to the occasional bravado act, it was predominantly an economic resource for those struggling to make a living. So, let us review the evidence.

---

1   OBP, February 1735, Ann Ward, Sarah Bream (t17350226-10).
2   *The Great Grievance of Traders and Shopkeepers, by the Notorious Practice of Stealing their Goods out of their Shops and Warehouses, by Persons commonly called Shoplifters; Humbly Represented to the Consideration of the Honourable House of Commons* (1699).

Occasional thieves

Crime historians have long been faced with the difficulty of discerning whether indicted thieves were professional or amateur at the time of the offence. This is certainly no straightforward task, for to eighteenth-century shoplifters these oppositional terms were highly mutable. As Heather Shore has stated for this period, 'The definition of the professional criminal was inherently problematic, based as it was upon the fuzzy boundaries between the economy of crime and the economy of makeshift.'[3] Court testimony and criminal histories present lifetime accounts of offenders moving effortlessly between legitimate and illegitimate activity as circumstances dictate. However, the evidence indicates that for the great majority of indicted offenders, shoplifting was casual. Presenting as the ultimate part-time crime, it offered an accessible means to supplement earned income or provide an urgent subsidy at times of unemployment. Subject to the constraints of internal and social controls, and the compulsion of impending destitution, it could be employed with varying degrees of regularity.

An examination of the environmental circumstances and demographic characteristics of these intermittent shoplifting offenders goes far to explain their attraction to the crime, and particularly in London. Making a living in the metropolis was a challenge for a major proportion of its inhabitants, notably women, children, and the semi-skilled or unskilled workers that Leonard Schwarz has estimated formed two-thirds of the male working population.[4] Londoners were largely dependent on small-scale domestic manufacturing or service trades, such as building and dealing, occupations that were subject to the instability of the market and seasonal variations in demand. Workers might be laid off at times of economic downturn or financial crisis, which were regular occurrences during a century of continual wars. Demand for certain services would fall when the upper classes left London to spend summer on their estates and adverse weather halted outdoor trades such as building each winter. It was common for men only to be occupied in their main trade for part of each year, resorting to casual or labouring work at other times. While some areas of the north were experiencing growing prosperity, there too workers were victim to the same insecurities. London wages were generally higher than in the rest of the country but this was offset by the higher cost of living.[5]

Certain sectors of the population were particularly vulnerable. Women were formally or customarily excluded from most trades and restricted to a narrow range of low-paid occupations, most commonly domestic service,

---

3   Shore, 'Crime, Criminal Networks', p. 150.
4   Schwarz, *London in the Age of Industrialisation*, p. 56.
5   Schwarz, *London in the Age of Industrialisation*, pp. 49–51.

needlework and types of dealing. Huge numbers of young women were attracted to London to fill the demand by upper and middling families for domestic servants, but the majority were obliged to leave their residential situations in their twenties upon marriage. As real wage rates fell from mid-century, few families could survive without wives and children contributing to the family budget. Amy Erickson in her study of eighteenth-century married women's occupations found that those appearing at the Old Bailey between 1728 and 1800 were almost universally employed, almost two-thirds in needle trades or hawking, carrying and retailing.[6] Children were a second vulnerable group. Their plight was particularly dire if they had lost parents or their families were economically overstretched; the latter more frequent as family sizes increased towards the end of the century with a gradual decrease in infant mortality.[7] And further, London attracted large numbers of migrant workers from the provinces or abroad and could be a particularly hostile environment for those without the economic fail-safe of employment, family or friends. Sarah Holmes had come to London from Nottinghamshire in 1769 to take up a post as a servant but lost it after three days due to illness. Eight weeks later, having failed to find another place, she stole three handkerchiefs from a City linen draper.[8] Borrowing, pawning and relying on credit were all forms of makeshift for those struggling to survive, and for many theft was simply another practical expedient *in extremis*. A systematic analysis of the shoplifters in the sample by gender, age and occupation reveals a bias towards precisely these most economically vulnerable groups.

Shoplifting was widely practised by both sexes, and consequently by a far higher proportion of women than for the majority of eighteenth-century property crimes. Table 1 shows roughly equal participation in London until the final sampled period. The greater discrepancy here may simply be reflective of the enlistment of men at a time of war, or their entering the services as an elective alternative to prosecution, but could also reflect a toughening of attitudes towards female offenders.[9] In the Northern circuit cases, women are more prominent comprising nearly two-thirds of offenders.

Establishing the age and marital status of offenders is more difficult as these are infrequently recorded or disclosed in court transcripts prior to the late eighteenth century. They are only readily accessible from October 1791 when the government directed that ages should be routinely recorded in calendars of prisoners. For an initial period the Keeper of Newgate prison

6   Amy Louise Erickson, 'Married Women's Occupations in Eighteenth-Century London', *Continuity and Change* 23/2 (2008), 267–307 (pp. 277–8).
7   Schwarz, *London in the Age of Industrialisation*, p. 228.
8   OBP, September 1769, Sarah Holmes (t17690906-9).
9   Peter King, *Crime and Law in England, 1750–1840: Remaking Justice from the Margins* (Cambridge, 2006), p. 212; and see p. 21 below.

Table 1. Shoplifting prosecutions: gender constituency of offenders appearing at the
Old Bailey and Northern Circuit assizes

	London		Northern circuit (1726–1829)	
	Male	Female	Male	Female
1743–54	110 (48%)	121 (52%)		
1765–74	146 (50%)	148 (50%)		
1785–89	143 (49%)	148 (51%)		
1805–07	108 (41%)	155 (59%)		
Total	507 (47%)	572 (53%)	68 (36%)	119 (64%)

Source: Combined sample

also registered the occupation or marital status, and place of birth, of all
prisoners awaiting trial at the Old Bailey.[10] In practice this information was
not listed consistently for every offender, but it is sufficiently comprehensive to
allow reliable profiling of the London population that engaged in shoplifting.

The date of the earliest recording in October 1791, while not precisely
overlapping with any of the sample periods used in this study, is close enough
in time to that of 1785–89 to act as a surrogate. Examining the Newgate
Criminal Registers for the three years from October 1791 to September 1794,
we find ages listed for 96% of the 169 defendants in the *Proceedings* who were
tried for shoplifting at the Old Bailey during the same period. This sample of
169 is seemingly anomalous in its smaller proportion of women defendants,
and an unexpected finding given the commencement of war in 1793 and the
likely reduction in male crime due to enlistment. A probable explanation is
that for a period between December 1790 and October 1792 the *Proceedings*
omitted any cases where the defendant was acquitted, the court invariably
treating women more leniently in this respect.

An age analysis of the sample (Table 2) reveals that while the majority of
offenders were under thirty, there was a distinct difference between the mean
ages of male and female defendants. Male shoplifting peaked in the late
teens and early twenties while female offenders were generally older. Around
half of female offenders were in the 25–39 age range. As the average age at
first marriage in London at this period was below twenty-five it might be
anticipated that a high proportion of offenders were married. Peter King,
examining all female offenders recorded at the Old Bailey in 1792, found only
41% had been married, leading him to conclude that they were generally

---

10   TNA, HO 26, Home Office, Criminal Registers, Middlesex (Ancestry.co.uk, *England &
Wales, Criminal Registers, 1791–1892*, accessed 22 November 2011).

Table 2. Age analysis of shoplifting offenders tried at the Old Bailey, October 1791–September 1794 (where age specified)

Age	Male	%	Female	%	Total	%
14 and under	9	8	1	2	10	6
15–19	26	23	7	12	33	20
20–24	35	32	8	14	43	25
25–29	12	11	11	19	23	14
30–34	9	8	12	20	21	12
35–39	5	5	9	15	14	8
40–44	5	5	2	3	7	4
45 and over	7	6	4	7	11	7
Not given	2	2	5	8	7	4
Total	110	100	59	100	169	100

Source: OBP; TNA, HO 26/1–3, Home Office, Criminal Registers, Middlesex

less vulnerable to prosecution than single women. However, the Newgate Registers do record marital status for three-quarters of the sample of female shoplifters and of these, 62% were married.[11] The same profile over a longer period is very apparent in the Northern assize records. With the benefit of the more routine recording of marital status in depositions there is information for 82% of the female sample, of whom 72% were married.

This clearly points to shoplifting being a crime that attracted an older cohort of women, at a life-cycle stage when the financial demands of maintaining a home and family would be most pressing.[12] This is compounded by the fact that male abuse or desertion is frequently hinted at, and many women may effectively have been single parents, dependent on their own resources. When soldier's wife Elizabeth Boyd was brought before the court in 1743, her friend testified how she had begged the shopkeeper to show mercy, explaining, 'she has three small children; her husband is in Flanders'.[13] Ruth Frostick, prosecuted in 1771, had four children and was reported to have taken refuge at the house of one of her witnesses 'when she was absent from her husband, who used her very ill'.[14] A number of offenders are identified as

11   See King, 'Female Offenders', pp. 69–70.
12   Deirdre Palk observed a similar female age bias in her study of shoplifting trials at the Old Bailey in nineteen sample years between 1791 and 1823, in Gender, Crime and Judicial Discretion, p. 57, Table 5.
13   OBP, May 1743, Elizabeth Boyd (t17430519-13).
14   OBP, April 1771, Ruth Frostick (t17710410-2).

widows. In a character reference for Margaret Carr sent to the Cumberland assizes in 1819, her employer wrote, 'she has a very large family of 4 small children without any father and an old mother who has no strength or ability and no person to do anything for them'.[15] Of course, this demographic bias could also be a function of situation. King contends that young single women would normally be seeking work in service and, 'Once employed, servants were surrounded by an abundance of temptations great and small.'[16] Married women, obliged to leave service, would have found such opportunities for domestic theft from their employers or fellow employees denied to them.

There were fewer openings for men than women in domestic service and the relative youth of many of the male defendants, two-thirds being aged under twenty-five, and half of these in their teens, may reflect their economic disadvantage as they competed to enter the workforce and establish themselves in a trade. Prosecutions frequently feature children or young adolescents, predominantly boys, working together in groups of two or three to steal. Children, obliged by the death or poverty of parents to fend for themselves, had limited options. As Shore has observed, only the lowest-paid, least secure and seasonal work was available to them.[17] However, this male bias may not entirely reflect the prevalence of child crime. King concluded that there was greater leniency shown by tradesmen and magistrates towards young offenders in this period and that this operated more strongly in favour of girls.[18] Certainly, there are examples of such young offenders being given considerable leeway in the hope of reform. Between the ages of eleven and fourteen, Mary Moon, otherwise Moore, appeared four times at the Old Bailey, charged on each occasion with shoplifting. Twice set free with admonishments from the bench to 'let this be a warning to you' and to 'be careful in future', Moon ultimately received the relatively lenient sentence of a year in the House of Correction.[19] Even so, court sympathy was prone to evaporate in the face of apparent incorrigibility. Fourteen-year-old George Reynolds was sentenced to death in 1785 for shoplifting twelve hats valued at £6. The jury recommended mercy, to which the judge responded, 'Gentlemen, there is one thing that is necessary for me to state to you, that this is not the first, second, third, or fourth time that this boy has been here.'[20]

---

15   TNA, ASSI 45/52, Assizes, Northern and North-Eastern Circuits, Criminal Depositions and Case Papers, 16 August 1819, Margaret Carr.

16   King, 'Female Offenders', p. 75.

17   Heather Shore, *Artful Dodgers: Youth and Crime in Early Nineteenth-Century London* (London, 1999), p. 42.

18   King, 'Female Offenders', p. 67.

19   *OBP*, December 1783, Thomas Knight, Mary Moore (t17831210-72); September 1785, Mary Moon (t17850914-180); May 1786, Mary Moon (t17860531-87); July 1786, Mary Moore, Ann Holloway (t17860719-54).

20   *OBP*, September 1785, George Reynolds (t17850914-10).

Table 3. Age analysis of shoplifting offenders tried at the Old Bailey, January 1805–December 1807 (where age specified)

Age	Male	%	Female	%	Total	%
14 and under	11	10	6	4	17	6
15–19	16	15	43	28	59	23
20–24	21	20	28	18	49	19
25–29	14	13	24	16	38	15
30–34	8	7	15	10	23	9
35–39	8	7	9	6	17	6
40–44	8	7	12	8	20	8
45 and over	22	21	16	10	38	14
Total	108	100	153	100	261	100

Source: London sample

It is possible that a hardening of attitude towards young offenders, irrespective of gender, accounts for an increasing proportion of younger female defendants being prosecuted in the early nineteenth century.[21] Eleanor Condy, Mary Marney and Sarah Sullivan, aged fifteen, fourteen and eleven respectively, accused of stealing a length of printed cotton in 1805 in what may have been an escapade – the constable reported that 'they only laughed' when caught – were each found guilty and sentenced to transportation.[22] Correspondingly, an age analysis of the 1805–07 sample (Table 3), by which time defendants' ages were routinely noted in the *Proceedings*, reveals a markedly younger female age profile.

While youth predominated, a significant percentage of offenders were aged over forty. Ill health and incapacity were an increasing risk to livelihood with age. William Trueluck, aged sixty-four, who stole a pair of corduroy breeches from a shop door, claimed he 'was in a good deal of distress', and eighty-year-old George Wright, indicted the same year for stealing handkerchiefs from a Barbican linen draper, explained in his defence that he had found parish relief wanting.[23] Moorfields broker Richard Wright, prosecuting Elizabeth Collegan for stealing a flat iron, stated, 'The prisoner is a cripple; she has frequently come to my door a begging.'[24] Disability could prevent individuals

---

21 Palk, *Gender, Crime and Judicial Discretion*, p. 50; King, *Crime and Law*, pp. 108–9.
22 OBP, April 1805, Eleanor Condy, Mary Marney, Sarah Sullivan (t18050424-111).
23 OBP, September 1806, William Trueluck (t18060917-128); December 1806, George Wright (t18061203-7).
24 OBP, April 1765, Elizabeth Collegan (t17650417-58).

Table 4. Occupations of female shoplifting offenders recorded in sampled Old Bailey
and Northern Circuit shoplifting trials, 1726–1829

Occupation	Number	%
Domestic service – servant, char, washerwoman	39	37
Street/market hawker	33	31
Needle worker	21	20
Other (shopkeeper, penciller, wireworker, silk winder, weaver, stay maker, midwife, labourer, prostitute)	13	12
Total	106	100

Source: Combined sample

benefiting from wider regional prosperity. Although openings for women in
the Manchester cotton industry were apparently plentiful in 1806, Isabella
Mathum, labelled a 'notorious shoplifter' by the *Lancaster Gazette*, was
described by a prosecuting shopkeeper as 'lame of her right arm'.[25]

Occupational information reinforces the impression of shoplifters'
economic marginality. As women were customarily defined in legal documents
by their marital status, limited information is provided on female occupations,
although such that there is confirms their restricted employment options
(Table 4). An occupation is given for only 17% of the 572 London and 9% of
the 119 Northern female defendants sampled for this study, and of these 88%
are within three main work areas most commonly accessible to eighteenth-
century plebeian women: domestic service, needlework, and hawking.

Information on male occupations is equally sparse for the four London
sampled periods, but reasonably comprehensive occupational information is
included in the Newgate Registers.[26] An analysis for the period October 1791
to September 1794 reveals that male shoplifters worked in some of the lowest-
paid or seasonal trades and sectors (Table 5). A third were categorised as
labourers. Five worked in building trades, committing their crimes at times of
the year when work would have been scarce through adverse weather, or lack
of demand outside London's November to June social season. When eighteen-
year-old painter, John Barber, stole 8 yards of Irish linen from Charing Cross
draper William Prater in February 1794 he was treated leniently by the court.
However, in September 1794, 'coming from Mr –, a painter and glazier',
perhaps in search of work, he was once again tempted to remedy his financial

25   TNA, PL 27/8, Palatinate of Lancaster, Crown Court, Depositions, 23 January 1806,
Isabella Mathum, Ann Wilson; *Lancaster Gazette*, 22 March 1806, p. 3.
26   TNA, HO 26, Home Office, Criminal Registers, Middlesex.

Table 5. Occupations of male shoplifting offenders recorded in Newgate Registers, October 1791–September 1794

Occupation	Number	%
Agriculture/mining	0	0
Manufacturing trades	36	39
Service trades (including building)	16	17
Soldier/sailor (including militia)	7	8
Dealing/selling	4	4
Labourer	29	31
Other	1	1
Subtotal	93	100
Unknown	17	
Total	110	

Source: OBP; TNA, HO 26/1–3, Home Office, Criminal Registers, Middlesex

situation by stealing muslin from a Cheapside shop, this time with a less fortunate outcome.[27]

The percentage of occupations given for male shoplifters in the north of England is higher at 54%, although the sample is small (Table 6). As in London, a third were classified as labourers, but rather less worked in service trades and more as travelling dealers or pedlars, reflecting differences in the economy of the two regions. A plotting of incidents in northern England between 1726 and 1779 clearly shows how the majority occurred along established trading routes, often in centres associated with markets or fairs. Nevertheless, similar economic conditions could obtain. Joseph Powell, the accomplice of a shoplifter indicted in Sheffield in 1789, asserted that he was 'by trade a joiner and carpenter but has not worked at his trade for about two months past'.[28]

The frequent incidental mention of offenders' livelihoods in their own testimony and that of their character witnesses reinforces the proposition that shoplifting was for most a form of makeshift, supplementing an inadequate or irregular employment income. Sarah Davis, identified in the press as 'an old offender' when prosecuted in 1745, was solidly defended by

27 OBP, February 1794, John Barber (t17940219-19); September 1794, John Brown, John Barber (t17940917-62).
28 TNA, ASSI 45/37/1/209, Criminal Depositions and Case Papers, 27 November 1789, Samuel Salt.

Table 6. Occupations of male shoplifting offenders recorded in Northern Circuit depositions, 1726–1829

Occupation	Number	%
Agriculture/mining	2	5
Manufacturing trades	6	16
Service trades (including building)	2	5
Soldier/sailor (including militia)	7	19
Dealing/selling	8	22
Labourer	12	33
Other	0	0
Subtotal	37	100
Unknown	31	
Total	68	

Source: Northern sample

her employer: 'the prisoner is a mantua maker, she has worked for me a great many years, and I never knew any thing of her, but what was pretty, modest and virtuous'.[29] Alice Burk, twice found guilty of thefts from china shops in the same year, was similarly supported in court. Mary Innys testified on her behalf:

> I have known the prisoner these three years, she has worked with me a year and an half at a time, at quilting and mantua-making, and worked from six to six. I have trusted her with valuable silks, and other things, and she never wronged me of any thing. I never knew her to wrong any body of a half-penny.[30]

The ability of even prolific shoplifters to maintain the trust of employers suggests that protecting their livelihood and identity as a worker was of paramount value to them. Dishonest conduct at work would inevitably entail a loss of the reference essential at that period to their future hiring. Put succinctly by another defendant's sympathetic employer, 'The prisoner lived in our family as a chamber-maid, between two and three years, and has been gone about three months; we never mistrusted her honesty, if we had, we should not have kept her so long.'[31]

29   *General Advertiser*, 29 May 1745, p. 1; OBP, May 1745, Sarah Davis (t17450530-3).
30   OBP, April 1743, Alice Burk (t17430413-6).
31   OBP, May 1743, Ann Rhodes (t17430519-5).

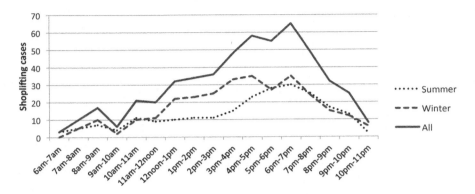

Chart 1. Time that crime was committed in four sample periods, 1743–1807
Source: London sample

Other defendants refer to casual work in their evidence, frequently hawking, in explaining their happenstance at the time and scene of the crime. Sarah Dalton, accused of stealing from a Covent Garden silversmith said, 'I had been out all day selling cauliflowers', and Elizabeth Jones caught mid-afternoon taking muslin from a Houndsditch draper, declared, 'I had but just done selling my fruit'.[32] In fact a seasonal analysis of the recorded time that prosecuted incidents took place persuasively suggests that offenders did work and shoplift concurrently. The number of cases in the *Proceedings* where a time of offence was given increased significantly from 35% in 1743–54 to 78% in 1805–07. An aggregated analysis of all the sample periods (Chart 1) produces a preferred time for theft of early evening, between 4 p.m. and 7 p.m. This is not totally unexpected as these may have been the busiest trading hours in the local shops predominantly targeted by thieves, when staff were most distracted. And dusk was a favoured time for shoplifters, expediting surreptitious theft and escape. However, if darkness was a dominant factor we would expect to see a significantly later time profile in the summer months, which is not the case. An alternate reading of the chart is that much theft was perpetrated at the end of the working day. And while relative privation might account for higher theft levels in winter months, the disproportionate increase in daytime thefts is consistent with seasonal unemployment.

It would be satisfying if it could also be established that goods were routinely shoplifted to support the continuance of legitimate work. Casual thefts of shoes or breeches, which comprised 7% of all items stolen, may indeed have been to meet the basic requirement of working clothes.

---

32 *OBP*, July 1767, Sarah Dalton (t17670715-45); October 1787, Elizabeth Jones, Elizabeth Cummins (t17871024-21).

Examining female offenders in this period, King concluded that most of the older, married shoplifters in his sample were 'needle- and clothing-workers stealing raw materials for use in their trade'.[33] Certainly in Mary Hodwell's trial in 1792 for stealing ribbon from an Oxford Street haberdasher, a witness described her sighting of the goods: 'I had occasion to have a bonnet made, and I called upon Mary Hodwell, and she shewed me some green ribbon'.[34] But it is necessary to enter a caveat here. Such use as raw material is many times outweighed by evidence of the conversion of the same order of goods into cash through pawning or sale. The market in textiles and second-hand clothes was so active and unregulated that these were easily the most economically rational targets for theft.

While the data substantiates a greater propensity to shoplift among those whose livelihoods were least secure, it is worth noting that employment circumstance may have particularly drawn some to this crime. For example, James Stewart's accomplice in the theft of a diamond from a store in the Strand was a jeweller. Similarly, Richard Manley, who stole seven books from bookseller Thomas Cadell in June 1789, worked as a journeyman book binder, a trade described by Campbell in his *London Tradesman* of 1747 as being 'out of business half the year'.[35] Although domestic servants only formed a small percentage of shoplifters, they were often ideally placed to shoplift, regularly being sent by their employers to shop for goods that would be beyond their means to acquire personally (or credibly being able to claim they were so commissioned). Sarah Hirst, who in 1781 visited Joseph Nollans' haberdasher's shop in York to match some black lace for her mistress, stole a 20 yard piece when the shopwoman was called to the door to serve a lady in her carriage.[36] Sarah Staniforth was likewise sent to match a piece of muslin in Sheffield in 1790, with a corresponding outcome.[37]

Not unexpectedly, a number of shoplifters had retailing experience. With such inside knowledge they may have been more familiar with a store's potential for criminal exploitation or simply more at ease operating in a familiar environment. Above all, however, they are likely to have had access to routes of disposal and indeed many such shoplifters may also have acted as receivers. At Ann Galloway's trial in 1786, Richard Tinkler testified:

> I am shopman to Mr. Steele, the prosecutor, he is a mercer in the parish of St. Ann, Soho, the prisoner came to my master's shop, the 15th of February,

---

33 King, 'Female Offenders', pp. 80–1.
34 *OBP*, May 1792, Mary Hodwell (t17920523-24).
35 *OBP*, April 1769, James Stewart (t17690405-39); June 1789, Richard Manley (t17890603-8). R. Campbell, *The London Tradesman* (London, 1747), p. 135.
36 TNA, ASSI 45/34/2/33, Criminal Depositions and Case Papers, 23 July 1781, Sarah Hirst.
37 TNA, ASSI 45/37/2/194, Criminal Depositions and Case Papers, 2 August 1790, Sarah Staniforth.

about five in the evening, and asked to look at some childrens great coats, she said she kept a shop in Monmouth-street, and wanted some to sell again.[38]

And over the course of four separate prosecutions in October 1795, it emerged that Mary Clarke had visited linen drapers across the city to steal goods to stock her husband's small Whitechapel drapery, where the proceeds were found 'open for sale in the shop'.[39]

There are also cases where dealers or hawkers were accused of stealing from their regular suppliers, particularly in the north of England where they were a vital element of the retail network. Their opportunity for such theft was clearly enhanced by familiarity, trust and repeated access. John Donaldson, convicted in 1760 of stealing toys and metalware valued at 75 shillings from three York hardware dealers, was described by one as 'a dealer in hardware and used to frequent this informant's said shop to buy goods of him'.[40] Luke Palfreyman, a Sheffield hosier, who accused Richard Davison of the theft of four pairs of men's cotton stockings, stated that Davison 'had frequently dealt with the informant before' and had in fact just bought stockings worth a guinea and a half before pocketing the disputed goods.[41] Employment and shoplifting were not only concurrently practised, but in many cases closely related.

While most of the shoplifters who came to court were part-time thieves, a minority appear to have made a substantive living from their theft. We will next consider the potential extent and nature of their operation.

Professional thieves

Shopkeepers' accusations that shoplifting was a form of organised crime were periodically vindicated by an apparent shoplifting 'ring' being brought to court. In 1726, during a period of heightened public alarm at criminality, a group of female shoplifters came to notoriety. Jane Holmes, Katherine Fitzpatrick, Sarah Turner and Mary Robinson were convicted and subsequently executed on the evidence of their sometime accomplice Mary Burton.[42] Mr Justice Vaughan, the committing magistrate, recorded that

---

38 OBP, February 1786, Ann Galloway (t17860222-16).
39 OBP, October 1795, Mary Clarke (t17951028-28; t17951028-29; t17951028-55; t17951028-57).
40 TNA, ASSI 45/26/5/7D, Criminal Depositions and Case Papers, 30 August 1760, John Donaldson.
41 TNA, ASSI 45/38/1/53, Criminal Depositions and Case Papers, 5 February 1793, Richard Davison.
42 OBP, August 1726, Jane Holmes (t17260831-21); August 1726, Katherine Fitzpatrick (t17260831-22); August 1726, Sarah Turner, Katherine Fitzpatrick (t17260831-23); August 1726, Mary Robinson, Jane Holms, Hannah Briton (t17260831-24).

Holmes 'would fain have been an evidence, and named I believe near 40 robberies, that she had been concern'd in', and in court, Mary Robinson spontaneously referred to shoplifting as 'our profession'. The group were also tainted by their admitted past association with thief-taker, Jonathan Wild, who had been discredited for criminal collusion and hanged the previous year. As in most such cases, receivers were closely implicated and four women were subsequently tried for purchasing their stolen goods.[43] A myth-making literature swiftly developed, in which the commercial nature and scale of their operation was emphasised. Writing of the condemned prisoners, the Newgate Ordinary described how Holmes had returned to London after previous transportation for shoplifting, where 'she renew'd her acquaintance with her old friends the ladies who deal in shop-lifting, in which way of merchandizing she equall'd most of her partners'.[44] Some ten years later the popular publication, *Lives of the Most Remarkable Criminals*, related how the action against the group in the summer of 1726 'seems to have pretty well broke the neck of this branch of thieving ever since'.[45]

Twenty years on, another ring was dismantled on the evidence of thirteen-year-old Sarah Bibby. Henry White, John Price and Elizabeth Stavenaugh, alias Howell, were convicted of shoplifting, and their associate, Sarah Soames, of receiving.[46] The testimony builds a picture of a tightly run enterprise. Bibby described White's business as thieving: 'he harbours thieves; and takes children away from their friends; he took me away from my mother. I had lived with him about a fortnight before this happened – I had lived with Howell before.' Elizabeth Howell shared White's house in Shoe Lane, Holborn. A witness, Elizabeth Buckley, complained that Howell 'harbours children to run them: my child has gone a thieving with her, and is transported'. Bibby claimed that she and thirteen-year-old Jack Price, convicted of stealing razors from a City shop, were threatened by White and Howell if they did not co-operate. The Shoe Lane property clearly had a reputation as a clearing house. In court, constable Charles Shuckborough testified that 'Last Saturday was seven-night, Mr. Seawell had an information that he had lost some goods, and got a search warrant; we went to Harry White's house, Mr. Seawell did not find any of his goods, but found these linens.'

This pattern was not restricted to London. The teenaged Hannah Ellison and Mary Widdup, caught shoplifting in Hull in 1804, were key contributors

43   *OBP*, October 1726, Jane Keatly (t17261012-41); October 1726, Isabel Lewis (t17261012-49); December 1726, Elizabeth Higgins, Ann Green (t17261207-72).
44   *OBP*, *Ordinary's Account*, 12 September 1726 (OA17260912).
45   *The Lives of the Most Remarkable Criminals, who have been Condemn'd and Executed*, 3 vols (London, 1735), vol. 2, p. 299.
46   *OBP*, April 1745, Henry White, Sarah Soames (t17450424-13); April 1745, John Price (t17450424-39); May 1745, Elizabeth Stavenaugh (t17450530-8).

to a thriving family business. They were found guilty of stealing ten separate lengths of calico and muslin from two linen drapers over a two-month period, four of which had subsequently been sold to local residents by Widdup's mother and the remainder pawned.[47] Similarly in York, infamous receiver Isabella Thirkill employed a ring of young thieves in the city, including two of her sons, for several years until transported in 1817.[48] And professional shoplifters did not necessarily specialise in the crime. Patrick Savage, giving evidence in the 1791 shoplifting trial of his two associates, John Wood and William Haslam, disclosed that in the six weeks leading up to the theft from a Warrington shop, Wood had stolen a bale of goods at Northwich fair, handkerchiefs from a corner shop in Liverpool and buckles from another, while Haslam had picked an old man's pocket of silver and stolen a watch from a house in Stockport.[49]

Apart from the exposure of such cases, there are other indications in transcripts and depositions that advertise defendants deriving their living from shoplifting. Aliases were inherently suspicious, and their repetition in court, *Ordinary's Account* and published criminal histories was clearly intended to emphasise this. As the court reporter slyly commented in a 1742 case: 'Davis had not one person to her character, though she had a great many last Sessions, when she was tried by the name of Mary Shirley, for robbing Mr Setcole, linnen-draper in Smithfield'.[50] Ingenuity or competency of tactics could also mark out the dedicated offender: the genteelly dressed thief who distracts a watchmaker in dismantling his watch for 'cleaning' while he helps himself to others from the shop display, or the browsing shopper who admits to having posted accomplices outside the shop to receive the stolen goods.[51] The choice, value and quantity of targeted goods were also indicative. Caught stealing over £5 worth of highly marketable cotton in 1805, Sarah Gladman came fully equipped, the constable testifying, 'there was twenty-eight yards of print in one pocket, and twenty-five yards in the other, they are extreme large pockets'.[52] Employment of defence counsel, increasingly common from the 1780s, but financially beyond the reach of the more destitute, also infers a profitable living from crime. When Jane Gavin's accomplice was captured on a shoplifting foray in 1823 Carlisle, she immediately pawned some stolen

47   TNA, ASSI 45/42, Criminal Depositions and Case Papers, 4 February 1804, Hannah Ellison, Mary Widdup.
48   TNA, ASSI 45/50, Criminal Depositions and Case Papers, 1 March 1817, John Fowler, James Thirkill; 24 March 1817, William Jennings, John Ullathorne.
49   TNA, PL 27/7, Lancaster, Crown Court, 12–15 December 1790, Patrick Savage, John Wood, William Haslam.
50   OBP, September 1742, Catherine Davis, Jane Canwell (t17420909-29).
51   OBP, December 1750, Charles Speckman (t17501205-74); June 1747, Henry Stephens (t17470604-27).
52   OBP, February 1806, Sarah Gladman (t18060219-41).

goods to raise 3 shillings to hire her friend an attorney.[53] Such suspicions were enhanced by press reporting of a repeat pattern of offending, or in some cases the response, verdict and sentencing of the parish law enforcers, magistrates and judiciary that reveal or imply a fuller knowledge of the offenders' history and previous criminal record. Even so, only a small proportion of shoplifters prosecuted, perhaps less than 20% of the cases sampled in this study, can be securely identified as professional criminals.

Middling thieves

Having determined that poverty motivated the bulk of shoplifting cases here, we can finally spotlight the minority of indicted shoplifters whose main inducement was not economic, particularly those from middling or genteel backgrounds. Not that we can entirely preclude financial motivations even here, for those of the middling sort could experience monetary crisis. John Leminghau, whose father was chaplain to Catherine the Great, stole from a bookseller when he found himself penniless in England. A family friend advised the court:

> I knew his father in Russia, who is a man of great character in the Russian church: His father left him here for his education, and furnish'd him with apparel and money; but the young man was guilty of some extravagancies … and I believe this thing was merely out of necessity.[54]

Character witnesses in other trials related histories of business failure. Elizabeth Ross lived 'in good repute' as the wife of a periwig maker, 'but her husband failed about half a year ago' and Lewis Sharkey 'did keep a publick-house, but he has failed in trade'.[55] And pure economic advantage may have driven some middling thieves. When milliner Sarah Tonge was accused of stealing lace and gauze from two Cheapside haberdashers in 1773, evidence given in court and contemporary press reporting revealed that shoplifting was a strategic and well-worn element of her business model.[56]

However, there are some, albeit rare cases where we sense individuals may have been acting in response to social, cultural or even psychological impulses. The illicit thrill of shoplifting, particularly when done in company,

---

53   TNA, ASSI 45/56, Criminal Depositions and Case Papers, 28 January 1823, Jane Gavin.
54   *OBP*, January 1750, John Leminghau (t17500117-35).
55   *OBP*, May 1766, Elizabeth Ross (t17660514-3); December 1774, Lewis Sharkey (t17741207-3).
56   *OBP*, April 1773, Sarah Tonge (t17730421-2); *Morning Chronicle and London Advertiser*, 29 April 1773, p. 3.

may have had the same attraction as that recognised by criminologists in more recent times.[57] When John Wilkinson stole *Memoirs of a Young Lady of Family* from a bookseller off Fleet Street, his employer protested in court, 'I am a carver and gilder; he was at work for me at the time; I take this to be more of a frolick than anything else, that seems plain to me'.[58] There are also apparent impulse thefts where attractive goods may have proved irresistible to those on constrained budgets. Twelve-year-old peruke-maker's apprentice Edward Ashington, sent out to deliver a wig in 1766, snatched a watch from a Fenchurch Street shop. In his defence his master avowed that the boy 'had been trusted with many thousands of pounds value in his shop, and was he at liberty, he would be very glad to take him again; and that he looked upon the prisoner, by circumstances he had observed, to have a particular fancy to a watch'.[59] Daniel Marshall, shopping for some plated buckles in 1786, was spied pocketing a silver shirt buckle. 'What is [the] value of it, without fashion?', his counsel quizzed the shopkeeper.[60]

Sociologist Colin Campbell has argued that the eighteenth-century middle-rank ideals of sensibility and romanticism fostered a hedonistic, but morally sanctioned, desire to consume.[61] This may account for the apparently insouciant attitude to illegal acquisition glimpsed in the few identified prosecutions of middling defendants. What are we to make of the confession of Eleanor Richardson in 1741 who admitted a joint theft with her mistress from a Penrith milliner:

> That she ... did feloniously take and carry away out of the shop ... one piece of cambrick about three yards and three quarters in length and that the same day she saw her mistress Mrs Hannah Brisco take the other piece of cambrick ... and this examinant further saith that her said mistress gave her one half of the piece or they divided it equally between them and ... that part of both pieces of cambrick were made into caps and aprons by Elizabeth Collinson a milliner in Penrith.[62]

A yeoman's wife, Brisco alone was prosecuted, clearly as much for transgressing the expectations of an employer as for the theft. And at the Old

57 Jack Katz, *Seductions of Crime: Moral and Sensual Attractions in Doing Evil* (New York, 1988).

58 *OBP*, October 1766, John Wilkinson (t17661022-9).

59 *OBP*, October 1766, Edward Ashington (t17661022-55).

60 *OBP*, May 1786, Daniel Marshall (t17860531-80).

61 Colin Campbell, 'Understanding Traditional and Modern Patterns of Consumption in Eighteenth-Century England: a Character-Action Approach', in *Consumption and the World of Goods*, ed. J. Brewer and R. Porter (London, 1993), pp. 40–57 (pp. 48–9, 53–4).

62 TNA, ASSI 45/22/2/116D, Criminal Depositions and Case Papers, 15 October 1741, Hannah Brisco.

Bailey in 1789. Elizabeth Fellows expressed outrage at her charge after being caught stealing stockings from a Leicester Square hosier. Possibly the daughter of magistrate Thomas Fellows, she declared, 'I had no intention to rob him of them; the gentlemen of the jury know me perfectly well; my father is here'. Although found guilty she was later 'recommended by the jury and prosecutor knowing her father'.[63]

Categorising middling theft is problematic, however, due to the extreme rarity of such prosecutions. In keeping with the consideration shown Fellows, this lack may simply reflect shopkeepers' refusal to prosecute in such cases. Trial transcripts repeatedly record the reluctance of shop staff to detain, or even suspect any customer dressed genteelly. 'I had no suspicion of them because they were well dressed', admitted John Barbe in 1744, and when in 1778 Joseph Wateridge was told that his sister suspected two 'very genteelly dressed' customers of stealing his lace, his immediate reaction was to say, 'no; he did not think they looked like any thing of the kind'.[64] In the same year Daniel Dartnell, an Oxford Street silversmith, was asked by a fellow jeweller to hold a man from whom he had bought goods stolen from his shop, 'Though I had been desired by Mr. Cartwright to stop the man of whom I bought the seals, the prisoner had so much the appearance of a gentleman, that I could not prevail upon myself to stop him.'[65] Another jeweller was equally hesitant when a customer lifted a diamond stud from his display case in 1779: 'I said it was a dangerous thing to stop him, as he had the appearance of a gentleman'.[66] Their anxieties were not entirely without foundation. The *London Evening Post* reported In January 1767 that a £1,000 suit was being brought against a Westminster shopkeeper for falsely accusing an army officer's wife of shoplifting.[67] That shopkeepers did frequently tolerate middling theft or deal with it informally, in the interests of customer relations, is intimated by the testimony of a Long Acre goldsmith, a defence witness in the trial of Sarah Tonge, the shoplifting milliner we encountered earlier. On the stand, John Burcher parried fierce cross-examination. Had he heard Gunston swear that he retrieved his lace from under Tonge's stays, the judge demanded. Did he think it had got there by mistake? 'We have had many mistakes in my shop', responded Burcher, 'and ladies have carried things into their coach ... in their laps some how.' The judge was incredulous. 'Now suppose a fine lady was to come into your shop, and you should miss some jewels, and find them afterwards, half way down their stays, would you think that a mistake', he retorted. 'We have found this mistake', said Burcher, 'and taken them out.'[68]

It is apparent from such evidence that while we can safely determine the demographic characteristics and economic motivations of the majority of shoplifters in this study, we are on far weaker ground with middling thieves. This is particularly the case for those shoplifters who retailers failed to recognise as thieves or detain. We will be revisiting some of the economic, social and cultural factors contributing to this in the coming chapters.

This chapter has questioned who shoplifted. It argues that while a proportion of those prosecuted were likely to have been professional criminals, a demographic analysis of defendants strongly indicates that the majority of shoplifters were occasional thieves, struggling to survive the low incomes and intermittent employment patterns that were the common lot of working households. The significant numbers of older women, children and the infirm among offenders confirms their particular vulnerability and, while there is evidence that most still worked, a time of crime analysis points to concurrent thieving. It concludes by highlighting the rarity of middling prosecutions and suggests this was exacerbated by the extreme reluctance of retailers to prosecute members of a class that primarily sustained their livelihood.

68   *OBP*, April 1773, Sarah Tonge (t17730421-2).

2

The Extent of the Crime

The incidence of shoplifting was so extensive that it was crippling London's retail trade. This was the unequivocal message that the capital's traders intended to convey to Parliament in the late 1690s as the country's lawmakers debated the need for dedicated legislation. Petitioning Parliament, they related a litany of ills. Shoplifting was the daily experience of all London shopkeepers, they declared, 'against which their strictest diligence cannot secure them'. They bewailed that due to the shoplifter's cunning and the inadequacy of sentencing under the law, those actually prosecuted were but a fraction of the shoplifters plying the crime: 'Experience shews, that burning and whipping increases their number, and ripens their invention; so that few offenders are taken; when taken, not one in ten prosecuted.'[1] But how accurate were their accusations: was shoplifting indeed as frequent, pervasive and under-prosecuted as they asserted? In this chapter we interrogate that view, examining the extent of the crime.

We begin by projecting the true prevalence of the crime, calculating its scale from prosecution, retailer and offender evidence. An examination of the many factors impeding the stopping and prosecuting of perpetrators lends credence to the traders' claims. The chapter then explores the geography and topography of the crime, identifying the location of incidents over time and the significance of their spatial patterning. It shows how retail specialisation and the casual nature of most offending, imparted in the last chapter, was formative to its spread. The exercise reveals that the shopkeepers most at risk were not those that previous historiography may lead us to expect. Perhaps surprisingly, shoplifting had a greater impact on local neighbourhood shops than the elite stores that were most emblematic of England's consumer renaissance.

Assessing the prevalence of the crime

In attempting to accurately quantify shoplifting we must grapple with a problem that has long frustrated historians. Only a proportion of actual thefts

---

1 *The Great Grievance of Traders and Shopkeepers.*

will ever be detected and prosecuted. The remainder, termed the 'dark figure' of unreported crime, can be as elusive today as in the eighteenth century. British self-report surveys in the last fifty years have suggested that only between one in forty and one in 250 shoplifting incidents result in a conviction or caution.[2] But modern criminological studies are fortunate in being able to supplement prosecution rates with police and retailer reports, and by strictly controlled self-report and observation studies. We can only build a fuller estimate by carefully piecing together fragmented historical evidence to provide a surrogate of these additional sources. And in doing so, we find that shoplifting was a crime that had some peculiar disincentives to prosecution.

We should first look, however, at what prosecution figures can tell us of the levels and trend in customer theft over the period. The trial transcripts contained in the *Proceedings* of the Old Bailey are the most easily accessible record of shoplifting incidents in the capital. Whether prosecuted as a crime under the 1699 Shoplifting Act or as grand larceny, shoplifting was a felony and, as such, offenders were conventionally tried at London's highest criminal court, the Old Bailey. It was not unknown in England for justices and prosecutors to collude in reducing the severity or value of the charge to enable cases to be heard in local quarter sessions courts or even summarily, but there is no evidence that this was widely practised in London. Beattie even found the opposite to be the case in the early part of the century, with a few petty larceny cases referred to the Old Bailey each year.[3]

If we take Old Bailey prosecutions as an underlying indicator of the number of shoplifting incidents within the London population it is apparent that, even adjusting for population increases, the incident rate rose steadily over the course of the century (Table 7). This does not in itself confirm that more crimes were being committed. Retailers may have become more adept at identifying thieves, or simply more willing to prosecute those caught. However, Beattie has suggested that the major driver for increased prosecutions was fear prompted by public awareness of escalating crime rates and, as such, prosecutions were an indirect barometer of crime.[4]

This rapid amplification of the rate towards the end of the century was not evident from previous studies of the crime that have looked solely at prosecutions under the Shoplifting Act. In her study of indictments under the Act, Deirdre Palk has calculated that an average of thirty cases a year were heard at the Old Bailey between 1780 and 1823. Annual totals fluctuated between nineteen in war periods and fifty-six in peacetime but the yearly

2   David P. Farrington, 'Measuring, Explaining and Preventing Shoplifting: A Review of British Research', *Security Journal*, 12 (1999), 9–27 (pp. 15–17).

3   Beattie, *Policing and Punishment*, pp. 12, 24; Petty larceny was theft of goods valued at under a shilling. Such cases were traditionally tried in lower courts.

4   Beattie, *Crime and the Courts*, pp. 202, 218–19.

Table 7. Frequency of London shoplifting as indicated by Old Bailey prosecutions

Years	Estimated population[1]	Average yearly cases[2]	Incidents per 1000 population
1743–54	690,000	17	0.02
1765–74	750,000	25	0.03
1785–89	850,000	49	0.06
1805–07	1,100,000	79	0.07

Source: London sample

Notes

1 Figures extrapolated from those given in John Landers, *Death and the Metropolis: Studies in the Demographic History of London, 1670–1830* (Cambridge, 1993), p. 180.
2 Rounded to nearest whole number.

mean remained remarkably constant.[5] This finding is verified by the London sample, with an annual average of 28.3 in the two later periods. However, a graph by charge (Chart 2) demonstrates that by the 1800s indictments under the Act constituted a declining proportion of all prosecutions for customer theft.[6] Shopkeepers' improved surveillance, and therefore inability to meet the 'privately stealing' qualification of the Act, will have contributed to this reduction. But more significant, as we shall see in chapter 6, was many retailers' increasing unease at employing legislation that carried a capital penalty.

The experience of London was exceptional. Far fewer shoplifting cases were heard at the Northern Circuit assizes; the sample average of less than two cases a year is similar to that Beattie found for another provincial assizes, Surrey.[7] While the low number, dispersed nature and lower confidence in the comprehensiveness of the Northern case records preclude a similar calculation of offence frequency rates to that of London, the movement in prosecution rates over time (Chart 3) hints at a similar trend. However, we cannot safely assume that this reflects an increased rate in relation to population. The region was undergoing rapid economic change with exponential population increases in many northern manufacturing towns during this period.[8]

5 Palk, *Gender, Crime and Judicial Discretion*, p. 43.
6 The criminal law under which each defendant was indicted has been derived from information given in the text of the *Proceedings*.
7 Beattie, *Crime and the Courts*, p. 178.
8 The population of Sheffield expanded from around 3,500 in 1700 to 35,344 inhabitants by 1801, Liverpool from 5,714 to 88,358 during the same period, Manchester from under 10,000 to 75,000, while that of Leeds quadrupled and Newcastle doubled. Population figures taken from Christopher Chalklin, *The Rise of the English Town, 1650–1850* (Cambridge 2001), pp. 77–9.

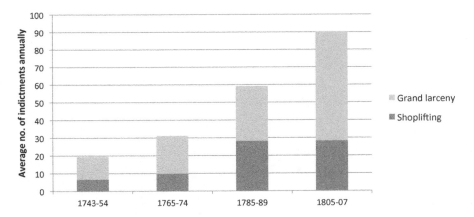

Chart 2. Yearly average of offenders indicted for shoplifting and grand larceny in Old Bailey shoplifting trials during four sample periods, 1743–1807
Source: London sample

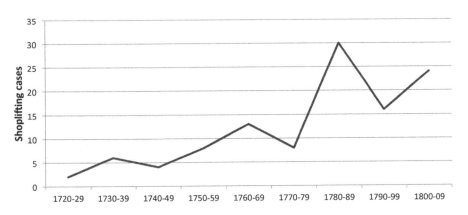

Chart 3. Trials for shoplifting heard at Northern Circuit assizes, 1720–1809
Source: Northern sample

Comparing the pattern of offending in the north with that of the shoplifting cases heard at the Old Bailey during the same period is, however, instructive. For in spite of London's accelerated economic development and substantially greater number of cases, a plotting of its prosecutions produces a remarkably similar curve (Chart 4). Historians have long debated the causes of the consistently recurring pattern of property crime in the eighteenth century. Beattie identified war and dearth as prominent factors, in particular highlighting the classic spikes that accompanied the ending of the century's

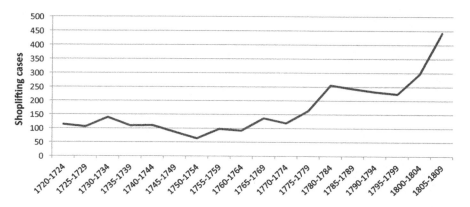

Chart 4. Trials for shoplifting heard at the Old Bailey, 1720–1809
Source: OBP

many wars.[9] The influx of demobilised soldiers and sailors to the job market at these times was perceived to lead to distress from a shortage of work and downward pressure on wages. This in turn heightened the fear of crime and created moral panic, increasing the propensity to prosecute.[10] Certainly the visible peaks on the two charts in the 1760s and 1780s do correspond with recognised crime waves at the end of both the Seven Years War (1763) and the American War of Independence (1783), but a similar crime surge in the late 1740s after the War of the Austrian Succession is absent. As prosecutions for other property crime rose steeply, those for shoplifting perversely fell. Examining the pattern of property crime in a number of English counties, King has argued for a more discriminating approach, showing that war and dearth impacted regional crime rates to different degrees and at different times.[11] The similarity of the two regional shoplifting curves, however, cautions us against treating property crime in aggregate. It is perhaps time to recognise that discrete crimes could have their own unique pattern. Wars may have been less significant to a crime with a high female profile and prosecuting retailers may have been less influenced than most by moral panics, which were undoubtedly more strongly associated with violent crime.

In order to make a comprehensive assessment of the number of shoplifting cases prosecuted, we need consider briefly the extent to which offenders may have been dealt with by lower courts, due to stolen value or other judicial

---

9   Beattie, *Crime and the Courts*, pp. 213–37.
10   Robert Shoemaker, 'Worrying about Crime: Experience, Moral Panics and Public Opinion in London, 1660–1800', *Past and Present* 234/1 (2017), 71–100 (p. 74).
11   King, *Crime, Justice and Judicial Discretion*, pp. 145–61.

policy. London shoplifting prosecutions for low-value pilfering were certainly heard at the City, Middlesex and Westminster quarter sessions during the course of the century but determining their number is problematic as court minute books and indictments, where they survive, seldom distinguish petty larceny by type. However, court recognisances, which state the occupation of the prosecutor, suggest that at times these may have been comparable in number to those heard in the higher courts. In 1785, a year when thirty-two shoplifting cases were heard before Middlesex juries at the Old Bailey, recognisances for the Middlesex Sessions record that thirty-two shopkeepers prosecuted for theft. All but one were for goods costing 10 pence or less and the items stolen, predominantly food or single items of clothing, were likely to have been genuinely valued. Although there is no way of knowing how many of these petty larceny cases were for pocket-picking or household theft, the prosecutor only coincidentally being a shopkeeper, the numbers are indicative of the scale of prosecutions.[12] However, a further analysis of recognisances for a later year, 1805, when eighty cases were heard at the Old Bailey, suggests quarter session cases became increasingly less significant as a proportion of prosecutions. Documents survive for both Westminster and Middlesex Sessions for this year, but it has been possible to identify only thirty-seven shopkeepers prosecuting for theft, an average of five per session in Westminster and hardly more than two in Middlesex. Case numbers showed more fluctuation across the eight Middlesex Sessions, there being notably fewer cases in sessions burdened by higher numbers of assault and public order prosecutions.[13] The types of item stolen were similar to those of 1785, which may imply that as inflation eroded value, shopkeepers had little interest in prosecuting for such minor losses.

The same recording limitations make it difficult to confirm how many shoplifting cases were heard at quarter sessions in the north of England. Though again, indications from two regions are that these were restricted. An examination of surviving papers for the West Riding Quarter Sessions between 1786 and 1792 reveal no shoplifting cases were heard for Sheffield during this period (in contrast to twelve sent from the town to the Yorkshire assizes), although Calendars of prisoners held in Wakefield Gaol indicate there was the occasional case at Huddersfield, Selby, Halifax and Leeds.[14] Similarly, presentments for the Newcastle Quarter Sessions between 1767 and 1785 contain only four relating to shoplifting among sixty-eight for property

12   LMA, MJ/SR/3453, 3455, 3457–3458, 3460, 3462, 3464, 3466, Middlesex Sessions of the Peace, Court in Session collection, Session Rolls 1785.
13   LMA, MJ/SR/3712, 3714, 3716–3717, 3719, 3721–3722, 3724, 3726, 3728–3729, 3731, Middlesex Sessions of the Peace, Court in Session collection, Session Rolls 1805.
14   West Yorkshire Archive Service (Wakefield), QS1/125–132, West Riding of Yorkshire Quarter Session Rolls 1786–1792.

offences.[15] Although survival is patchy, there is no reason to believe that among these indictments, those for shoplifting would have been disproportionately destroyed.

There is perhaps even less evidence of shoplifting cases being dealt with by magistrates summarily. In his study of summary justice in the City of London, Drew Gray identifies shopkeepers among those instigating cases, but these actions were more frequently for other offences, including employee theft and thefts from carts.[16] The eighteenth-century Minute Books of the City Justice Rooms, from which Gray derived his material, are a particularly valuable resource as they identifiably record most offences charged. An examination of the surviving Guildhall Justice Room Minute Books for 1775–81, a period earlier than that examined by Gray, reveals that charges of shoplifting were periodically brought to these sittings, but that when this did happen defendants and accusers were invariably bound over to appear at the Old Bailey Sessions.[17]

In the hundred years from 1715, approximately four thousand shoplifting cases were tried at the Old Bailey and we can also project that around two hundred were heard at Northern assizes over the same period. If we conclude that a somewhat lesser number of predominantly petty larceny cases came before magistrates in quarter sessions and summary courts, these numbers are still far from representing a crime that was the 'daily experience of all shopkeepers', as London retailers claimed. In order to appreciate why so much crime apparently went unpunished, we need to turn to the evidence of retailers themselves. Testimony given by shopkeepers in court indicates a far higher incidence rate. We hear of depredations they were unable to prevent and on occasion their conscious avoidance of prosecuting those they did detain.

Shopkeepers complained repeatedly in court of the frequency of their losses, adding substance to linen draper William Conran's outburst in 1743, 'we are pester'd with these creatures'.[18] Katherine Quantem, prosecuting in 1746, claimed she had been robbed eleven times, and James Bayley, bringing a case the following year, asserted that he had been a victim nine or ten times previously.[19] Similar reports pepper later periods. In February 1785, Seven Dials shopkeeper

---

15 Tyne and Wear Archives, QS.NC/74–77, 79–84, 87/2, 89–100, Newcastle Borough Quarter Sessions, Sessions Papers 1767–1785. Presentments are Grand Jury statements confirming that a crime had been committed and that an indictment should be drawn up.

16 Drew Gray, *Crime, Prosecution and Social Relations: The Summary Courts of the City of London in the Late Eighteenth Century* (Basingstoke, 2009), pp. 71, 73, 77.

17 LMA, CLA/005/01/004–015, Guildhall Justice Room, City of London collection, Minute Books, 1775–81.

18 *OBP*, May 1743, Mary Johnson (t17430519-12).

19 *OBP*, October 1746, Jacob Holloway (t17461015-41); September 1747, Ann Gregory (t17470909-28).

Thomas Hobbs declared, 'I have lost so much goods lately out of my shop', and in December 1805, haberdasher Thomas Lloyd admitted suffering 'daily depredations'.[20] While it was clearly in shopkeepers' interest to exaggerate their affliction in court, there is no instance of defence counsel challenging such testimony, and indeed regular attrition does seem to have been a driver in encouraging retailers to prosecute when they did apprehend a shoplifter. Linen draper David Lewis resisted thirteen-year-old Mary Hinder's pleas for mercy when caught stealing his calico, testifying that he told her, 'I had so many things of the kind lately, that I could not forgive it'.[21] Retailers thus openly acknowledged the occurrence of a considerable amount of successful, undetected shoplifting. And even defendants unconsciously endorsed this perception as they sought to discredit their captor's motives in court. 'He said he had had a great many losses and he would lay all his revenge upon me', accused Rachael Dinder, charged with stealing cloth from a Fleet Street linen draper.[22]

But undercounting was not merely due to those who 'got away'. In spite of their low apprehension rate, some shopkeepers were clearly moved by the plight of those shoplifters they did catch, raising the possibility that such sentiments may have led to others escaping prosecution entirely. Smaller shopkeepers in particular, chandlers and sale shop owners, must have been very aware of the precarious financial circumstances and makeshift existence of many London residents. Such attitudes might account for the testimony of Elizabeth Compton, a clothes shop proprietor, when Elizabeth Phillips stole a petticoat from her door in 1744: 'I would have had the Justice have sent her to Bridewell to be lashed, but he would oblige me to prosecute'.[23] Even more explicit was linen draper's assistant Richard Twydale, giving evidence in the prosecution of Mary Walker for stealing twenty linen handkerchiefs in the winter of 1787:

> Your master felt a great deal of pity for her and her two children, one of four years of age, and the other at the breast? – My young master was very sorry for her.

> He did not wish to indict her capitally, I believe, if he could have helped it? – No.[24]

Magistrate Henry Fielding, writing in the shadow of the 1740s crime wave, was particularly scathing about retailers who were 'tender-hearted, and cannot

20 OBP, February 1785, Elizabeth Chapman (t17850223-83); December 1805, Mary Wilson, Mary Morgan, Elizabeth Walker (t18051204-3).
21 OBP, February 1772, Mary Hinder (t17720219-47).
22 OBP, September 1769, Rachael Dinder (t17690906-38).
23 OBP, April 1744, Elizabeth Phillips (t17440404-9).
24 OBP, February 1787, Mary Walker (t17870221-31).

take away the life of a man'. He warned 'a benevolent and tender-hearted temper often betrays men into errors not only hurtful to themselves, but highly prejudicial to the society'.[25] However, his chief criticism was directed at the financial disincentives to prosecution embodied in the current judicial system:

> It is true that the necessary cost on these occasions is extremely small; two shillings, which are appointed by Act of Parliament for drawing the indictment, being, I think, the whole which the law requires; but when the expence of attendance, generally with several witnesses, sometimes during several days together, and often at a great distance from the prosecutor's home; I say, when these articles are summed up, and the loss of time added to the account, the whole amounts to an expence which a very poor person, already plundered by the thief, must look on with such horror (if he should not be absolutely incapable of the expence) that he must be a miracle of public spirit, if he doth not rather choose to conceal the felony, and sit down satisfied with his present loss.[26]

No mechanism for state prosecution existed in the eighteenth century and victims of theft were therefore obliged to bring a private prosecution at their own volition and expense. Although court fees were generally within the means of traders, the consequential loss of time and business could be onerous. Retailers' ensuing reluctance to prosecute seriously compromises any reliance on case numbers as an indicator of prevalence.

If, as Fielding recognised, time and expense was a disincentive to retailers in London, it was far more so in the provinces. Northern assize sessions were held in York, Kingston upon Hull, Durham, Newcastle, Carlisle, Appleby and Lancaster, a considerable distance for shopkeepers from other localities to travel. Contemplating the need to support their own and witnesses' costs for several days awaiting the case being called, the difficulties in staffing their shops in the interim and potential loss of business in their absence, retailers might readily choose not to prosecute. The obstacles that a small shopkeeper could contend with are illustrated by the case of Ann Turner, from whose Leeds shop Elizabeth Cahill stole eleven silk handkerchiefs in September 1732. Selling the goods en route, most beyond trace, Cahill was not apprehended until she reached her home in Selby, 25 miles distant. Unable to leave her shop, Ann Turner was obliged to send her sister to Selby to press charges but, bound by recognisance, could not avoid the 60 mile round trip to York, in the still wintry harshness of the following March, to prosecute the case.[27]

25　Henry Fielding, *An Enquiry into the Causes of the Late Increase of Robbers &c with some Proposals for Remedying this Growing Evil* (London, 1751), pp. 106, 108.
26　Fielding, *An Enquiry*, pp. 109–10.
27　TNA, ASSI 45/19/3/9, Criminal Depositions and Case Papers, 19 September 1732, Elizabeth Cahill.

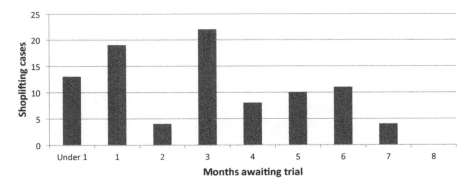

Chart 5. Time period between committal and hearing of shoplifting cases at Northern Circuit spring assizes, 1726–1829
Source: Northern sample

And northern shopkeepers faced further potential deterrents. In contrast to the eight sessions annually at the Old Bailey, assize sessions were convened only twice a year at York and Lancaster, in spring and summer, and a single summer session held in the more northern counties. The long gap between sessions could prove both an expense to the municipal authorities, obliged to support a defendant in gaol until trial, and a burden on retailers who could lose access to their stolen goods, held as evidence, for a considerable period. The higher rates of prosecution found where crimes were perpetrated in the period immediately preceding an assizes implies a consequent reluctance of retailers to prosecute offences that would entail a long wait for hearing, or that cases were being diverted to lower courts, though as we have seen the latter was an infrequent practice.

Chart 5, depicting the time period between the date of the crime and the date of hearing at the Northern Circuit spring assizes (February–March), clearly indicates that the majority of cases heard related to crimes perpetrated in the three months immediately preceding the assizes. While it might be objected that this simply reflects a higher incidence of cases in winter months when hardship caused by seasonal work shortages and higher fuel and food costs may have driven more offenders to crime, the seasonal crime pattern (Chart 6) rebuts this argument. It displays a similar peak of cases in the months approaching the summer assizes (July–August). Delays between sessions were patently a discouragement to prosecution that contributed to an under-recording of detected incidents. It is hardly coincidental that there was a more than threefold increase in shoplifting cases prosecuted at the Carlisle and Newcastle assize sessions in the decade from 1819 when spring assizes were first extended to the more northern counties.

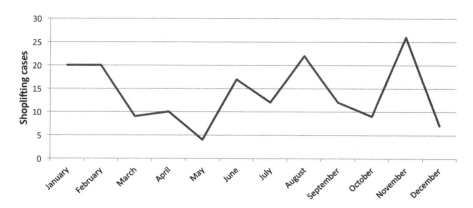

Chart 6. Seasonal pattern of prosecuted shoplifting cases in the Northern Circuit
assize courts, 1726–1829
Source: Northern sample

Measures were introduced mid-century to counteract financial disincentives but these only partially addressed retailers' needs. Legislation authorising the reimbursement of court expenses to impecunious prosecutors and witnesses on conviction for felony was introduced in the 1750s and extended to all, irrespective of circumstances or the outcome of the case, in 1778.[28] This was welcome to some retailers, particularly those obliged to prosecute. If a shopkeeper had been drawn into the judicial process by involving parish law enforcers in the offender's arrest and subsequent committal before a justice of the peace, they would invariably be bound over by recognisance to appear in court. But such compensation was rarely generouss so, if the retailer alone was aware of the theft, there was always a temptation to turn it into a sale, possibly at a ransomed price. John Farrow, who stole a watch valued at 36 shillings from William More's shop in 1768, claimed in court that More 'wanted me to give him two guineas and a half for the watch, and he would say nothing about it'.[29] And Kenerth M'Kenzie, stealing from a hosier in the Strand five years later, stated that the shopkeeper 'said if I would pay for them he would not hurt me; I had not money to pay for them, so he said he would keep my hat'.[30] Such an informal arrangement with the offender for recovering the value of their goods was strictly illegal. It was an offence to 'compound' a felony by agreeing not to prosecute in return for restitution of goods or any other consideration. As might be expected, shopkeepers routinely denied

---

28   25 Geo II, c. 36, s. 11 (1752); 27 Geo II, c. 3, s. 3 (1754); 18 Geo III, c. 19, ss. 7–8 (1788).
29   *OBP*, September 1768, John Farrow (t17680907-20).
30   *OBP*, February 1773, Kenerth M'Kenzie (t17730217-34).

claims such as made by Farrow and M'Kenzie in court, but they are suggestive of such transactions masking a substantial amount of unrecorded customer theft. And even shopkeepers who were concerned to observe the law might ultimately consider the most pragmatic option to be simply releasing the shoplifter on recovery of the goods.

We cannot know how widespread such simple dismissal of offenders was, but court testimony suggests that it was a frequent recourse, particularly where the shopkeeper felt the theft was a rash or aberrant act, or had some sympathy with the plight of the offender. When Mary Buck caught Christian Pronor stealing a hat from her shop in 1743 she related how she had upbraided her: 'girl, I believe you have stole something; if you have, you had better lay it down; and she slid it down on the counter; I would have had her have gone about her business, but some busy neighbour would have us prosecute her. It may be the first fact'.[31] In similar fashion, linen draper Richard Fitzgerald was surprised to observe Elizabeth Ross stealing a piece of his muslin in 1766, explaining 'she was pretty well dressed, I thought she was some tradesman's wife'. Inviting her into a back room, he said, 'you have got something of my property about you, deliver it, and you shall go about your business'. Only when she failed to do so, did he summon a constable.[32] And when in 1807 pawnbroker Thomas Hill was alerted to two women attempting to steal a cloak he had for sale in his shop, his initial instinct was simply to send them packing: 'I turned the other woman out of the shop, and desired her not to come any more, and I was turning the prisoner out but she was so insolent, I was obliged to send for the constable'.[33]

Apart from their financial concerns, shopkeepers faced yet a further obstacle to prosecution: the potentially confusing and regularly modified processes of the judicial administration system. Linen drapers Thomas and Joseph Slack were defeated by procedure when attempting to prosecute a shoplifter in February 1788. In an affidavit sworn to protect their recognisance, they explained:

> that not having employed any solicitor and being totally unacquainted with the necessary steps to be taken in the prosecution and not having received any notice for that purpose these deponents did not appear at Hicks's Hall Clerkenwell at the proper time to prefer a Bill of Indictment against the said Phoebe Williams for the said felony: And these deponents further say that they both attended at Justices Hall in the Old Bailey from day to day during all the days of the said February Session in order to prosecute and

---

31 *OBP*, June 1743, Christian Pronor (t17430629-34).
32 *OBP*, May 1766, Elizabeth Ross (t17660514-3).
33 *OBP*, December 1807, Elizabeth Probert (t18071202-68).

give evidence against the said Phoebe Williams but the said Phoebe was discharged for want of a Bill being preferred against her.[34]

As the century progressed and the law on, or affecting, shoplifting was gradually interpreted and defined by the courts, even parish law officers could be unequal to the demands of an increasingly complex legal system. Haberdasher Robert Earl, a nevertheless undaunted and successful prosecutor, testified in court how 'the constable informed me, that I could do nothing with it, that I had better let her go about her business'.[35] John Langbein has suggested that from the 1780s shopkeepers were also discouraged from prosecuting by the aggressive style of cross-examination employed in court by defence counsel.[36] Court appearances did carry the risk of public discredit. When Ralph Steel brought a case in 1783, he even incurred the displeasure of the judge:

> Court to Jury. I cannot, but remark, I think it my duty to remark upon the conduct of Mr. Steel, that it is such as does him no credit, and such as would not give force to his testimony, if the proof of this robbery depended on his single testimony, for there appears a degree of inveteracy in him, which is very improper in any prosecutor.[37]

Although he did in fact bring six further shoplifting cases in the three years following this case, Steel never appeared personally again, letting his shopmen give evidence on his behalf.

Retailer testimony confirms that prosecutions alone substantially undercount the amount of active shoplifting, but we must turn to a third indicator of prevalence to give some sense of degree. The confessions of perpetrators are the closest we have to modern self-report studies. John West, a seventeen-year-old with a history of robbery was capitally convicted for shoplifting in 1755. West is described in the *Ordinary's Account* as 'one of the most artful little rogues in the ways of contriving to bring about a design of shop-lifting of any of them all', and identified as a daily offender. In the course of his confession to the Newgate Ordinary he is reported as stating:

> 'Tis six years ago ... since he first began to go a thieving; and shop-lifting was the chief attempt of him, and his companions, in which he had been so very successful (tho' scarce a day past he was not concerned in one of the greater, and less account) that yet he never once got into trouble as he

---

34   LMA, OB/SP/1788/10/012, Gaol Delivery Sessions at the Old Bailey post-1754 collection, Session Papers, Statements and Informations, King v. Phoebe Williams, affidavit of prosecutors re their failure to appear.
35   *OBP*, February 1786, Mary Jones (t17860222-29).
36   Langbein, *The Origins of Adversary Criminal Trial*, p. 296.
37   *OBP*, February 1783, Elizabeth Hart (t17830226-15).

called it (the usual phrase of these sort of people when apprehended for felony) till last October sessions.[38]

While the didactic intent of the *Ordinary's Account* may cause us to suspect the authenticity of this admission, it is corroborated by similar statements collected from defendants at the time of arrest. John Ullathorne who was charged with stealing silk handkerchiefs from two York shops in 1817 voluntarily confessed to more than fifteen other undetected offences over the previous year.[39] And to fully grasp the potential scale of the crime we turn to a London case.

In November 1773 habitual shoplifter Hannah Mumford learned that a pawnbroker had stopped a 28 yard length of linen that she had been party to stealing. Seeing the writing on the wall, Mumford surrendered herself at the local Rotation Office in Litchfield Street and offered to turn Crown evidence. Some days later, in a lengthy information taken on oath, she disclosed that she and three accomplices had between them carried out twenty-six thefts from London linen drapers over the preceding ten months.[40] Three were from the same St James Market shop on successive days, giving credence to retailers' complaints of repeated thefts. Twenty-six was almost certainly an economical account. In the week preceding her detention, the period most easily recalled, Mumford admitted five thefts. Thus at a conservative estimate the members of this shoplifting ring were stealing at an annual rate of thirty thefts to one prosecution. But if we take the final week before arraignment as more typical, this rate could be as high as 250 to one, strangely resonant of the twentieth-century estimate quoted at the start of the chapter.

Having examined the extent of the crime in numerical terms, we move on now to explore the geography of shoplifting. While acknowledging the scale of the crime, we are obliged for this purpose to rely on known incidents, represented by our sample, as examples of type.

The geography and topography of the crime

When we survey the location of recorded thefts in the two regions that are central to this study it becomes apparent that the crime's spatial patterning was principally a function of the types of shop targeted and the opportunistic nature of most offending. Looking first at the smaller Northern sample, we see

---

38   *OBP, Ordinary's Account*, 12 May 1755 (OA17550512).
39   TNA, ASSI 45/50, Criminal Depositions and Case Papers, 24 March 1817, John Ullathorne.
40   LMA, OB/SP/1773/12/006, Gaol Delivery Sessions, Hannah Mumford statement in the case against Esther Peters, Ann Chatham, Ann Bartlett and Thomas Wright charged with various felonies.

the significance of custom and proximity. At the start of the period (1726–79) incidents were most frequent in settlements along the traditional inland trade routes, and often in centres associated with markets or fairs.[41] However, by the later period (1780–1829) this is far less marked as the north underwent rapid, if uneven, economic development. Multiplying fourfold, incidents became concentrated in the increasingly populous industrial, manufacturing and trading areas of south Yorkshire and Lancashire, Tyneside and the Cumbrian coast. The highest numbers of incidents were recorded in Newcastle, York and Sheffield with an emerging or increasing problem in some other towns, including Manchester, Liverpool, Whitehaven, Carlisle and Hull. The number of shops in England had trebled between 1688 and 1759 with over twenty thousand shops in the six northernmost English counties at that date.[42] This was a continuing trend; Hull alone saw a 66% increase in its number of shops, from 403 to 669, between 1791 and 1810.[43] The growth of these towns as the industrial revolution took hold created new opportunities for retailers, but more importantly for retail specialisation. This development was significant for, as we shall now find, shoplifters did not target shops randomly.

In March 1764 Sarah McCabe, Mary Edgar and Elizabeth Young, three women also answering to a string of criminal aliases, were taken up and detained at London's principal magistrate's office. The following day the press reported:

> Yesterday ... three notorious shoplifters were examined before Sir John Fielding, in Bow Street, and committed for further examination. ... it appeared by the account of an accomplice, who is admitted as evidence for the Crown, that these offenders ... have let few shops escape them, within London and Westminster, in the linendrapery, hosiery, mercery, haberdashery, millinery and jewellery way.[44]

Confirming this bias, we find shops with identifiable trades within the two samples were overwhelmingly stores selling textiles, haberdashery or clothing. In London these accounted for 69% of thefts (Table 8). The disproportionate victimisation of this sector is evident from Mui and Mui's functional analysis of London trade entries in the 1783 *Bailey's Directory*, which calculated that such retailers formed a mere 35% of all shops in the capital.[45] A further 16% of thefts were from food shops or those selling jewels or precious metal ware.

The same range of shop type was targeted in the north of England (Table 9) although these included a higher proportion of drapers and fewer clothes

41   See p. 23 above.
42   Mui and Mui, *Shops and Shopkeeping*, pp. 44, 295–7.
43   Ann Bennett, *Shops, Shambles and the Street Market: Retailing in Georgian Hull, 1770–1810* (Wetherby, 2005), pp. 35–6.
44   *Public Advertiser*, 3 March 1764, p. 3.
45   Mui and Mui, *Shops and Shopkeeping*, pp. 67–9.

Table 8. London shops targeted by shoplifters during four sample periods, 1743–1807

Type of shop	No. of cases	%
Linen draper, mercer, woollen draper	275	37
Clothes and shoe shops (hosier, glover, hatter, tailor, sale, slop, shoemaker)	175	23
Haberdasher, milliner	68	9
Food shops (cheesemonger, butcher, grocer etc.)	67	9
Goldsmith, silversmith, jeweller, watchmaker, toyshop	50	7
Ironmonger, broker	27	4
Other	85	11
Subtotal	747	100
Not given	187	
Total	934	

Source: London sample

Table 9. Northern shops targeted by shoplifters, 1726–1829

Type of shop	No. of cases	%
Linen draper, mercer, woollen draper	86	60
Haberdasher, milliner	14	10
Goldsmith, silversmith, jeweller, watchmaker, toyshop	9	6
Clothes and shoe shops (tailor, shoemaker)	7	5
Food shops (grocer)	3	2
Ironmonger, broker	2	1
Other	23	16
Subtotal	144	100
Not given	23	
Total	167	

Source: Northern sample

shops. This may in part reflect the fact that specialist shops such as glovers and hatters were less in evidence: Mary Orr's theft of ten pairs of gloves in 1819 was from a Whitehaven draper.[46] But probably of more significance to this finding were regional differences in sourcing clothes. Sir Frederick Eden, examining the domestic economy of the poor in the late eighteenth century, drew a distinction between the customary home-manufacturing of clothes in the north, and the standard purchasing of clothes from shops in the south.[47] This does not conclusively account for the lower figure of clothes shop thefts. John Styles has questioned Eden's distinction, contending that there was an extensive market for ready-made outer garments in the north at this time.[48] He does acknowledge, however, that this frequently operated on an informal basis. So whereas in London a high proportion of plebeian clothing was obtained second-hand from sale shops, in the north this trade would have been more frequently conducted outside the fixed shop network.

The geographical configuration of the crime in the north of England can be understood in large part by offenders' predilection for such merchandise. Economic development created a sufficient customer base to support the specialist shops such as linen drapers, mercers, haberdashers and jewellers that were a primary attraction for shoplifters. The close correlation between such shops and number of recorded incidents can be demonstrated by a comparison of York with Lancashire. Mui and Mui identified the latter county as populous but not yet urbanised in 1759, with a correspondingly low incidence of shops (one shop for every 90 people in contrast with a northern regional ratio of one shop for every 58 people), suggesting a limited number of specialist shops.[49] Not unexpectedly, few shoplifting cases were heard at the Lancaster assizes before the 1760s.[50] By contrast, the City of York with 486 shops assessed for Shop Tax in 1785, around a third of which specialised in cloth and clothing, recorded the highest number of cases in the period.[51]

When we turn our attention to London, we can trace the distribution of shoplifting more precisely than in the north. The information given in transcripts, supplemented by deposition evidence and early business directories enables us to pinpoint a street location for 63% of the shops in the 1743–54 sample, and 85%, 90% and 94% of those in the samples for 1765–74,

---

46   TNA, ASSI 45/52, Criminal Depositions and Case Papers, 30 March 1819, Mary Orr.

47   Sir Frederick Morton Eden, *The State of the Poor: or an History of the Labouring Classes in England*, 3 vols (London, 1797), vol. 1, pp. 554–5.

48   Styles, *Dress of the People*, p. 162.

49   Mui and Mui, *Shops and Shopkeeping*, pp. 41–2, 296.

50   Jon Stobart and Andrew Hann, in 'Retailing Revolution in the Eighteenth Century? Evidence from North-West England', *Business History* 46/2 (2004), 171–94 (p. 185), calculate that between 1760 and the 1790s the number of retailers in Liverpool increased from 132 to 891, and in Manchester from 162 to 737.

51   Mui and Mui, *Shops and Shopkeeping*, pp. 121–3.

1785–89 and 1805–07 respectively. It is clear from this plotting exercise that over the seventy-year span covered by the sample there were some radical changes in the set of streets most popular with shoplifters. Of London's two main east–west shopping arteries, the southern route of Cheapside, Fleet Street and the Strand lost precedence by the end of the century to the more northerly spur from Newgate Street and Holborn to the heavily raided Oxford Street. Forays in the 1740s into the elite shopping district around Covent Garden were supplanted from the 1780s by sorties on the shops of Piccadilly and St James but these remained only a tiny proportion of overall thefts. Incidents in the fashionable West End area south of Oxford Street were rare and by the end of the century the leisure shopping areas of the city, the Strand and Covent Garden had also visibly fallen out of favour with thieves. Particularly notable over time was the relentless spread of incidents northward and eastward to the fringes of the capital. This expansion reflects in part the greater opportunities for theft provided by the increasing extent and density of housing in the metropolis as aristocratic estates were developed and speculative building engrossed small settlements and farmland on London's borders.[52] With this new custom, shops proliferated in suburban back streets and specialist retailers expanded into the main thoroughfares of freshly populated neighbourhoods. By the first decade of the nineteenth century it is apparent from the location of incidents that many of these poorer and less fashionable northern and eastern neighbourhoods, namely Shoreditch, the area east of the Tower of London, and perennially Holborn and St Giles, had become some of the most popular haunts for shoplifters.

This situational evidence that shoplifters were operating predominantly in London's less prestigious areas is reinforced when we analyse the size and class of shops found in the sample. Visitors to eighteenth-century London wrote admiringly of its shopping streets, most notably Cheapside and the Strand earlier in the century, and later Oxford Street.[53] The capital's shops were lauded for their finery and, as consumer demand grew, many expanded into back and upper rooms or even adjoining premises to advance their market share.[54] Yet contemporary prints and directories suggest that it was common for even major shopping streets to retain a mixture of large and small businesses. The best indicator we have of the size spectrum of the shops included in the sample is their staff complement and constituency. An analysis of the information disclosed in court on staff numbers present at the time of the crime (Table 10) reveals that most shops targeted in London were, ostensibly, small family concerns. Even by the early nineteenth century, the majority of shops suffering

52   Jerry White, *London in the Eighteenth Century: A Great and Monstrous Thing* (London, 2012), pp. 68–76.
53   White, *London in the Eighteenth Century*, pp. 186–7.
54   Walsh, 'Shop Design and the Display of Goods', p. 32.

Table 10. Staffing size of London shops during four sample periods, 1743–1807

Size	1743–54		1765–74		1785–89		1805–07	
	No.	%	No.	%	No.	%	No.	%
Small *(Shopkeeper, sole or with spouse, and one or no members of staff)*	150	75	175	69	139	57	152	65
Medium *(Shopkeeper, sole or with spouse/partner, and two members of staff)*	11	5	28	11	35	14	19	8
Large *(Shopkeeper, sole or with spouse/partner, and three or more members of staff)*	1	1	3	1	16	7	10	4
Unknown *(Insufficient information given to reliably gauge staffing numbers)*	39	19	48	19	53	22	55	23
Total	201	100	254	100	243	100	236	100

Source: London sample

depredations were staffed by the owners alone or, at most, one employee. We do need to concede a potential undercounting of medium and large shops in this later sample. A high proportion of the shops recorded as having insufficient information on staffing in this period were drapers that had lost goods from external display, and drapers at this time were generally more heavily staffed than other stores. And certainly some thieves may have deliberately sought out larger concerns on occasions when they were understaffed, but the overall ratio is too striking for this to undermine the general conclusion.

These staffing figures are indicative because it is reasonable to infer an intuitive relationship between staff complement and store size. Many London shops were cramped by today's standards and would hardly accommodate more than a single shopkeeper. Martha Braithwaite's goldsmith shop, reconstructed by Claire Walsh from Chancery Masters' inventories, measured a mere 15 by 7 feet.[55] Conversely larger stores, in extended premises, could not function practicably without several shop assistants. Allowing that the staffing profile is a defensible surrogate for the physical size of the properties in the sample, we need to ask how representative their smaller size profile was of London shops generally during this period. In particular, how representative they were of those drapers and mercers predominantly targeted by London shoplifters. When seeking their preferred merchandise were shoplifters

55   Walsh, 'Shop Design and the Display of Goods', p. 161.

actively selecting smaller shops of the type? Unfortunately, the statistical
evidence available to answer this query effectively is limited. Assessments for
the Shop Tax in 1785 classified London's shops by rental value, with almost
half falling into higher rental categories of £25 to £305.[56] But we cannot
assume these were necessarily large shops. Rental values were as reflective
of the geographical location of the shop as its size, rents in the City and
Westminster being generally higher than in other areas of the metropolis.

A second source, however, is more promising. A report commissioned in
1797 by William Pitt to review the potential for raising further tax, categorised the shops of the metropolis into five assessment classes.[57] Shopkeepers'
tax assessments were largely contingent on two factors: the annual rent and
number of windows, this latter measure potentially having more relationship
to building size. The assessments were at ward or parish level but fortuitously
a few, more detailed, street-level reports survive for certain parishes, giving
a breakdown of assessed taxes by individual property.[58] Mui and Mui have
analysed these reports, revealing in the process the number of windows and
tax class typically pertaining to different shop trades.[59] Admittedly their study
is based on a small sample of the London-wide assessment and can therefore
only be indicative, but it shows a consistent relationship between the assessed
class of a shop and its size in terms of number of windows. Further, there is
a clear distinction in terms of shop type between the three lower assessment
classes, containing only 'petty shops' such as chandlers and slop shops, and
the two higher classes where we find the specialist shops including the drapers,
mercers and haberdashers favoured by shoplifters. While 69% of London
shops overall were placed in the three lower classes, the collectors of taxes
assigned 31% of shops to these two classes of generally larger stores. So while
most London shops were still small in 1797, those with a similar merchandise
profile to the shops in our sample in Table 8 were generally among the larger.
Though in no way conclusive, this finding suggests that, given the findings in
Table 10, our sample contains a somewhat smaller proportion of medium and
large shops than a statistically random sample of the same type of London
shop at this period would lead one to expect. It is consequently difficult to
avoid the conclusion that there was little tendency for shoplifters to seek out
the greater choice and range of goods that larger stores might offer. More
germane might be simpler shop layouts, fewer staff to observe attempted theft

---

56   Mui and Mui, *Shops and Shopkeeping*, p. 87. Shops with an annual rent below £5 were
excluded from the tax.
57   TNA, PRO 30/8/280, William Pitt, 1st Earl of Chatham, Papers, 2nd series, papers relating
to Revenue and Finance, fols 1–289, Schedules of houses & shops in London with their assessed
Taxes. The five tax assessment classes are: Class 1, 'under £1'; Class 2, '£1 to under £2'; Class 3,
'£2 to under £5'; Class 4, '£5 to under £10'; Class 5, '£10 to £20'.
58   TNA, PRO 30/8/281, William Pitt, Papers, Assessment papers.
59   Mui and Mui, *Shops and Shopkeeping*, pp. 111–16.

or perhaps unpretentious shops predominantly catering to a poorer customer base, where their presence would not arouse any unwonted suspicion.

Of course, we cannot assert this conclusion on the basis of shop size alone as there is no neat equation between size and class of shop. Martha Braithwaite's bijou shop was a high-class goldsmith while Flint and Palmer, a large, heavily staffed London Bridge draper's shop, is recorded as catering to 'customers ... of an inferior class'.[60] Firmer evidence that London shoplifters tended to eschew higher-class stores is provided by the 1797 assessments. Returns survive for the majority of wards and parishes in the metropolis, supplying an assessment class profile of the shops in each reported area which broadly reflects their relative wealth and retail status. Only 8% of shops within the north London parish of Clerkenwell were placed in the top two assessment classes (4 and 5) with one Collector representing this area as 'very poor shopkeepers scarcely able to live'.[61] By contrast, the fashionable West End parish of St Marylebone, containing much of Oxford Street, had 72% of its shops assessed at those higher levels. A comparison of these profiles with the geographical location of shoplifting cases in the two later samples, the dates of which bracket that of the assessment, is telling. Over 70% of the cases heard at the Old Bailey within these periods were located within the recorded wards and parishes.[62] The analysis of these cases by assessment class profile in Table 11 displays a clear statistical tendency for thieves to operate in areas with fewer prestigious shops.

But perhaps the most convincing evidence of shoplifters preferring less prestigious shops can be construed from some research on the London shopping habits of the elite. In an illuminating case study, Jon Stobart has analysed the spending patterns of the Honourable Mary Leigh (1736–1806), the daughter of a wealthy aristocratic family. For most of the period between 1750 and 1774 Leigh was a London resident and even later, when she became responsible for the family estates at Stoneleigh Abbey, she continued to patronise London suppliers. As clothing items comprised a major proportion of her expenditure, particularly in her earlier years, much of her purchasing was from the types of shop most popular with shoplifters.[63] However, the physical distribution of her retailers seems almost inversely related to that of retailers who suffered shoplifting incidents. Stobart has been able to geographically locate around half of Leigh's suppliers. Between

60   Robert Owen, *The Life of Robert Owen, Written by Himself* (London, 1857), p. 19.

61   TNA, PRO 30/8/280, William Pitt, Papers, fol. 139 (Collector, St James Clerkenwell Middle District).

62   Reports have not survived for three parishes in which 17% of shoplifting cases occurred: St Giles in the Fields (8%), St James (5%) and St Martin in the Fields (4%).

63   Jon Stobart, 'Status, Gender and Life Cycle in the Consumption Practices of the English Elite. The Case of Mary Leigh, 1736–1806', *Social History* 40/1 (2015), 82–103 (pp. 85–7).

Table 11. Tax class profile of London tax collection areas with reported shoplifting cases, 1785–89 and 1805–07

	No of Cases	% of Cases	Tax collection areas included
Tax collection areas with over 66% of shops in top assessment classes, 4 and 5	88	25%	St Marylebone, St Anne Soho, Cheap, St Paul Covent Garden, St George Hanover Square
Tax collection areas with between 33% and 66% of shops in top assessment classes, 4 and 5	120	35%	Farringdon, Bishopsgate, Portsoken, St Pancras, St Clement Danes, Aldgate, Langbourn, Aldersgate, Queenhithe, St George the Martyr
Tax collection areas with less than 33% of shops in top assessment classes, 4 and 5	137	40%	St Andrew Holborn, Shoreditch, St George in the East, Cripplegate, Whitechapel, Clerkenwell, St Luke Old Street, Wapping, East Smithfield, St Margaret Westminster, Tower Hamlets, Shadwell, Ratcliff, Norton Falgate, Christ Church Spitalfields, Islington, St Luke Chelsea, Bethnal Green
Total cases where tax collection area reported	345	100%	
Total cases in period	479		

Source: London sample, TNA, PRO 30/8/280, William Pitt, Papers

1750 and 1769 two-thirds of Leigh's expenditure was with retailers in the West End areas of the Strand, Covent Garden, Piccadilly, Grosvenor Square and Hanover Square.[64] Shops near her West End residence in Grosvenor Square furnished her with a wide range of goods including gloves, lace and millinery, and one of her key suppliers was a mercer in Henrietta Street, Covent Garden. Although the new shops in Oxford Street had a reputation for fashion, Leigh preferred to source dress materials from an established City firm. She continued to patronise suppliers in these same high-class shopping areas until her death in 1806. Leigh did have a major grocery supplier, Francis Field, on Holborn Hill, a hive of shoplifting, but grocers were almost immune from pillage. Only seven of seventy thefts from food shops were from grocers, shoplifters' customary targets being butchers, cheesemongers and chandlers. This geography of elite shopping in the capital is consonant with that of her

64   Stobart, 'Status, Gender and Life Cycle', pp. 92–6.

contemporary, Durham gentlewoman Judith Baker.[65] When in London, Baker shopped extensively in streets around Piccadilly, Hanover Square and Berkeley Square, including New Bond Street and Jermyn Street. So, while the dearth of shoplifting incidents in the fashionable West End area south of Oxford Street might lead one to conclude it contained few shops, this was clearly not the case. Rather, the prestigious shops here were consciously avoided by shop thieves. We can conjecture that shops such as those on Oxford Street that relied on a more passing trade, where an unfamiliar face would not be potentially suspect, were safer stalking grounds.[66]

The general tendency for shoplifters to target specialist shops, but predominantly in less prestigious neighbourhoods, significantly explains the developing spatial pattern of the crime, both in London and the north. But why should this pattern obtain? A principal answer relates closely to the nature of offending that we examined in the last chapter, most importantly that the majority of shoplifters in responding to economic circumstance were casual and opportunistic.

Criminologists have theorised that thieves will invariably operate within, or on the fringes of their 'awareness space', the geographical area that encompasses routes they are familiar with through their routine activities around home, work and entertainment. Crimes are more likely to be committed in those parts of an offender's awareness space where there are many targets and they feel safe. But time and distance deter, so shops closer to the potential offender's normal area of activity more readily become a target.[67] This will, to some extent, account for shoplifters' cleaving to shops and streets they patronised daily. But how true is it that the working populace of London operated in restricted local areas, those where they lived? Robert Shoemaker, in his examination of consistory court records and Old Bailey narratives for the hundred years prior to 1750, found that Londoners were rarely limited to the bounds of their parishes in their daily lives, with the poor being the most mobile.[68] He argued that this was particularly the case for women whose occupations, and generally short-term hiring, as nurses, washerwomen and servants required them to move between districts. So a high proportion of

---

65   Helen Berry, 'Prudent Luxury: The Metropolitan Tastes of Judith Baker, Durham Gentlewoman', in *Women and Urban Life in Eighteenth-Century England: 'on the Town'*, ed. R. Sweet and P. Lane (Aldershot, 2003), pp. 131–56 (pp. 146–8).

66   Dorothy Davis, *A History of Shopping* (London, 1966), pp. 196–7.

67   Patricia L. Brantingham and Paul J. Brantingham, 'Notes on the Geometry of Crime', in *Environmental Criminology*, ed. P. L. Brantingham and P. J. Brantingham (London, 1981), pp. 27–54 (pp. 30, 35, 42).

68   Robert Shoemaker, 'Gendered Spaces: Patterns of Mobility and Perceptions of London's Geography, 1660–1750', in *Imagining Early Modern London: Perceptions and Portrayals of the City from Stow to Strype, 1598–1720*, ed. J. F. Merritt (Cambridge, 2001), pp. 144–65 (pp. 156–9).

London shoplifters are likely to have had the geographical familiarity to venture farther afield. Even in northern England, stealing from local shops was not inevitable. Margaret Carr shunned the shops of her home town of Whitehaven to steal in the smaller town of Workington, 6 miles away.[69] Perhaps a major reason for choosing local shops was their convenience for personal reconnaissance, the process of evaluating a shop's contingent risk and attraction.

While all shoplifters targeted the same broad range of shops, there is a clear divergence between the tactics of the more professional and those of the general mass of casual shoplifters. Studying cases, it is apparent that the average offender stole repeatedly from the same, often local, shops. John Hawkesworth, shopman to an Aldgate haberdasher, explained in court how he had come to suspect servant, Anne Stafford:

> She came on the 18th of February, between seven and eight, to buy some blond lace. I shewed her a box, and she bought about as much as came to 1 s. by noon, after she was gone, we missed a card of blond lace; I was very sure I had not shewed any lace to any body but her, and was resolved to lay wait for her the next time she came; and on the Monday morning, the 23d of February, she came again much about the same time to buy some white ribbon; I shewed her some, and observed every parcel that lay in the drawer; the piece of white was in the corner next to her; it was missing. I charged her, and she was committed to the Poultry Compter; I went and confronted her with all these goods, after we had searched her box, and shewed her them; she confessed to all, and said she took them all in the shop; she did not say when, but we believe she took them from time to time; she has been an old customer.[70]

In small northern settlements with few shops it was almost inevitable that shoplifters would return to the same outlets. When prosecuted by a Yorkshire mercer for stealing camlet, stuff and tammy from his New Malton shop, Sarah Robinson confessed that 'at different times she hath stolen the goods ... out of the shop of the said Thomas Menell'.[71] Similarly Henry Wood, in a detailed confession, itemised how he had stolen two remnants of velveret from his local village store in Slaidburn and a week later had taken a length of yellow cotton from the same shop.[72] But this pattern was just as common in London where there was no such imperative. Perhaps the ultimate example

69 TNA, ASSI 45/52, Criminal Depositions and Case Papers, 2 June and 19 August 1819, Margaret Carr.

70 *OBP*, April 1767, Anne Stafford (t17670429-20).

71 TNA, ASSI 45/27/1/73, Criminal Depositions and Case Papers, 15 December 1762, Sarah Robinson.

72 TNA, ASSI 45/36/1/280, Criminal Depositions and Case Papers, 3 March 1787, Henry Wood.

of reckless theft to the extent of compulsion was Elizabeth Saunders' visits to a Smithfield oil shop. Three times in a single day she called at the shop for small items, a quartern of tea or halfpennyworth of sugar, and on each occasion pilfering a cake of soap from a pile in the shop.[73] This habitual practice of repeatedly thieving from the same shops may account for some shoplifters' pleadings. Anne Jones was caught stealing handkerchiefs from a milliner's shop in 1754. A witness reported that 'After she had acknowledged the robbery, she told Mrs. Vincent, that if she would forgive her, she would never come there again.'[74] Jones obviously expected this undertaking to carry weight.

What is remarkable about these cases is that the impulse to steal, most likely to allay need, was stronger than the desire to protect themselves through anonymity. These were individuals familiar to their local shopkeeper, who if not caught in the act would be subject to a growing suspicion, depleting their immunity. Catherine Saunders, whose husband worked for an auction house in the Strand and who confirmed in court that she lived in the same neighbourhood, was accused of stealing lace from Moses Leny's lace warehouse in Round Court, off the Strand. 'Saunders had been at my shop before, and I suspected her not to be honest', testified Anne Leny, 'she came in with the other prisoner on the 5th of May, and said she had brought me a new customer; I desired my servant to look sharp.'[75] Abraham Key was caught stealing from a butcher in Whitecross Street, the London back street where he had worked for the previous six years. John Tyler described how, having missed joints of meat from his shop, he left it untended and watched from a Yorkshire warehouse opposite, catching Key red-handed.[76] Another shoplifter was caught when she stole a pair of shoes from a Whitecross Street shoemaker, pawned it a few doors down and sold the ticket to a woman in an adjoining court.[77]

Casual theft was opportunistic. Occasional thieves were unlikely to have ready access to the networks of information relied on by those more established in the trade. For instance, Sarah Stear, who in 1752 turned Crown evidence, recalled that one of her associates, Elizabeth Bush, had initially alerted her sister and brother-in-law to their chosen target: 'there is a great hosier's shop facing Great St. Helen's; there is a great number of stockings by the side of the door'. For the Southwark-based Bush family this shop, directly north from London Bridge, offered ideal access and a safe escape route.[78]

73   OBP, April 1765, Elizabeth Saunders (t17650417-28).
74   OBP, January 1754, Anne Jones (t17540116-36).
75   OBP, June 1767, Catherine Saunders, Mary Gibbons (t17670603-1).
76   OBP, January 1769, Abraham Key (t17690112-35).
77   OBP, April 1805, Susannah Rands (t18050424-87).
78   OBP, June 1752, Martha Bush, Elizabeth Bush, Margaret Bush (t17520625-63).

Professional shoplifters certainly also revisited shops where they had had success, but with the benefit of such wider criminal intelligence. Hannah Mumford, the prolific shoplifter discussed earlier in this chapter, recorded in her deposition of November 1773:

> That in August last a day or two before Barnet Races this informant and Ann Chatham went to a linen drapers shop near Saint James Market where they took sixteen yards of printed linen ... That the next day they went together to the same shop and took twenty yards more of printed linen ... That the next day they went to the same shop and took forty-four yards of muslin.[79]

From the location of this and her other confessed thefts, it is clear that she and her criminal confederates actively avoided shops in their immediate neighbourhood where the risk of recognition was greatest. Though we are rarely given residence information for London shoplifters, circumstantial evidence given in her deposition, and that of other witnesses, suggests Mumford lived north of Holborn; her criminal contacts were located in the rookeries of St Giles and the infamous haunts around Chick Lane.[80] Yet all the shops she and her associates targeted were at some distance from these neighbourhoods, including several in the higher-class areas of Piccadilly, Bond Street and the City.

In contrast to the majority of defendants, career criminals manifestly took a degree of care to avoid detection. In March 1817 John Fowler and James Thirkill persuaded John Greenwood, a boy in the York Workhouse, to break curfew and accompany them to a hosier's shop in the centre of the city. Greenwood was instructed to distract the shopkeeper by asking for a pennyworth of worsted while Fowler, lurking near the entrance, helped himself to some handkerchiefs and Thirkill waited outside. It is likely that Thirkill and Fowler were already known to York shopkeepers. Unable to depend on the anonymity of distance in the smaller city, they employed other means to minimise identification. Fowler had bought a new coat before venturing into the shop and this was returned to the vendor with a demand for a refund the following morning.[81]

Finally in this chapter we might reflect on the city as an environment for

79 LMA, OB/SP/1773/12/006, Gaol Delivery Sessions, Hannah Mumford statement.
80 Between 1685 and 1745, trial accounts do regularly state a parish of residence for defendants, but this information is unreliable as it was routine practice for clerks in drawing up indictments to list the defendant's place of residence as the parish where the crime took place. Beattie, *Crime and the Courts*, pp. 21, 255; LMA, OB/SP/1773/12/006, Gaol Delivery Sessions, Hannah Mumford statement.
81 TNA, ASSI 45/50, Criminal Depositions and Case Papers, 1 March 1817, John Fowler, James Thirkill.

the crime. Whether stealing near to home or at a distance, shoplifters needed to be streetwise. Not only the geography but also the topography of their area of operation was a hazard to be negotiated. The breadth and narrowness, crowds and activity, mud, dirt and poorly defined carriage-ways and walkways of London's streets were the daily contingencies of crime. Pavement stall-holders, hackney coachmen and lamplighters featured among witnesses giving evidence against shoplifters. Street traffic was a mixed blessing. In New Bond Street Samuel Cooley melted into the morning crowd after stealing a case of mathematical instruments from Nicholas Meredith's shop; a neighbouring shopkeeper stated regretfully, 'I looked to see where he went, but could not, for the people who were walking backward and forward'.[82] But crowds could equally hamper a getaway. As the newly popular shops of Oxford Street became a magnet for shoplifters, their immediate paths of escape were the simpler grid patterns of the better-paved and less-peopled streets to the north. After stealing a bolt of cotton and linen check from David Peyton's shop in Oxford Street, Lewis Lang zigzagged in vain through the adjoining streets to throw off his pursuers, choosing the rapid passage across the open expanse of Cavendish Square rather than doubling back into the Oxford Street throng. These same crowds had prompted a foreign visitor to London three years earlier to comment, 'there are as many people along this street as at Frankfurt during the fair, not to mention the eternal stream of coaches'.[83] Easily spotted and caught, Lang was handed over to one of Westminster's patrol officers. Three months earlier he had been fortunate to escape a charge of stealing a pair of boots from outside a shop in Covent Garden. Discretion had perhaps driven him to operate in this new and unfamiliar hunting ground.[84]

Further east, the mass of courts and yards leading off London's older streets offered refuges for thieves and temporary hiding places for stolen goods. James Hammond was found in Bull Inn Alley off the Strand, James Brown was pursued to Vinegar Yard in St Giles and Charles Knight hid in Cecil Court off St Martin's Lane.[85] Having stolen four silk handkerchiefs from a Holborn shop, Ann Smith and Elizabeth Bayley were pursued down Drury Lane, along the Strand and into Fleet Street until finally stopped and found to have nothing on them. The goods were later traced to a pub yard in Ragged Staff Court at the top of Drury Lane where the pair had nimbly stowed

82   OBP, May 1788, Samuel Cooley (t17880507-9).
83   Sophie von la Roche, 'Sophie in London' 1786: Being the Diary of Sophie v la Roche, trans. Clare Williams (London, 1933), p. 142.
84   OBP, January 1789, Lewis Lang (t17890114-38); September 1788, Lewis Lang (t17880910-80); LMA, OB/SP/1788/09/071–072, Gaol Delivery Sessions, Information, Edward Davis, John Dore and Robert Frear v. Lewis Lang – stealing boots.
85   OBP, January 1750, James Hammond (t17500117-40); April 1749, James Brown (t17490411-26); February 1768, Charles Knight (t17680224-56).

them mid-chase.[86] Guarding against the hazards of running on London's muddy streets may also have been in their mind. When Ann Ross and Mary Sullivan were pursued from a Piccadilly linen draper to cries of 'stop thief', Ross smartly took up the cry herself to deflect attention to her partner, but then disaster struck. Susannah Smith, wife of the draper, recalled, 'It being a slippery day the prisoner Ann Ross slipped; I saw the print fall from under her; she had attempted to conceal it under her gown.'[87]

From region to conurbation to street, this chapter has examined the dimensions of the crime, assessing its scale of incidence and defining its geographical extent. Prosecution totals from the Old Bailey and assize courts indicate that the rate of shoplifting increased steeply over the course of the century. Yet projecting the extent of the crime from retailer and offender reports suggests that this grossly underestimates the crime's prevalence. The referral of cases to lower courts only marginally explains this discrepancy. A more important factor, this book contends, was retailers' reluctance to prosecute even detected crime, given the potential financial and reputational penalties to their business. Plotting where shoplifting occurred in London and the north reveals the significance for its geographical spread and patterning of the type of shop targeted and opportunistic nature of most shoplifting. An analysis of the types of shop in which shoplifters operated shows a tendency for thieves to actively seek out specialist shops dealing in textiles, clothes and haberdashery while avoiding the larger or more prestigious stores. A closer scrutiny of the size and class of shop principally victimised serves to endorse these findings. Predominantly drawn from plebeian backgrounds, shoplifters apparently chose smaller, more local shops as their main hunting grounds, suggesting that familiarity, lesser surveillance and lack of conspicuousness were primary considerations. Only a minority of more professional shoplifters are identified as deviating from this trend. Finally, the chapter looked at the impact of London's topography on the execution of the crime.

86 *OBP*, May 1786, Elizabeth Bayley, Ann Smith (t17860531-32); LMA, OB/SP/1786/05/037, Gaol Delivery Sessions, Information, Abraham Underdown, Jacob Freeman and Ann Clemments v. Ellizabeth Bailey and Ann Smith – stealing handkerchiefs.
87 *OBP*, December 1806, Ann Ross, Mary Sullivan (t18061203-49).

3

Shoplifting in Practice

For the shoplifting crew are so vigilant and dextrous and come under so
many disguises, that the tradesman cannot be too watchful, and in spight
of all their sharp-sighted servants, they are sometimes out-witted and
over-reach'd.[1]

Daniel Defoe, writing his early-eighteenth-century trade manual, had no
doubt that shoplifting was a battle of wits between shopkeeper and thief. In
this chapter we draw on the wealth of information found in contemporary
court transcripts to anatomise the tactics that shoplifters employed in order
to steal, and the measures store owners took to resist their incursions. To
better understand their respective stratagems and the dynamics of these
encounters we turn to an explanatory framework developed in modern criminology. Routine activity theory seeks to define criminal behaviour in terms
of the routines of the participants. It specifies that for a crime to occur there
needs to be an offender, a target and the absence of an effective guardian
against the crime. The target will be an object of high value to the thief:
visible, accessible and portable. The crime will occur in a place which has
a manager: for a shop, this will be the shopkeeper. Guardians, in the case of
shoplifting, may be shop staff, police or very commonly other shoppers and
the general public.[2] This theory provides a useful model for illuminating the
tactical manoeuvrings of eighteenth-century shoplifters and shopkeepers in
their competing struggle for advantage. Repeatedly we find the evidence from
the London and Northern sample cases endorses its validity for explaining
patterns of customer theft behaviour in this earlier period. So, first, how did
offenders identify the personal value and accessibility of their target object?

Planning the crime

While some thefts may have been on impulse, witness evidence suggests that
thieves commonly took great care to size up the risks and potential rewards

---

1   Daniel Defoe, *The Complete English Tradesman*, 3rd edn, vol. 1 (London, 1727–32), p. 402.
2   Marcus Felson, 'Preventing Retail Theft: An Application of Environmental Criminology',
Security Journal, 7 (1996), 71–5 (p. 72).

offered by individual shops. Birkhead Hitchcock noticed Thomas Smith 'pass and repass the shop two or three times', before stealing cloth from his open shop window, while Alexander White was spotted observing his chosen hosier's shop for an hour and a half.[3] Shop interiors were also thoroughly scouted to assess what was on offer and the ease with which it might be stolen. Linen draper John Humphreys watched Elizabeth Cole and Mary Johnson reconnoitre a number of Shoreditch shops in April 1786, describing to the court how he followed them from his own shop to a neighbouring haberdasher, before the pair elected to re-enter his store. One then distracted his staff while the other covertly slid a parcel of stockings under her cloak.[4]

Shoplifters contrived to choose a day and time that would minimise their chance of being detected or later identified. Sparsely patronised or staffed shops implied fewer potential observers, but an hour when the store was crowded and staff distracted might be more propitious, particularly if the lighting was poor. Linen draper John Thwaites was unaware that he had lost a length of brown linen until informed by the local justice. His shopman speculated, 'on the evening these were supposed to be stolen, we were busy, and I suppose it might be taken at the time the lamps were dull, and the shop was rather dark'.[5] Dusk provided an effective screen. Draper's apprentice Edward Clements was only able to swear to the identity of a shoplifter in court by reference to her distinctive dress, admitting, 'I did not see her face, because it was getting dark'.[6]

We know from a previous chapter that most theft was accomplished in the early evening, but was there a definitive weekly trend? In the north of England the busiest shopping day of the week was invariably Saturday, commonly a market day in urban settlements. An analysis of the days on which shoplifting incidents were perpetrated in the north clearly demonstrates this weekly bias (Chart 7). Markets drew in local customers and those from the immediate hinterland. In larger towns, they might attract consumers from an even wider geographical area, increasing the crowd cover for theft in a locus of high temptation. For example, in May 1764 Sarah and Mary Burgess, the wife and daughter of a husbandman, travelled 12 miles from the village of Etton to their nearest large centre, Kingston upon Hull, bypassing the smaller town of Beverley en route. Deposition evidence reveals that they visited both shops and stalls in the market and made some legitimate purchases, before being arrested for stealing a length of stuff from linen draper Edward Coulson.[7] By

3   OBP, February 1785, Thomas Smith (t17850223-88); May 1751, Alexander White (t17510523-18).

4   OBP, April 1786, Elizabeth Cole, Mary Johnson (t17860426-27).

5   OBP, June 1789, William Green, Charles Pinkstan (t17890603-30).

6   OBP, January 1807, Mary Crawley, Ann Bolton (t18070114-22).

7   TNA, ASSI 45/27/2/10–12, Criminal Depositions and Case Papers, 4 May 1764, Mary Burgess, Sarah Burgess.

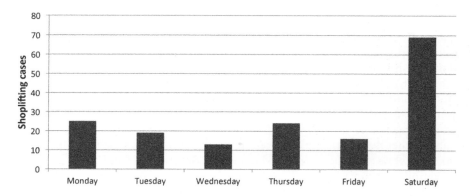

Chart 7. Days of the week on which the crime was perpetrated – Northern sample,
1726–1829
Source: Northern sample

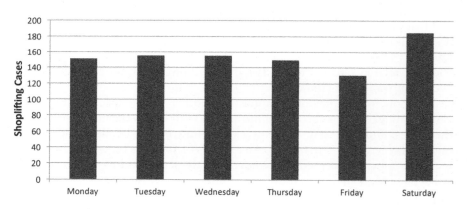

Chart 8. Days of the week on which the crime was perpetrated – London sample
periods, 1743–1807
Source: London sample

contrast, London shopping was not market-led as shops were plentiful and to
hand. Every street of any size had its shops and long trips to lay in stores were
unnecessary. The thousands of London residents could shop little and often,
and popular shops would be busy week-round. While Saturday was still the
most common day for thefts, its predominance was marginal (Chart 8).[8]

8   Sunday thefts were negligible, the combined sample recording none in the north and only
ten in London.

Table 12. Whether shoplifters engaged with staff

Level of Engagement	Male		Female		Total	
	No.	%	No.	%	No.	%
Engaged with staff	250	42	529	71	779	59
No engagement with staff	287	49	130	17	417	31
Not specified	52	9	86	12	138	10
Total number of defendants	589	100	745	100	1334	100

Source: Combined sample

In their approach to the crime, eighteenth-century shoplifters conventionally adopted one of two broad stratagems. There was the snatch raid, most often practised by men, where the game plan was to remove the goods without communicating with shop staff, either unobtrusively or by grabbing and fleeing the scene before staff could mobilise pursuit. The alternative was the stealth theft, in which the shoplifter simulated a customary shopping exchange, seeking to engage and distract staff while clandestinely taking, concealing and removing the stolen goods. This method was ostensibly more common, though the greater number of reported incidents could be indicative of its higher risk of capture (Table 12).

Only a minority of thefts were accomplished by men and women working together, and where this did happen they were often married couples or family groups. Hawker John Carroll, together with his wife and sister-in-law, shoplifted goods from two London drapers in 1765, and further north, husband and wife John and Jane Cook worked together in 1820 to steal doilies from a Scarborough mercer.[9] More commonly, thefts were carried out by men or women working alone or in same-sex groups, a practice enduring from the seventeenth century, a period for which Garthine Walker observed the same pattern in indictments for larceny.[10]

Accomplishing the theft

For the snatch thief, an empty but unlocked shop was an ideal opportunity. Small neighbourhood shops relied on a degree of trust to operate, where a

9 OBP, February 1765, Mary Carroll, John Carroll, Mary Carroll (t17650227-23); TNA, ASSI 45/53, Criminal Depositions and Case Papers, 27 March 1820, John Cook, Jane Cook.
10 Garthine Walker, *Crime, Gender and Social Order in Early Modern England* (Cambridge 2003), p. 172.

sole trader might leave his shop untended for brief periods while taking meals or visiting the courtyard privy. His regular clientele would know to avoid the shop at certain times, or be punctilious in alerting the shopkeeper on entering. Richard Marsh described in court how 'I went to an eating-house over-against my house, but I kept my eye upon my shop: I had left this piece of flowered lawn upon the counter, I saw somebody go into the shop pretty quick, I went over and took this piece of lawn upon the prisoner'.[11] Tailor John Sanderson of Howden was less vigilant, bemoaning how he had 'put a hat in his shop window about eleven o'clock in the morning and having occasion to leave his shop he did so and was absent but a few minutes and on his return he missed the hat'.[12] Thomas Griggs, already known in court as an old offender when convicted of stealing books from Thomas King's shop in 1747, claimed disingenuously, 'I knocked three or four times, could find nobody, and came out again from the shop'. King demurred, explaining he had been within earshot in an adjoining room.[13]

Small shops had vulnerabilities that shoplifters readily exploited, explaining in part their disproportionate attraction. A quarter of merchandise thefts where the shoplifters avoided engaging with staff were from temporarily untended shops. Apart from this obvious risk factor, another was the fact that many were still 'open' shops, having no permanent glazing. Whether sold through the window or merely exposed for view, goods on open display were prime targets for opportunist thieves. Prosecuting Daniel Williams in 1765 for stealing a ribbon, handkerchief and linen cap, Hannah Waites testified:

> I keep a cloaths shop in Field-lane; the things mentioned in the indictment were hanging on a line, on the inside of the window; the window was not glaz'd; two of the shutters were up, and two down; I was stooping down behind the counter, and heard the line break: I looked, and missed the things; I went to the door, and saw the prisoner looking at the cap, by the light of a candle at my neighbour's window[14]

Equally exposed were goods displayed on stalls, or 'on the bulk', an attribution used both for a counter board attached to the window opening or a wooden structure outside the store, an arrangement such as that described by Richard Carr, who lost fourteen pairs of worsted stockings in April 1743: 'I keep a publick-house at the sign of the Bell in Sidney-Alley, by Leicester-Fields, and sell stockings besides. – They lie out upon a place like a bulk

11   OBP, February 1744, Joseph Doody (t17440223-20).
12   TNA, ASSI 45/52, Criminal Depositions and Case Papers, 30 September 1818, John Bayley.
13   OBP, January 1747, Thomas Griggs (t17470116-17).
14   OBP, January 1765, Daniel Williams (t17650116-8).

under the window.'[15] In January 1754 the servant of a Fenchurch Street hosier related how he 'was within the shop, about two or three yards from the door. I saw a man's face, and two hands take a truss of stockings, as it stood on the bulk.'[16] Open windows and bulks, legacies of simpler shop styles from the sixteenth and seventeenth centuries, became rarer as the eighteenth century progressed and glass was increasingly affordable, even for small shopkeepers. However, while textile and clothes shops enthusiastically embraced new trends, many food shops preserved traditional methods into the nineteenth century and remained susceptible to snatch thefts (Plate 1).[17] Butcher John Mortimer's experience, losing a piece of mutton on a November evening in 1807, was typical. The meat was 'laying about a yard in the shop window, the window was open', he told the court, 'I heard some one run from the door; I looked out, I could not see who it was'. He later traced the thief, William West, to a public house.[18]

It should perhaps be noted here that even glazed windows were a magnet for snatch thieves; goods placed so near to the street offered easy access and rapid escape. So although a protection from the environment, glass was by no means a panacea against theft. At one Sessions alone in September 1785 the Old Bailey jury heard that Mary Moon had been seen at the window of Thomas Ham's linen draper's shop in Fleet Street before putting her hand round the door-frame to take an apron; of Ann Ravenhill's loss of nine silk handkerchiefs from her shop window, her shopman being at dinner when he saw someone run hastily down the steps; and how John Neale had looked through the glass of John Hubbard's shop window before taking off with two dead fowls that lay there.[19]

Given the stress that routine activity theory places on the importance of visibility and accessibility of merchandise to thieves, a late-century development played to their advantage. As competition increased, drapers in particular sought more effective ways of attracting the attention of the buying public. Window displays remained important but, in spite of the risk, doorways were also increasingly a site for exhibiting wares. Displays of goods started to creep outside the shop propped on stools, tables or chairs; nailed or hooked to door-posts; pinned or tied to window furniture, iron bars and rails (Plate 2). The argument of counsel for Elizabeth White, prosecuted for shoplifting in June 1785, hinged on whether the printed linen she let fall

15 Cox and Walsh, 'Their Shops are Dens', pp. 78–9; *OBP*, April 1743, James Guttery (t17430413-2).

16 *OBP*, January 1754, William James (t17540116-29).

17 Cox and Walsh, 'Their Shops are Dens', p. 79.

18 *OBP*, December 1807, William West (t18071202-11).

19 *OBP*, September 1785, Mary Moon (t17850914-180); September 1785, William Hayward (t17850914-25); September 1785, John Neale (t17850914-83).

Plate 1   *Monmouth Street Mutton*, 1798: butcher and second-hand clothes shop

from under her cloak by the shop door could have fallen from one of the
horses fastened on either side, through which a person might 'just steer clear'.
The shopman had no hesitation in dismissing such a ridiculous suggestion:
'We never put any such common goods on the horses, this was a linen, we
never put any on the horses but callicoes.'[20] Such external display of goods
had traditionally been the practice of clothes or sale shops (see Plate 1), but
for drapers to willingly expose their goods to the grime and dust of London
streets demonstrates the competitive pressure they felt themselves to be
under. This was particularly so in rising retail areas. Between 1805 and 1807,
two-thirds of the shoplifting cases instigated by Oxford Street stores involved
thefts from external displays.

Street display was, of course, a boon to shoplifters who could acquire a
wide range of goods without having to enter the more closely superintended
interior of the store. The high proportion of external thefts in the 1805–07
sample (Table 13) reflects this development in retail practice, and may even be
a contributory factor in the marked increase in prosecuted cases during this
period. This new practice even disturbed the judiciary. In 1806, trying a case

20   *OBP*, June 1785, Elizabeth White (t17850629-82).

Plate 2 *Charing Cross*, 1830 (detail): goods hung on rails outside and at the entrance to a linen draper's shop

Table 13. Location of goods in London shops at time of theft

Size	1743–54		1765–74		1785–89		1805–07	
	No.	%	No.	%	No.	%	No.	%
Counter	70	50	84	48	89	51	53	30
Other display area within shop	29	21	51	29	31	18	35	20
Window	30	21	26	15	33	19	21	12
Hanging outside shop/ on bulk or stall	11	8	13	8	21	12	68	38
Subtotal	140	100	174	100	174	100	177	100
Unspecified	61		80		69		59	
Total	201		254		243		236	

Source: London sample

brought by a Holborn linen draper, the judge remonstrated, 'If you choose to put your property at the door, so as to tempt these poor unfortunate creatures that walk the streets, it is your own fault; why do not you keep them within the shop as it was formerly.' The *Proceedings* fails to record the shopkeeper's response.[21]

Shoplifting techniques were adapted to these new developments. A lamplighter described in court how he had observed two women eyeing a piece of print fixed to an iron rail outside James Teasdale's draper's shop:

> the prisoner at the bar, and an elderly woman, were together, the elderly woman stood right fronting the door, and the prisoner stood on the left-hand side; they went away about twenty yards, and they had a little bit of discourse, … they came back again to the same place, and looked at the same print, and the prisoner at the bar unpinned it, and then went away about twenty yards again; they came back again to the same place, and looked at the same print they had unpinned; the elderly woman still kept her place towards the door, for a little while, and the prisoner at the bar snatched it off.[22]

Modern shop assistants would recognise the shoplifter who removes the tags from a rail of clothes before returning when the coast is clear to sweep them past security. Salesman William Haywood noticed two men lurking by his door and then saw one 'pull something out of his pocket, and cut the gaiters

21   *OBP*, January 1806, Mary Smith (t18060115-44).
22   *OBP*, January 1805, Martha Needham (t18050109-41).

Table 14. Location of goods in Northern shops at time of theft

Size	1726–89		1790–1829	
	No.	%	No.	%
Counter	10	29	33	61
Other display area within shop	7	21	8	15
Window	6	18	7	13
Hanging outside shop/on bulk or stall	11	32	6	11
Subtotal	34	100	54	100
Unspecified	44		35	
Total	78		89	

Source: Northern sample

from the door post; they were hanging on a nail'.[23] Four women taken with a piece of print stolen from the door of an Oxford Street linen draper were discovered to be carrying scissors.[24]

This tendency towards external display was not replicated in the north, where developments in marketing inevitably lagged behind those of the capital. We only have location details of the goods stolen for half the cases in the Northern sample but these indicate a reduction in thefts from external bulks and market stalls over the same period, as an increasing percentage of goods were sold from fixed shops (Table 14).

Although theft from the outer environs of a store was expedient, the interior offered shoplifters the promise of greater choice and more valuable pickings, albeit at the expense of somewhat higher performance skills. In August 1782 a warning on shoplifters' tactics appeared in *The Hue and Cry*, the nationally distributed monthly newspaper launched by Sir John Fielding in 1773 to foster the spread of criminal intelligence.[25] As with a series of previous alerts placed in the *Public Advertiser*, the article was intended to enlist both retailers and the general public in detecting and reducing crime:

> Their plan in SHOP LIFTING is nearly similar, there are generally two or three also concerned in this exploit, and frequently one of them is a female,

23   *OBP*, January 1807, James Barker, William Saunders (t18070114-47).
24   *OBP*, May 1805, Juliet Shaw, Johanna Bukk, Mary Howell, Mary Jones (t18050529-50).
25   John Styles, 'Sir John Fielding and the Problem of Criminal Investigation in Eighteenth-Century England', *Transactions of the Royal Historical Society*, 5th series, 33 (1983), 127–49 (p. 137).

Table 15. Whether shoplifters were accompanied or worked alone

Whether accompanied	Engaged staff		Did not engage staff		Unknown	
	No.	%	No.	%	No.	%
Worked with others	248	41	86	23	26	22
Worked alone	363	59	288	77	90	78
Total crimes	611	100	374	100	116	100

Source: Combined sample

in a cloak or cloathes adapted to the purpose of concealing the things to be stolen: where they observe a shop suited to their purpose, either from having so many buyers therein, as seem to keep the sellers busily employed, or from any other circumstance favourable to their design, they step in one after the other, seemingly unconnected, as chaps wanting to buy something, Mrs Dextress takes the first opportunity of placing herself next to the thing that lies most conveniently to be carried off, whilst the other or others, by pointing to, desiring to look at, and pricing goods in some other part of the shop, endeavour to draw all attention that way, till Mrs Dextress carries off the booty.

Therefore when a chap cheapens a variety of articles, and seems difficult to be pleased, and perhaps at length buys a trifling article of small value, and offers a piece of money, or a bill to be changed, in order to pay for it, then is the time for suspicion and a sharp lookout; if anything is miss'd, detain the suspected cheapeners, and quickly pursue the marcher off, get assistance and deliver them over to a constable to be carried before a magistrate[26]

While this description of shoplifters' modus operandi was not unfamiliar to London shopkeepers, the judiciary were primarily concerned with organised, professional shoplifting. It was in fact untrue that shoplifters routinely worked with others. Two-thirds of those in the sample (Table 15) acted alone and a proportion of the remainder may have been with companions unaware of their intentions, rather than complicit. Further, criminologists warn that statistics of the percentage of shoplifters working in groups can contain a positive bias as multiple offenders have a higher likelihood of being detected.[27]

Nevertheless, the higher proportion of those who worked as a team when the theft entailed engaging with shop staff, 41% to 23%, suggests that this

26   As reprinted in the *Newcastle Courant*, 3 August 1782, p. 1.
27   Lloyd W. Klemke, *The Sociology of Shoplifting: Boosters and Snitches Today* (Westport, 1992), p. 99.

arrangement had utility. It could be particularly effective in small, sparsely staffed shops. Daniel Defoe had indicated as much in 1727:

> For such is the slippery dealings of this age, especially in mercers and drapers business, that the shop-keeper ought never to turn his back towards his customers; and this is the reason why the mercers and drapers in particular are oblig'd to keep so many journeymen, and so many apprentices in their shops, which were it not for the danger of shop-lifting, would be a needless, as it is a heavy expence to them.[28]

And there is a clear synergy between the portrayal of shoplifting tactics in *The Hue and Cry* and the behaviours that shopkeepers chose to present in court as identifying and typifying offenders. Reading trial transcripts and depositions one swiftly concludes that shopkeepers were perpetually suspicious, although this trait might naturally be more prominent among the subset that succeeded in detecting and prosecuting shoplifters. Retailers were alert to shoppers who were 'difficult', who took an excessive time choosing or bargaining, asked for goods unlikely to be available, or displayed one of a raft of other well-recognised diversionary behaviours. Joseph Starky described how two boys came into his shop 'about candle-light' and 'asked for out of the way handkerchiefs; ... I immediately suspected that they were thieves. They asked for blue birds-eyes handkerchiefs, which, perhaps, are not to be found in one shop in fifty. They commonly ask for something that would puzzle one.'[29] Bargaining at too low a price was another danger signal. Covent Garden linen draper Ann Viguers was wary of the two women who asked to see some lawns: 'I shewed them several pieces; they bid me less than they cost me, and that made me suspect them'.[30] Bidding low could also conceal the fact that a shoplifter had no money – often taken by magistrates as conclusive proof of criminal intent. Mary Russel and Joyce Millam 'had not a farthing to buy anything with' when brought before the justice for stealing 4 yards of cotton.[31] Many shoplifters tried to defray such suspicion by stretching their resources to make a small legitimate purchase, but this needed to be plausible. 'They said they only wanted half a quarter of a yard', recalled Henry Pyrke, shopman to a Cheapside linen draper, 'Their asking for so small a quantity made me suspect them.'[32] When Catherine Henry asked Holborn draper John Mackey for a nail of lawn[33], she was told that it was not customary for him to cut so small a quantity, but suspicions had already been raised 'By her shuffling

28 Defoe, *The Complete English Tradesman*, p. 401.
29 *OBP*, December 1746, Edward Vaughan (t17461205-3).
30 *OBP*, October 1770, Elizabeth Clinch, Ann M'Daniel, Mary Brown (t17701024-2).
31 *OBP*, December 1746, Mary Russel, Joyce Millam (t17461205-20).
32 *OBP*, July 1770, Mary Salmon, Sarah Harris (t17700711-7).
33 A nail was a cloth measurement of a sixteenth of a yard or two and a quarter inches.

about the counter, and about her clothes.'[34] Three months later, another Holborn shopman was of similar mind when Ann Smith and Catherine Johnson 'tumbled the things over the counter more than generally is the case, and asked for a number of things from the poles, which induced me to turn round'.[35] Being asked to fetch goods from high shelves, inner rooms or the far end of the shop were all means of diverting staff attention.

Some retailers' suspicions could be psychologically astute. Modern observation studies have confirmed a key behavioural clue in detecting a shoplifter is their practice of scanning the store to spy potential observers and countermeasures, rather than concentrating on examining the merchandise.[36] A Fleet Street shopkeeper's wife testified how her husband 'called for a drawer of black lace; I immediately went out and handed it to him; the prisoner was talking about the lace, but looking at Mr. Pudner's face, that made me suspect that she was not an honest woman'.[37] Others relied on native shrewdness. George Scott, a North Shields shoemaker, suspected at once that Thomas Robinson intended to steal when he saw him leave his shop abruptly after overhearing Scott say he was going to South Shields that morning. Scott changed his plans, 'placed himself behind a screen in his ... shop', and two hours later did indeed catch Robinson red-handed, pocketing three pairs of his shoes.[38]

But we should also acknowledge that retailers could be quick to label, their attitudes coloured by stereotypical prejudices. Red cloaks were customarily the wear of the poor, so when butcher John Berry testified, 'I was backwards sitting by the fire ... My wife was in the yard, and said to me, what does that woman in a red cloak want in the shop?', he knew his wife's words to be freighted with meaning.[39] Appearance counted. A haberdasher related how 'the two prisoners came into my shop, and asked me if I had got any hats to sell, I did not like the looks of them, so told them I had none for them'; another shopman reported that two shoplifters 'bid me 20d. I said I could take no such price. They said they were poor girls, and could not afford to give any more. I did not like the appearance of the girls, so I took the handkerchiefs off the counter.'[40] By contrast, a Covent Garden linen draper admitted, 'the prisoners came into my shop about eight o'clock in the morning; they

34   OBP, January 1787, Catherine Henry (t17870110-27).
35   OBP, April 1787, Ann Smith, Catherine Johnson (t17870418-84).
36   Dean A. Dabney, Richard C. Hollinger and Laura Dugan, 'Who Actually Steals? A Study of Covertly Observed Shoplifters', Justice Quarterly 21/4 (2004), 693–728 (p. 709).
37   OBP, December 1787, Alice Haynes (t17871212-6).
38   TNA, ASSI 45/34/3/87, Criminal Depositions and Case Papers, 21 March 1782, Thomas Robinson.
39   OBP, February 1765, Eleanor Boyd (t17650227-12).
40   OBP, June 1753, Mary Perkins, Elizabeth Evans (t17530607-25); June 1769, Mary Kynaston (t17690628-40).

asked for a quarter of a yard of clear lawn. Hodges looked so neat, that I had no suspicions of her.'[41] Preconceptions of shoplifter character and behaviour could have proved self-fulfilling, accounting for a narrower profile of offenders before the courts than the true prevalence of the crime would warrant.

Performance

If plebeian shoplifters struggled to pass undetected in neighbourhood shops, their task was intensified in the higher-class shops of London's fashionable districts. In these stores, where appreciable transactions were conducted on credit, a customer's perceived worth was of the essence. In an age of competitive social mobility, such retailers found themselves serving an expanding but increasingly anonymous clientele. Presumed status and social connections guided an owner's judgement of which shoppers to welcome through their door.[42] So we shall now take a short diversion from our examination of the routines of the majority of offenders to consider those few who employed dress and performance to achieve their ends. To some extent any shopping expedition in which the outward comportment was that of the authentic shopper, while the true purpose was to procure goods illegitimately, could be described a performance. However, these self-fashioners embraced the highest stakes and promised gains by masquerading as the middling sort or by simulating connections to the elite. Class was a blind spot in retailers' security awareness. Shopkeepers had been raised in a society that viewed criminality as primarily a moral failing and moral weakness as essentially a characteristic of the poor.[43] They were also perennially anxious to nurture and preserve relationships with middling and elite customers, on whose continued patronage their turnover primarily depended. Plebeian shop thieves knew that if they could appear genteel then suspicion would be allayed, defences lowered and they could shop inconspicuously in fashionable shops which purveyed the finest goods.

Such tactics were particularly advantageous in the theft of items from jewellery shops, their wares being almost by definition beyond the reach of plebeian shoppers. William Williamson, who in July 1773 stole a pair of diamond earrings from George Farquharson, a jeweller in the Strand, was described as dressed in sky blue with a showy embroidered waistcoat. A second jeweller, targeted by Williamson three days later, confessed that 'being

41   OBP, September 1770, Theodosia Hodges, Harriot Matthews (t17700912-86).
42   Craig Muldrew, The Economy of Obligation: The Culture of Credit and Social Relations in Early Modern England (London, 1998), pp. 149, 166; Margot C. Finn, The Character of Credit: Personal Debt in English Culture, 1740–1914 (Cambridge, 2003), p. 47.
43   Beattie, Policing and Punishment, p. 51.

a man of a genteel appearance I had no suspicion of him'.[44] It also eased disposal. Thomas Ford played up his background when attempting to dispose of a watch stolen from a City shop, telling pawnbroker John Piercy that he was a member of Lord Portmore's household. Discretion overcame Piercy's suspicions:

> I said, I think it is very odd your ambition should induce you to wear a gold watch? and asked him what he was, but he did not care to satisfy me in that particular; so I did not press him. He was actually very genteely dressed, as any man could well be.[45]

Claire Walsh highlights the theatricality of shops and a select few rose to this challenge, adapting their creative talents to this stage.[46] Mary Cummins played the role of Mrs Forbes, a Winchester milliner, flawlessly when she presented herself at Robert Dyde's shop on New Year's Day, 1787. His large Pall Mall haberdashery, shortly to reach its stylish apotheosis under the new ownership of Messrs. Harding Howell & Co (see Plate 3), was accustomed to act as a wholesaler for country shopkeepers.[47] One of his staff even thought that he remembered her from the previous year. Cummins happily maintained her front for an hour and a half, picking out a consignment of £60–£70 worth of goods that she knew would never see delivery. As Dyde later said, 'she passed entirely, and acted in looking out the goods, as a woman that knew business exceeding well'. As shop staff fetched samples from around the store, Cummins methodically secreted a card of lace and eight separate pieces of ribbon about her person.[48]

Alice Trueman, a sailor's wife from Ratcliff Cross, adopted the guise of Mrs Jemmit, the wife of a Fleet Street grocer, who being virtually housebound in the final weeks of pregnancy was unlikely to appear and undermine her alibi. Visiting shops across the capital, she ordered goods to be sent to the Jemmit home with bills to be settled on receipt. Giving evidence, the wife of one Newgate Street linen draper described how 'she agreed for two pair of sheets and many other articles; she behaved very much like a gentlewoman; I asked her, if she would go backwards and drink a dish of tea'. This classic ritual of client hospitality extended Trueman's visit in the shop to two hours. One might speculate whether her gratification extended beyond the 16 yards of muslin she

44   OBP, September 1773, William Williamson (t17730908-7).
45   OBP, July 1745, Thomas Ford (t17450710-19).
46   Walsh, 'Shops, Shopping, and the Art of Decision Making', pp. 157–8.
47   Kathryn A. Morrison, English Shops and Shopping: an Architectural History (New Haven and London, 2003), pp. 39–40.
48   OBP, January 1787, Mary Cummins (t17870112-2); LMA, OB/SP/1787/01/039, Gaol Delivery Sessions, Information, Robert Dyde, Isaac Smith and Thomas Richardson v. Mary Cummings – stealing ribbon.

managed to purloin; whether in an age of societal ambition there was pleasure in enjoying the privileges of middling society for those two hours.[49]

Certainly in a later case we can sense, reading between the lines of witness testimony, a certain relish in acting out a pastiche of middling manners. Two trials heard in 1783 afford us an insight on the June day that Mary Hill, Sarah King and William Richardson spent shoplifting in some of Covent Garden's more select stores.[50] They had prepared meticulously and, as the Old Bailey jury heard a year later, their appearance was far from that they presented in the dock: 'They had their hair just-dressed; and had large hoops on, one was in pink silk; they were in quite a different stile to what they are now; Richardson had a blue coat, round hat, and a pair of boots.' Clad in the high fashion of the day, they sought to blend seamlessly with other polite shoppers in the Piazza. But although they had taken care to dress the part, they could not entirely suppress their plebeian manners. 'I thought they were strange people, because they called me my dear, in a very sociable way', the shop assistant testified. Nevertheless this odd manner perhaps accounted for one shopman's vivid recall of the defendants' conversation:

> I shewed her [King] several pieces; she then made choice of this sattin striped, which I have here, and asked the prisoner Richardson if he liked it, he said, if she liked it he did, the prisoner Hill said to Richardson, I hope you do not think anything of the expence of a gown for your wife, the striped silk was for King; Richardson said, he did not mind anything about the expence; ... Hill observed to King, will not you have something to line it with; she said she would, and desired to look at some white persian, which I shewed her, she desired me to cut off a yard and a half; I then observed to her, that was a small quantity; she turned round to the other woman and said, she would have a yard and three quarters, she always liked to have enough and to spare; Hill said to Richardson, you will pay for it, Richardson answered he would, but was prevented by King's saying, no, my dear, you shall not pay for it, I will pay for it, for you will not have enough money where you are going; they did not mention where they were going; King and Hill asked Richardson if he would go with them, he then said, he would go any where with them provided they did not go to a milliner's. shop, they said, they would not; I then said to Richardson, Sir, you seem to have a dislike to go to a milliner's shop, he said, he had, for there was so much trouble in trying on caps and such like.

This was a discourse echoing that of Frances Burney's comedy, *The Witlings*, written three years earlier. The first act is set unconventionally in a milliner's shop which, as Deidre Shauna Lynch has observed, lampoons the discomfort

49 *OBP*, January 1751, Alice Trueman (t17510116-71).
50 *OBP*, July 1783, Mary Hill, Sarah King, William Richardson (t17830723-3 and t17830723-4).

of the polite male characters at finding themselves within this 'zone of female mysteries'.[51]

Hill, King and Richardson were representatives of a band of more enterprising and probably more worldly-wise professional shoplifters who specialised in stealing from the larger fashionable stores. Higher stakes required higher investment. Mary Arbin and Sarah Young who stole from John Fisher's Mayfair store, described as 'two genteel young women' by a witness, were seen alighting from a coach before entering the shop.[52] Ann Wheeler, accused with Elizabeth Barnsley of stealing from a Bond Street linen draper, wore a fur-trimmed white silk cloak, a very large muff and told the shop staff who detained her that 'she was acquainted with Lady Spencer, that she was a customer at the shop, and had frequently come with her servants'. Barnsley had paid for some small purchases with a £10 note.[53] Sarah Lister and Jane Williams stole lace from the private room of a New Bond Street lace dealer, a room, the retailer conceded, 'we seldom admit any body into, unless we know them, or unless they are people of fashion'.[54] Where these women acquired their apparent familiarity with fashionable society is unclear. There is a suggestion from transportation memoirs and clemency petitions that Barnsley and her husband may have once aspired to a more respectable class, even though she boasted of her highwayman ancestors and he was at that time on the *Ceres* prison hulk in the Thames awaiting transportation for theft.[55] Others could have seen service in elite households in their youth. And they had access to the theatre, where farces such as *High Life below Stairs* depicted servants emulating their masters.[56] Even those who could not afford the cheaper gallery seats of the London playhouses might attend summer performances at London fairs.[57]

With the theft by Mary Wilson, Mary Morgan and Elizabeth Walker from a large Pall Mall shop in 1805, we see again the creative facility with which these plebeian shoplifters credibly situated themselves within elite society:

The prisoner Mary Morgan came into our shop and asked if I had a bonnet that would suit the old woman, the prisoner Wilson, she called her nurse.

51   Frances Burney, 'The Witlings', in *The Witlings and the Woman-Hater*, ed. Peter Sabor and Geoffrey Sill (Peterborough, Ontario, 2005), pp. 43–172; Lynch, 'Counter Publics', p. 225.
52   *OBP*, July 1787, Mary Arbin, Sarah Young (t17870711-39).
53   *OBP*, February 1788, Ann Wheeler, Elizabeth Barnsley (t17880227-54).
54   *OBP*, September 1798, Sarah Lister, Jane Williams (t17980912-68).
55   Sian Rees, *The Floating Brothel: the Extraordinary True Story of an Eighteenth-Century Ship and its Cargo of Female Convicts* (London, 2001), pp. 70, 97.
56   James Townley, *High Life below Stairs: a Farce of Two Acts* (London, 1759).
57   Lisa A. Freeman, *Character's Theater: Genre and Identity on the Eighteenth-Century English Stage* (Philadelphia, 2002), pp. 3–4; Benjamin Heller, 'The 'Mene Peuple' and the Polite Spectator: The Individual in the Crowd at Eighteenth-Century London Fairs', *Past and Present*, 208 (2010), 131–57 (pp. 142, 153).

... I hesitated for a moment; then the old woman, the nurse as she called her, Wilson, stepped forward and said it is for me ma'am. I said we have nothing of the kind that will suit you, for we never keep old ladies bonnets that is so plain as yours; Morgan said the fact is, my lady has sent nurse (calling Wilson the nurse) in the country for these last three months with the children, which was the reason she had not been before to order the bonnet; she said the lady wished nurse to look very nice.[58]

There were, of course, occasions when the performance failed. Elizabeth Needham, who was prosecuted for stealing two pairs of silk stockings from John Archer's Mayfair store, allowed her imagination to run to fantasy in spinning a story of her connections to the household of the Royal governess. Even after being rumbled by Archer, 'she said, she was servant to a perfumer in Bond-street, the corner of Bruton-street; there was no perfumer there I told her; then she said the corner of Grafton-street; I said there was no perfumer there', she continued to reiterate her story, ultimately as her defence in court.[59] And Margaret Bucknell and her companion had their efforts to simulate a higher class undone by the effects of alcohol. Asked in court if they were intoxicated, the shopwoman replied: 'It appeared to me so', but identified them as 'very genteel people'. A local manufacturer, who spotted them after they left the shop and had them taken up on suspicion, recalled 'she was apparently very well-dressed; she being very much intoxicated, abused the passengers as they went along; it attracted my attention, seeing a woman so well dressed, and so very abusive'.[60]

The eighteenth-century public associated theatre with the subversion of class roles and some performance was perhaps entirely malicious, a form of power play to delight in outwitting the shopkeeper.[61] In 1822, Matthew Renwick, a Newcastle linen draper, prosecuted two shoplifters, Sarah Rishton and Margaret Davison. He related:

that as the prisoners were leaving the shop, the prisoner Margaret Davison addressed herself to this informant, and pointing to the prisoner Sarah Rishton, said 'I have brought my mistress past all the shops, all the way from the Quayside to your shop' or words to that effect and under the impression that that they had bought something, informant thanked Margaret Davison and they went away.[62]

---

58   OBP, December 1805, Mary Wilson, Mary Morgan, Elizabeth Walker (t18051204-3).
59   OBP, July 1786, Elizabeth Needham (t17860719-15).
60   OBP, May 1805, Margaret Bucknell (t18050529-2).
61   White, London in the Eighteenth Century, pp. 309–10.
62   TNA, ASSI 45/55, Criminal Depositions and Case Papers, 21 November 1821, Sarah Rishton, Margaret Davison.

Such behaviour could be a form of agency, of exacting revenge within a social order that perpetually segregated those whom the shopkeeper would invite into their parlour and ply with tea, and those who would be automatically excluded from such middling niceties.

Removing the stolen goods

However they accomplished their theft, shoplifters shared a common problem, namely the unobtrusive removal of the stolen goods from the shop. It was now that another important factor in the routine of the shoplifter came into play: the portability of the desired object. Most made use of their person by transforming themselves into walking storage systems. In 72% of thefts, the stolen goods were concealed within or beneath clothing (Table 16). Pockets, aprons, petticoats and cloaks provided quick and convenient hiding places for goods picked off counters or plucked from window displays. This manoeuvre was simpler for women who customarily wore capacious tie-on pockets, hidden beneath their outer gown but accessible through placket holes.[63] They also had aprons, which could be looped up to carry goods, and floor-length petticoats under which prizes could be shuffled. Even when fashions became more svelte with the late-century adoption of the Empire line, inventiveness prevailed. A linen draper detaining Catherine MacNalty in 1806 observed,

> we took notice she appeared very pregnant we asked her if she was pregnant, she said yes; we took her into a little back room, the constable searched her, we found eight shawls in each pocket, she had drawn the shawls in her pockets before her, it appeared as if she was pregnant.[64]

Dedicated shoplifters customised their clothes. Ann Jones had a hook beneath her apron to hold the linen remnants she had stolen; draper Matthew Bell's printed cotton was fastened by ties under Ann Cuthbert's petticoats; Hannah Stevens had 'two pockets almost as big as sacks'.[65] When watchmaker Richard Howard suspected a customer of stealing he got him to strip and 'found my watch in a little pocket, seemingly made on purpose to conceal things in, at the bottom of one of the hind lappets of his waistcoat'.[66]

---

63   Barbara Burman and Seth Denbo, *Pockets of History: the Secret Life of an Everyday Object* (Bath, 2007), p. 19.
64   *OBP*, September 1806, Catherine MacNalty (t18060917-18).
65   *OBP*, April 1745, Ann Jones (t17450424-23); February 1748, Ann Cuthbert, Mary King (t17480224-8); July 1807, Hannah Stevens (t18070701-56).
66   *OBP*, May 1766, William Bletsley (t17660514-2).

Table 16. How stolen goods were removed from shop

Mode of removal	London		North		Total	
	No.	%	No.	%	No.	%
Under clothes	499	72	62	69	561	72
Carried openly	164	24	10	11	174	22
In basket/bag	16	2	15	17	31	4
Other	11	2	3	3	14	2
Subtotal	690	100	90	100	780	100
Not given	244		77		321	
Total crimes	934		167		1101	

Source: Combined sample

Men could successfully conceal small items in trouser pockets or under jackets, but whereas women employed cloaks to hide larger items, held underarm, men would be obliged to carry such items openly. They would hope their presence on the street would be dismissed as simply a porters' errand, and those detained commonly sought to explain away their possession of the goods as such.[67] Often the only practical way of transporting the astonishingly sized lengths of cloth stolen was underarm. Mary Ann Matthews, who managed to convey 70 yards of printed cotton from Taylor Courtman's shop in 1747, and Dorcas Talbot, who took 60 yards of printed calico in 1788, are just two of many who stole fabric lengths of 25 yards and upwards in one visit.[68] Admittedly eighteenth-century bolts were generally narrower than those of today and some textiles could be fine.[69] John Greenfield, asked in court how 100 yards of linen handkerchief pieces could have been stolen from his shop undetected, responded 'They will lie in a little room; I have pieces of handkerchiefs that cost ten guineas a-piece; you may put two pieces of them in one pocket.'[70] But more common textiles would have been heavy and bulky, straining to escape. The shopman who stopped Talbot in the street outside his store stated, 'I saw the callico hanging below her cloak, so far below it as to discover the pattern of it'.

67   For instance, *OBP*, September 1769, Abraham Peters (t17690906-53); April 1807, Richard Green, James Britten (t18070408-58).
68   *OBP*, December 1747, Mary Ann Matthews (t17471209-15); June 1788, Dorcas Talbot (t17880625-18).
69   Cottons, linens and worsted stuffs were generally produced in yard widths. Woollen broadcloths were the exception at 2–3 yards wide.
70   *OBP*, February 1765, Mary Carroll, John Carroll, Mary Carroll (t17650227-23).

Although routine, there were practical difficulties in insinuating an item
of any size beneath clothing, particularly if, as normally the case with cloth
or clothing, it was soft or textured. In fact, many shoplifting cases reflect the
frequency of failure, where an errant corner of material or length of lace was
spied protruding from its hiding place. Elizabeth Medows attempted to stow
26 yards of printed cotton while sitting at Edward Eyre's counter, but as the
shopman passed her he observed, 'part of a piece of printed cotton; about
eight inches of the selvidge lay upon the floor uncovered at her left side, the rest
of it was under her petticoats'.[71] A bulge under clothing or any awkwardness
in movement was equally suspicious. Mary Page who stole 16 yards of muslin
was seen walking 'as if she had some incumbrance about her', while Elizabeth
Jones, who had also taken muslin, stepped 'somewhat singularly; she could
not walk, but shuffled along'.[72] And there were some peculiar risks to hiding
goods underneath clothes. When caught, Elizabeth Ross quietly dropped to
the floor the muslin she had concealed in her stays but was betrayed by the
fact it was still warm from her body.[73] Inappropriate dressing could also be
a giveaway. Mary Miller wore a red cloak when she attempted to steal from
a linen draper in the Strand in August 1771; the shopkeeper recalled how he
'took hold of it and said, how can you wear so large a cloak so hot a day;
lifting up her cloak there was a piece of lawn under her left arm'.[74]

In spite of these drawbacks to clothing, it was rare in London for
shoplifters to conceal goods in external bags or baskets. In the north of
England 17% of cases involved the use of these receptacles. While this may
have been reflective of northern shopping practice, particularly of the market
shopping which is associated with many of the thefts, it is hard to believe
that London housewives did not carry baskets when provisioning. However,
this distinction is visibly reflected in late-eighteenth-century images; those of
rural market women show them bearing baskets, while the women in London
street scenes do not. The explanation is likely to be the ease of shopping in
the metropolis, fostering a custom of regular small-scale purchasing for which
large receptacles would be unnecessary.

How shopkeepers protected themselves

As 'place managers', retailers shouldered the burden of theft-proofing
their shops to prevent financial loss. They operationally responded to the

71   *OBP*, October 1751, Elizabeth Medows (t17511016-24).
72   *OBP*, July 1787, Mary Page (t17870711-66); October 1787, Elizabeth Jones, Elizabeth
Cummins (t17871024-21).
73   *OBP*, May 1766, Elizabeth Ross (t17660514-3).
74   *OBP*, September 1771, Mary Miller, Ann Dupere (t17710911-18).

experienced or perceived shoplifting threat by physically adapting their premises and enhancing store surveillance. In keeping with the principles of what is now termed 'situational' crime prevention, they sought to deter thieves by enhancing the risk of identification and capture.

Small, intermittently staffed shops were protected by fitting door-entry bells and glass spy-panels between shop and living quarters. John Fielding, always ready to pronounce on such matters, advised in 1757 that 'If a bell fastened to a spring, and made so as to take on and off, were to be fixed in the evening to the shop doors, it would give timely notice to the persons within, who are seldom farther distant than in a back parlour or counting house.'[75] Mary Furnas was sitting in the 'back shop or apartment' of her small Cumbrian store when 'hearing the tinkle of the bell at the front shop door she … immediately went into her … front shop and saw a woman standing with the door about half shut in her hand'. The opportune alert foiled Ann Gregg's escape from the shop with two stolen handkerchief pieces.[76] Pell Stutter of Wapping dock similarly recounted in court how he safeguarded his goods:

> I am a mercer. Yesterday morning between eight and nine o' clock, the prisoner comes into the shop; I have backward a pane of glass that commands my shop, and I saw the fellow look about him, and I think he gave a little knock with his finger, to find, I suppose, if any body was nigh, and immediately he whips up three yards and a half of damask, and he carries it out; thinks I I'll be after you presently; I ran after him, and catches him by the collar, and brought him back to the shop-door.[77]

Goods were monitored and displayed in ways that would instantly expose any loss. Goldsmith's wife Elizabeth Rooker told the court how their gold rings were kept on hooks on a velvet-covered board, as 'by that means we can presently perceive if any are missing', and shoemaker's wife Mary McPearson immediately spotted that a pair of her shoes had been taken as 'we always lay a pair to each pane of glass'.[78] Thomas Hobbs recognised that a card of lace had gone from his window as 'I have lost so much goods lately out of my shop, that I always desired my wife and shop-woman to count them'.[79]

The eighteenth century was an exhilarating time for the shop trade in London. Increased supply of imported and manufactured goods matched by demand for novelty and variety encouraged retail expansion. Higher-class

75 *Public Advertiser*, 26 January 1757, p. 2.
76 TNA, ASSI 45/33/1/54, Criminal Depositions and Case Papers, 15 February 1777, Ann Gregg.
77 *OBP*, September 1747, John Williams (t17470909-10).
78 *OBP*, February 1767, Susanna Hatfield (t17670218-48); May 1765, Daniel Wing (t17650522-10).
79 *OBP*, February 1785, Elizabeth Chapman (t17850223-83).

stores installed plate-glass windows and competed for custom by expanding sales areas and enhancing their general ambience with improved lighting, decor and fittings.[80] While it is unclear to what extent smaller shops followed suit, retailers who did have the means and enterprise to invest in shop improvements found these provided a perhaps unforeseen security bonus. New brighter patent Argand oil lamps, replacing candles, reduced the susceptibility of evening opening; decorative mirrors, placed behind the counter for customers to view purchases or simply to magnify the ambient lighting effect, gave staff eyes in the back of their head; and separate shop areas, divided by glass panels, enabled staff to keep an eye on, or isolate, suspicious customers (Plate 3). Thomas Ashby's Holborn drapery was divided into three 'shops'. A shopman described to the court the defendants' arrival at the store: 'they came into the front shop, and in consequence of there being a customer there, they were asked into the second shop'.[81] As the only customers in this shop when 20 yards of muslin went missing, they were irrefutably implicated.

Wooden counters protected stock, their bulk and positioning acting as a barrier to the removal of goods from the drawers or shelves behind. Mary Ann Forbes, a New Bond Street milliner who lost over £14 worth of goods to shoplifters, turned her counter round and abutted it to a wall for additional security after the theft.[82] Statistically the most vulnerable site for shop theft (Table 13), counters were increasingly enclosed and only accessible by negotiating a flap and gate entry. Such precautions were, however, in constant conflict with the customary practice of placing or leaving goods on the counter for marketing display. Shopkeeper Thomas Berry acknowledged this pregnability: 'The two Prisoners at the bar, Elizabeth Mitchel and Eleanor Conner came into my shop, they came to the further End of my compter, which at that time was very much tumbled with goods.'[83] John Greenfield, whose handkerchiefs were stacked chest-high on the counter of his Fleet Street linen drapers, claimed his view of the defendants' theft had been blocked by 'the piles of handkerchiefs that were between us'.[84]

While statistically less of a magnet for theft than the counter, the window and exterior of the shop were still significant areas of vulnerability. Hosier James Shannon entertained the court with his account of how he had attempted to introduce an early version of the loop system, explaining 'I was very desirous to set some of these thieves, for if we make a show in our windows, these people will take them away'. Having placed a parcel of

---

80   Walsh, 'Shop Design and the Display of Goods', pp. 166–7; Cox and Walsh, 'Their Shops are Dens', pp. 90–6.

81   OBP, January 1788, Sarah Roberts, Sarah Wilson, Mary Simpson (t17880109-32).

82   OBP, April 1783, Elizabeth Read (t17830430-48).

83   OBP, December 1746, Elizabeth Mitchel, Eleanor Conner (t17461205-5).

84   OBP, February 1765, Mary Carroll, John Carroll, Mary Carroll (t17650227-23).

Plate 3 *Messrs. Harding Howell & Co.: 89 Pall Mall*, 1809: shop fitting of a large linen drapers with separate shop areas divided by glass panels; counters are shown with goods on display

stockings in his window, he continued, he had 'tied a string to the parcel, and the other end of the string I had fastened to the bolt that fastens down into the threshold of the door'. He was soon gratified by his enterprise when he saw James Dollanson creep towards the door, grab the parcel, and be pulled up short by the attached cord.[85] When this episode appeared in *The Gazetteer* at the time of the arrest, Shannon was reported as reluctant to print details of his mechanical trap but 'very willing, for the general good, to shew it to any fellow sufferer, or any other person who may want to catch shoplifters, against whom it is almost impossible to be guarded, they being the most dangerous enemies to shopkeepers in general'.[86]

Goods displayed outside stores were frequently tied or pinned, although as we have seen this offered little protection from shoplifters armed with cutting equipment. Some shopkeepers did take elementary precautions. Cross-examined as to whether it was the custom of his shop to expose goods outdoors, the shopman of a City linen draper responded, 'Not after candle light.'[87] However, many West End streets were famed for their evening shopping. Foreign visitor Sophie von la Roche recorded in her 1786 diary

85 OBP, January 1768, Mary Anthony, Anne Claxton and James Dollanson (t17680114-24).
86 *The Gazetteer and New Daily Advertiser*, 15 December 1767, p. 2.
87 OBP, December 1806, Thomas Wright (t18061203-24).

entry: 'We strolled up and down lovely Oxford Street this evening, for some goods look more attractive by artificial light. Just imagine, dear children, a street taking half an hour to cover from end to end, with double rows of brightly shining lamps.'[88] Oxford Street stores would hardly wish to limit their displays after dusk. And true to expectation, a witness reported how he came across two men outside an Oxford Street haberdashery at half-past five on a November evening: 'I heard one say to the other, these things stand very easy to be taken away, now is the time to take them; the prisoner then jumped upon the thing at the door, and got the petticoat from the place where it hung; it hung in the door-way'.[89] Perhaps goods consciously exposed to the contamination of pollutants and weather had already been discounted from stock.

Marking goods was another method that could add some protection. It made goods less easily disposable. Dealer Anne Fare related how Elizabeth Bates had tried to sell her the fourteen pairs of children's worsted stockings that she had just stolen from a neighbouring hosier's shop. Suspecting they were stolen, Fare tried to detain her, but 'in the mean time she tore the mark off, and went into Mr Wilson's to pawn them'.[90] It also ensured that the ownership of any goods that were stolen could be proved in court and the goods returned. Marking the size, value and provenance of textiles and haber-dashery items to assist pricing was common from early in the century and almost ubiquitous by the end. Marks could be written on the items themselves but were more usually pieces of paper, sometimes referred to as tickets, attached by pins. In 1748 Susannah Urwin was charged with stealing cloth from William Portall's shop after his servant 'saw the ticket of the piece of lawn hang lower than her cloak'.[91] When Edward Gibbons lost a counterpane from his shop in 1788, he explained to the court how he knew it to be his:

> There was a mark on the paper that is torn out; I do not know it by the counterpane, but by the paper; there was a mark of the prime cost in letters, and also there was a small mark signifying the size of the counterpane, the one mark is entirely torn away, in the other there is a small part left.[92]

Although juries predominantly found in the prosecutor's favour, there was always the danger that unlabelled goods could undermine a prosecution. The court reporter in a 1793 shoplifting case tersely accounted for the defendant's acquittal: 'The shawl produced and deposed to, as the same that was taken

88   von la Roche, 'Sophie in London', p. 141.
89   OBP, December 1805, James Taylor (t18051204-28).
90   OBP, October 1747, Elizabeth Bates (t17471014-22).
91   OBP, April 1748, Susannah Urwin (t17480420-37).
92   OBP, December 1788, Moses Harris, Jacob Solomon (t17881210-16).

from the woman, but not having any private mark on it, the prosecutor could not swear to it.'[93]

So, who next were the 'guardians' that reinforced shopkeepers' efforts, and whose girding to the task was a constant mission for John Fielding? Staff alertness and surveillance was a crucial factor in the battle against shop thieves. To some extent this was exercised through careful and constant attendance, such as that described by Thomas Harrison, a linen draper's clerk:

> they came into our shop, and asked to look at some prints; I shewed them some, which they did not want; I had two other customers with me, I attended them also between whiles, when I gave the prisoners a second description of pieces to look at, which they had wished for, ... they did not seem satisfied, and immediately went to the door without buying any thing, and so hastily, that I followed them, to prevail on them to return;[94]

But commonly it was more deliberate. Isaac Malleson, suspecting a customer in 1741, related how he 'rapp'd with the yard on the counter for one of my servants to come down, and bid him go into the back shop to tie up some Irish cloth, at the same time giving him the wink to observe the motions of the prisoners'.[95] And as the century progressed, court cases increasingly mention the use of protocols and code words to alert colleagues. James Hennessey recalled that when he spotted Lydia Kenelly stealing from his employer in 1783, he 'cried, Devonshire, a word we use when we suspect anybody; then the people were all on their guard' and Edward Bowerbank testified that his shopman 'called to me for change, which I understood to be a signal or mark of suspicion'.[96] Certainly employers expected their staff to play this role effectively. 'What a careless young man you are,' one London hosier reprimanded his apprentice, on finding that he had failed to observe Elizabeth Needham stealing a pair of stockings from under his nose.[97]

It was particularly problematic for shopkeepers and their staff to give the shop floor their full attention when they had to attend to a routine flow of paperwork. In the eighteenth-century shop all receipts, credit sales and future orders were hand-written and recorded in day books and ledgers. There was also regular business correspondence. Joseph Golding, distracted writing a delivery note, described a close encounter in his ironmonger's shop:

---

93   *OBP*, February 1793, Adelard Hart (t17930220-76).
94   *OBP*, December 1788, Ann Clapton, Charlotte Marsh (t17881210-84).
95   *OBP*, February 1741, Ann King, Elizabeth Arm (t17410225-59).
96   *OBP*, September 1785, Lydia Kenelly (t17850914-40); December 1788, Ann Clapton, Charlotte Marsh (t17881210-83).
97   *OBP*, July 1786, Elizabeth Needham (t17860719-15).

I went to breakfast, and returned at ten, when I returned the prisoner was in the shop, I went to the desk, I then observed his hand over this parcel ... and I believe he saw me notice it, he drew his hand from the parcel, I then began to finish the direction I had began writing, but before I had finished I turned my head again, and he had hold of this parcel with his right hand, he took it, and I saw him put it into his pocket.[98]

Shopkeepers did periodically refer in their evidence to their having left an employee in the shop when they were occupied in their counting house or with business matters, but it was nevertheless a weak point.

Beyond the shop, retailers provided mutual support in their desire to protect their sector. Many cases coming to court disclose that shoplifters had initially been detected by neighbouring tradesmen who had then alerted the victim. Advantaged by the close proximity of shops in narrow urban streets, business solidarity and neighbourhood spirit trumped competitive rivalry. Shoplifter Elizabeth Smith failed to appreciate the risk presented by two Newcastle linen drapers being sited opposite one another. His staff having spied Smith whip something off the counter of the shop across the road, draper Joseph Alderson related that he had crossed the street, retrieved the black silk handkerchiefs she had dropped to the ground, and handed them to the proprietor John Verty.[99] Some shopkeepers went to exceptional lengths to serve the common interest. Thomas Ham, a Fleet Street linen draper, admitted in 1771 that he had trailed two of his customers that he suspected were shoplifters for three hours, through fifteen shops, eventually catching them half a mile away stealing 52 yards of muslin from a fellow draper in Ludgate Street.[100]

Even longer distances were seemingly no obstacle to such vigilantism. When John Higginbottom, 'a young man in the hosiery branch', spotted two boys looking through his South Moulton Street shop window in February 1787, he 'observed to a Mr. Dunn, that these were pickpockets, or shop-lifters'. He proceeded to follow them and a third associate for up to a mile on a circuitous route north of Oxford Street, noting their passing interest in the window of haberdasher James Hartshorn in Wigmore Street. Eventually he saw two of the boys enter Wigley and Bishop's hosiery store in Great Portland Street and one emerge with something under his coat. Not content with simply alerting the shopkeeper he then pursued and caught the culprits, retraced their steps to where they had dropped the stolen goods, and returned triumphant to the store (Map 1).[101]

98   OBP, July 1786, Thomas Burgess (t17860719-53).
99   TNA, ASSI 45/35/3/180, Criminal Depositions and Case Papers, 12 June 1786, Elizabeth Smith.
100 OBP, September 1771, Mary Jones, Ann Styles (t17710911-32).
101 OBP, February 1787, Thomas Wood, Thomas Riley, John Molloy (t17870221-38).

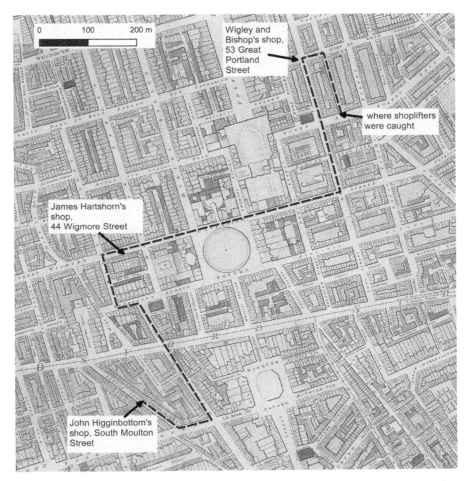

Map 1   Route taken by John Higginbottom when tailing the shoplifters Wood, Riley and Molloy, February 1787

While shopkeepers individually and collectively took every step within their means to guard their stores, they also found strong allies among the general public. Eighteenth-century shoppers and passers-by seemingly had little of today's detachment, their actions demonstrably indicating that they acknowledged the legitimacy of larceny laws. Trial reports and depositions repeatedly record instances of fellow customers alerting shop staff to observed theft, and not necessarily where they had an established relationship with the store. Robbed in 1783, draper Ralph Steel told the Old Bailey courtroom:

the first alarm that I heard was, I heard a gentlewoman that was in the shop say, why madam, you came into buy one cloak, how came you to steal another; the prisoner made no reply; but I instantly cast my eyes upon her, and the gentlewoman whom I saw pulling something from under the prisoner's petticoats, I did not know the gentlewoman.[102]

Customers often intervened fearlessly in their sense of outrage at such transgressing. Jane Clark was conversing with Newcastle linen draper Robert Oliver's wife when two men arrived next to her at the counter and asked to see some handkerchiefs. She related how she then

saw the prisoner William Campbell take the end of one of the pieces and hold it up, as if to examine it, and it was held in such a situation as to be between Mrs Oliver and the prisoner John Stewart, that while he was so holding up the piece, this informant distinctly saw the prisoner John Stewart in a hasty manner take up some of the pieces of silk handkerchiefs and put them into an inside pocket of his coat.

So incensed was Clark that when Robert Oliver was alerted to the ruse and preparing to search Stewart, Jane Clark pre-empted him and 'put her hand into his right hand inside pocket and pulled out three pieces of silk handkerchiefs'.[103]

There were instances of thefts being casually thwarted by the intelligence of passing foot and coach traffic or by the observation of neighbours, watching from their houses. Clearly a sense of community often prevailed. In January 1766, innkeeper Thomas Bramwell 'heard there were three or four men in the street, and it was imagined they were upon no good design'. He immediately left his pub and monitored the intruders' movements, his intervention foiling the theft of a ham from a neighbouring cheesemonger.[104] Many shoplifters who managed to leave the shop were chased and captured by the public on the street. There was long-standing legal duty for any member of the public observing the committal of a felony to apprehend the offender, although it seems unlikely that the individuals that did so were driven by a sense of legal obligation.[105] Nevertheless, the old tradition of 'hue and cry', while rarely invoked in the eighteenth century, may help to explain the alacrity with which the public responded to a shout of 'Stop, thief!'.[106]

102   OBP, February 1783, Elizabeth Hart (t17830226-15).
103   TNA, ASSI 45/54, Criminal Depositions and Case Papers, 16 July 1821, John Stewart, William Campbell.
104   OBP, February 1766, William Penson (t17660219-1).
105   Spencer Perceval, The Duties and Powers of Public Officers and Private Persons with Respect to Violations of the Public Peace (London, 1792), p. 8.
106   Shoemaker, The London Mob, p. 29.

Another incentive might have been the occasional reward on offer. In January 1756, following a local crime alarm, the St Clement Danes Vestry publicly advertised a two-guinea reward for the capture of any shoplifter.[107] In fact the passivity with which many escaping shoplifters returned to the store when requested by shop staff can be explained in part by their awareness that the alternative would be mob pursuit and capture. Although Shoemaker suggests that the public's willingness to assist in the chase and arrest of suspects declined after mid-century as voluntary participation in local watch and constable rotas became less common, there is scant evidence of this in the case of shoplifting.[108] When witness Charles Elliott described John Goldwell's shopman as being 'among the mob' chasing a shoplifter in 1789, he estimated it comprising two to three dozen people.[109] As late as 1807 a shopkeeper's wife declared, 'Being in a public situation, an hundred people came to my assistance. The man made no resistance, he came back with me.'[110] A public fascination with the crime was expressed in the huge crowds recorded as gathering around stores when a shoplifter was apprehended. Thomas Corp returned to his shop in 1748 to find 'there were thirty or forty people about the door; they said there was a shoplifter, and desired I would not hang her'.[111] And when William Williams was caught and brought back to Andrew Paterson's shop door, his assistant recalled how 'Master did not chuse to have a mob in the shop, so he desired he might be carried to an alehouse.'[112]

Naturally a sample of prosecuted cases is liable to contain a bias towards those in which the voluntary participation of the public produced a positive outcome. Occasionally we do get a hint that such willingness was not universal. John Goldby testified in 1745, 'I saw the prisoner take a white quilted petticoat off a post at the door, put it into her apron … I let her go because I was afraid of bringing myself into trouble'. Only when he spotted the thief for a second time three weeks later, did he alert shopkeeper Elizabeth Abbott.[113] Shoplifters' retorts on being stopped by the public also imply their expectation that disinterest would govern most people's behaviour. Ann Warring, selling fruit at the door of a Holborn linen draper, repeated how she challenged Margaret Carter as she emerged from the shop with stolen linen: 'I said to her, you have got more than your due; says she, does it belong to you, and be d—nd to you'; and in 1805 James Lane testified, 'I saw the prisoner take the piece of calico from the form which stood at the door; … I went after

107 *Public Advertiser*, 17 January 1756, p. 2.
108 Shoemaker, *The London Mob*, pp. 46–7.
109 *OBP*, April 1789, Maria Israel (t17890422-69).
110 *OBP*, February 1807, John Robinson (t18070218-28).
111 *OBP*, February 1748, Elizabeth Owen (t17480224-14).
112 *OBP*, January 1750, William Williams (t17500117-21).
113 *OBP*, January 1745, Frances Jones (t17450116-14).

him immediately, and asked him what he was about; he answered me, what is that to you'.[114] Hence, linen draper James Andrew's experience in 1807 was perhaps more common than the many examples of popular participation would lead us to believe. He disappointedly recounted how, after following two suspected shoplifters from his shop to that of a neighbouring furrier, he failed to secure both:

> the prisoner and another woman ... came out of the shop, I fell back towards St. Paul's church yard, I followed them but a few steps before I saw the end of the tippet hanging down between her legs, I ran after her and caught hold of it and pulled it down, and down came another along with it. I immediately got hold of her arm, I said you have stole the tippets. I called to several gentlemen going past to stop the other person, they did not.[115]

Even where a member of the public was potentially willing to assist in detaining a thief he might be bought off. Much as shoplifters sought to gain their liberty by compounding with retailers, they were also prepared to bargain with casual witnesses. A carpenter, passing by Simon Emanuel's shop as George Rainsforth took a coat and two pairs of stays from the doorway, testified to their exchange: 'I said to him, my friend, you have soon bargained for your lot; he said he had, did I see him; I told him I did; he asked me if I would go halves with him'.[116]

One prominent modern guardian, the police service, was only emerging in rudimentary form during the eighteenth century. Parish-appointed constables and night watches did little to prevent customer crime. Only towards the end of the century did shopkeepers begin to benefit from the increasing street presence of police patrols, particularly in protecting external displays. Concerns over public gatherings in the 1790s had led to increases in the numbers of constables hired in London and by the early nineteenth century many London parishes were organising day as well as evening patrols of their streets.[117] The parishes of St Marylebone, St James Piccadilly and St George Hanover Square covering Oxford Street and the west of London were some of the best equipped.[118] Mary Duff was found guilty of stealing from linen draper John Brookes in May 1805, her captor testifying, 'I am an officer of Marlborough-street: About five o'clock in the afternoon, I was going up

114   OBP, September 1753, Ann Jones, Margaret Carter (t17530906-23); September 1805, John Lemont (t18050918-102).

115   OBP, April 1807, Rosey Lovett (t18070408-15).

116   OBP, December 1805, George Rainsforth (t18051204-40).

117   Andrew T. Harris, *Policing the City: Crime and Legal Authority in London 1780–1840* (Columbus, 2004), pp. 59, 75.

118   Elaine Reynolds, *Before the Bobbies: The Night Watch and Police Reform in Metropolitan London, 1720–1830* (Basingstoke, 1998), p. 95.

Great Russell-street, and saw the prisoner at the bar take these handkerchiefs from the hook at the door, she was in company with another woman; I
pursued them, and took the prisoner'.[119] In similar fashion, Bow Street patrol
Edward Crocker arrested Juliet Shaw and her two companions when he saw
her steal a length of printed cotton from the door of a Holborn linen draper
the following winter.[120]

This chapter has examined how shoplifters planned and executed their
thefts and how shopkeepers, with the assistance of the public and to a lesser
extent judicial authorities and police, endeavoured to frustrate them. It
asserts that with an eye to both personal safety and likely pickings, customer
thieves were drawn to certain shops, times of the day and, in the north, a
particular day of the week; their opportunistic thefts from unstaffed and open
shops, bulks and stalls explaining some of the bias towards smaller shops in
prosecutions. Contrary to public perception, most shoplifters worked alone,
some choosing to engage with staff while others simply snatched goods from
shop displays. Statistically, the former tactic was more popular with women,
and also more common among those working in groups, accomplices often
playing a crucial role in distracting staff attention from the act of thieving,
their subterfuge again easier to achieve in less-staffed or busier shops. An
element of performance was desirable and, it is suggested, even necessary for
the few who preyed on higher-class stores. Faced with this persistent threat,
the chapter contends that shopkeepers did not simply rely on prosecution to
deter shoplifters, but used a range of situational techniques to protect their
goods and enhance the risk to thieves of detection. These comprised both
physical measures, including doorbells, spyholes, mirrors and lighting, and
practices such as the marking and counting of goods. Staff were trained to
be alert to potential thieves, although retailers' perception of likely offenders
could be stereotypical. And while court testimony indicates that traders
were mutually supportive, the wider endorsement of the legitimacy of their
action is demonstrated by repeated evidence of the willing participation of
customers and many members of the general public in the apprehending of
perpetrators.

119 *OBP*, May 1805, Mary Duff (t18050529-67).
120 *OBP*, January 1806, Mary Dow, Mary Jones, Juliet Shaw (t18060115-46).

4

What was Stolen

From fabrics to flat irons, shoplifters systematically sought items they valued. But did they privilege the same items that appealed to their middling and elite peers? Their choice can be of particular interest to historians who continue to debate what has been termed one of the conundrums of eighteenth-century consumption: how far down the social scale did the new goods and expanded consumption opportunities extend.[1] By examining what items shoplifters stole we can observe whether their 'alternative' mode of consumption played a part in distributing novel and fashionable goods more widely throughout the eighteenth-century population. If, as some economic historians have suggested, the working incomes of the poor remained at too low a level for them to meaningfully participate in the century's reputed consumer boom, did shoplifting serve an enabling function?[2]

However, suggesting that the crime brought unaffordable goods within financial reach begs a further and perhaps more interesting question: how actively did the poor avail themselves of this opportunity to acquire stylish attire and home embellishments? Historians have speculated that over the course of the century an appetite for consumer goods animated all levels of society. Jan de Vries has proposed that the desire for new home comforts was strong enough to encourage a greater industriousness in working households.[3] Beverly Lemire has also been prominent in affirming the importance of fashion to such communities, albeit in a more democratised and popular guise. She contends that demand for this was widely met by the second-hand trade, supplied in part by shop theft, and asserts that 'legal records abound with vivid depictions of the selectivity of ... shoplifters, who in turn reflect the preferences of the wider market for stylish clothes'.[4] But how sound is this conclusion? In its specific targeting of retail outlets, shoplifting was intriguingly different from other property theft. While burglars, housebreakers and pickpockets can rarely anticipate the exact content of their haul, this was a

1   Sara Horrell, Jane Humphries and Ken Sneath, 'Consumption Conundrums Unravelled', *Economic History Review* 68/3 (2015), 830–57 (p. 831).
2   See Introduction, pp. 8–9.
3   de Vries, *Industrious Revolution*.
4   Lemire, 'Peddling Fashion', p. 77.

type of thieving in which perpetrators could very deliberately take their pick from the same range of new manufactured and imported goods on display to better-off shoppers. It therefore offers us a unique opportunity to test the enthusiasm with which the poor sought to participate in the period's famed consumer revolution.

In this chapter we analyse in detail the type and range of goods stolen and look at the means employed by shoplifters to dispose of their gains. Through this mechanism we can gain insights into the rationale of the crime and develop an understanding of how the circumstances of the thieves operated to influence and determine their choice of goods. As we saw in the last chapter, practical issues such as accessibility and portability were certainly a factor but, in weighing up what to steal, shoplifters were primarily motivated by exchange value. It is apparent from the data that, of goods taken, very little was actually kept by the perpetrator of the crime. Admittedly we cannot be sure what percentage of these goods was destined for plebeian consumption. It is probable a proportion (and perhaps particularly of the more valuable silks, lace and silver) were sold informally to middling consumers. But evidence points for the most part to goods being converted or consumed within the thieves' own communities. As an item's remunerative potential was paramount to the thieves, the demand for fashion clearly figured in their calculation. Patterned cottons, silk handkerchiefs and coloured ribbons were regularly included in their haul, reflecting the degree to which such styles and accoutrements had become an established part of plebeian wear.[5] But if we define fashion as that which is most novel or in vogue, it appears less influential. Rarely do we observe the desire to chase high fashion, and only a proportion of goods stolen can be identified as the vanguard of plebeian style. In practice, much of what was taken reflects a residual conservatism of taste, implying a more contingent approach to exploiting the new consumer opportunities that shop theft might offer. As we shall come to see, shoplifters favoured those goods that were in greatest demand, less conspicuous and most easily negotiable in the communities to which they belonged. These requisites governed shoplifters' selection of fabric, clothing and haberdashery, food and household goods. Well-versed in the intricate social and economic relations that underpinned neighbourhood survival, they fed their spoils into formal and informal markets chiefly predicated on satisfying the pragmatic needs of daily living.

We start with an overview of what shoplifters stole. The combined sample records 1,030 separate items taken.[6] These have been divided by type into six main categories for analysis. Before examining the significance of the theft of these discrete types of goods, let us take a broad look at their preferences,

---

5 Beverly Lemire, 'Second-hand Beaux and "Red-armed Belles": Conflict and the Creation of Fashions in England c.1660–1800', *Continuity and Change* 15/3 (2000), 391–417.
6 Multiples of the same item taken in a theft are counted as one item.

Table 17. Types of goods stolen in London shoplifting cases during four sample periods, 1743–1807*

Type	1743–54		1765–74		1785–88		1805–07		All	
	No.	%	No.	%	No.	%	No.	%	No.	%
Cloth	56	27	62	24	72	29	81	34	271	29
Clothing	73	36	89	34	102	41	83	35	347	36
Haberdashery	24	12	26	10	16	7	9	4	75	8
Food	22	11	29	11	22	9	31	13	104	11
Jewellery/silver/toys	15	7	38	14	13	5	3	1	69	7
Household goods	14	7	16	6	16	6	20	8	66	7
Other	1	0	3	1	8	3	11	5	23	2
Total	205	100	263	100	249	100	238	100	955	100

Source: London sample

* This and succeeding tables in the chapter record the number of cases which fit the designated column and row criteria. In the vast majority of cases the goods stolen were of a single type and the defendants of a single gender. However, there are a very small number of cases in the sample, where defendants were tried for stealing more than one type of good, or type of material, or where the case involved both male and female defendants working jointly. Hence the totals given can vary between tables and may exceed the number of recorded crimes in the sample.

identifying differences between London and the north, changes over time and the extent to which gender had a bearing on choice. It is immediately apparent which goods were most attractive to shoplifters: textiles and clothing were overwhelmingly the most popular target. In London, these consistently accounted for around two-thirds of thefts throughout the period (Table 17). This dominance of clothing was not unique to shoplifting. It shows some co-relation with a large-scale study by Sara Horrell, Jane Humphries and Ken Sneath of items stolen in housebreaking and burglary during the period where clothing represented 42% of all items stolen. However, as we shall see, there were distinct differences in the individual types of clothing favoured by each crime.[7] Thefts of food remained constant at around one in ten, while those of haberdashery steadily decreased. The proportion of jewellery, silverware and toys stolen fluctuated over the course of the eighteenth century, but

7 Sara Horrell, Jane Humphries, and Ken Sneath, 'Cupidity and Crime: Consumption as Revealed by Insights from the Old Bailey Records of Thefts in the Eighteenth and Nineteenth Centuries', in *Large Databases in Economic History: Research Methods and Case Studies*, ed. M. Casson and N. Hashimzade (Abingdon, 2013), pp. 246–67 (pp. 254, 259).

Table 18. Types of goods stolen in Northern shoplifting cases, 1726–1829

Type	1726–89		1790–1829		All	
	No.	%	No.	%	No.	%
Cloth	50	60	35	38	85	49
Clothing	12	15	34	37	46	26
Haberdashery	6	7	12	13	18	10
Food	0	0	1	1	1	1
Jewellery/silver/toys	11	14	7	8	18	10
Household goods	2	2	2	2	4	2
Other	2	2	1	1	3	2
Total	83	100	92	100	175	100

Source: Northern sample

had diminished to insignificance by 1805. There was also a slow but steady increase in the percentage of thefts of household goods. In the north of England, cloth and clothing similarly dominated, comprising three-quarters of thefts (Table 18). Higher in the early period, the percentage of cloth thefts steadily converged with those of clothing, probably a consequence of the increasing sale of the latter from fixed retail outlets.

While similar numbers of men and women were indicted for shoplifting, there were marked differences in the types of goods they favoured. Contemporary print literature on crime already acknowledged this, if not entirely accurately:

> These Shoplifters have different provinces; the ladies are visitants of the linen-draper, mercer, haberdasher and laceman; … The men's business lies amongst lace shops, jewellers, and silversmiths; cloths, linens &c. being too cumbersome for their conveyance.[8]

However, an analysis of the gender distribution of thefts reveals a division that broadly conforms to this observation (Table 19). Cloth and haberdashery were predominantly stolen by women, and food, jewellery, silverware and toys, and household goods by men. Clothing was taken by both sexes in equal proportion. That women should primarily steal textiles, clothing and haberdashery is perhaps predictable. Garthine Walker has ascribed the similar

---

8   Richard King, *The New Cheats of London Exposed; or the Frauds and Tricks of the Town Laid Open to Both Sexes* (London, 1780), pp. 87–8.

Table 19. Types of goods stolen by gender – London and Northern England,
1726–1829

Type	Number of Thefts		Percentage of Thefts	
	Female	Male	Female	Male
Cloth	283 (75%)	95 (25%)	45%	17%
Clothing	201 (50%)	205 (50%)	32%	38%
Haberdashery	68 (71%)	28 (29%)	11%	5%
Food	26 (25%)	79 (75%)	4%	15%
Jewellery/silverware/toys	20 (23%)	68 (77%)	3%	13%
Household goods	24 (34%)	46 (66%)	4%	8%
Other	6 (23%)	20 (77%)	1%	4%
Total	628	541	100%	100%

Source: Combined sample

greater propensity of women to steal these items in the seventeenth century to
their daily familiarity with such materials in a household setting.[9] However,
her extension of this principle to household goods in general does not hold
true for shoplifting and, in spite of men's dominance in thefts of food and
jewellery, it is noticeable that they also more frequently stole clothing and
cloth. So let us turn first to these key potential conduits of eighteenth-century
fashion: cloth, clothing and haberdashery, investigating each in turn. What
was the nature of the items shoplifters stole and what do they indicate of the
incentives driving the theft?

Theft of cloth, clothing and haberdashery

Cloth was a staple in an age when much clothing was still hand-made and
ready-made clothes, though widely available new and second-hand, were
often ill-fitting.[10] Bolts were manufactured variously from wool, silk, linen
and cotton, or mixtures of these fibres. The thefts in the sample exemplify
the broad range of textiles sold by eighteenth-century drapers and mercers.
They include fifteen varieties of woollen cloth, twelve of linen and nine of

9   Garthine Walker, 'Women, Theft and the World of Stolen Goods', in *Women, Crime and the Courts in Early Modern England*, ed. J. Kermode and G. Walker (London, 1994), pp. 81–105 (pp. 87, 97).
10   Styles, *Dress of the People*, p. 161.

Table 20. Textiles stolen by London shoplifters during four sample periods, 1743–1807

Type	1743–54		1765–74		1785–88		1805–07		All	
	No.	%	No.	%	No.	%	No.	%	No.	%
Cotton/cotton mix	17	28	18	27	48	66	61	75	144	51
Linen	29	49	34	52	15	20	10	12	88	32
Wool/wool mix	12	20	8	12	7	10	10	12	37	13
Silk	2	3	6	9	3	4	1	1	12	4
Total	60	100	66	100	73	100	82	100	281	100

Source: London sample

silk. The terminology used in court indictments can be imprecise, in part reflecting common usage, and the fibre content of mixed fabrics might be adjusted to variously serve elite and plebeian markets, but neither factor is sufficiently significant to distort an overall analysis of the type of material stolen.[11] Dress historians have charted how cotton overtook traditional woollens in popularity, and increasingly linens, during the course of the eighteenth century.[12] Light, bright, washable cotton prints were fashionable and practical. Thick cottons replaced leather as the material of choice for men's breeches.[13] And falling production costs at the end of the century made cotton increasingly affordable.[14] This trend is clearly mirrored in shoplifting thefts (Table 20).

London thefts across the four sample periods decisively illustrate a shift to cottons from the 1780s, primarily at the expense of linens. Two-thirds of these cottons were described in the transcripts as printed cotton or calico, though values given were consistent with those for plebeian wear rather than the more expensive cotton chintz favoured by the gentry. The percentage of woollens stolen, although reduced by half from mid-century, remains fairly stable thereafter. Thefts of silk gown fabrics are few, suggesting a limited demand in the markets that shoplifters serviced. While a trend from heavy woollens to lighter draperies and cotton fabrics was observable in elite fashions also, silk was the core of genteel female wardrobes for much of the

---

11 Styles, *Dress of the People*, pp. 113, 118; Giorgio Riello, *Cotton: The Fabric that Made the Modern World* (Cambridge, 2013), p. 225.
12 Styles, *Dress of the People*, ch. 7.
13 Beverly Lemire, *Fashion's Favourite: The Cotton Trade and the Consumer in Britain, 1660–1800* (Oxford, 1991), p. 100.
14 Riello, *Cotton*, p. 214.

century.[15] Barbara Johnson, a member of a gentry family, kept a sample book of the fabrics used for her gowns between 1746 and 1825, the majority of which until 1770 were silks. By contrast, the swatches of fabric held in the London Foundling Hospital billet books for the same period, taken from the clothing of babies left there by poorer mothers and invariably cut down from their own gowns, are overwhelmingly cottons, linens and woollen stuffs.[16]

Issues of value and appearance similarly come to mind when we examine the clothes that shoplifters stole (Table 21). Those taken in the greatest numbers – handkerchiefs and stockings – were relatively small and light in bulk, easy to conceal and carry away. They comprised 51% of clothing thefts in London and 79% in the north. Both were most often stolen in multiples, partly due to the form of their merchandising, but also implying that they were intended for disposal rather than personal use. Half the handkerchiefs stolen were silk, with the remainder split between linen and cotton. For the thief, silk was prized as high value for size and weight. Shawls, stolen in increasing numbers from the 1780s were predominantly cotton but also attractive as the muslin fabric from which they were made, or their patterning, afforded them higher value.

Stockings were almost entirely a London interest, perhaps because home knitting was still common practice in the north during this period. Worsted stockings were the most popular target for thefts, although reducing from 76% of those stolen to 30% at the end of the century. From the 1760s they were exceeded by thefts of silk stockings, which in turn outnumbered those of the increasingly popular cotton. But by the early 1800s the number of stocking thefts had markedly declined, perhaps coincident with the change in men's fashion from breeches to longer trousers.

Leather shoes were the most common footwear stolen, boots only comprising 15% of thefts. The transcripts prior to 1800 regularly contained information on type and material, revealing that very few clogs, pumps and slippers were stolen and only one pair of women's stuff shoes. While women's shoes were generally made from textiles, working women wore leather.[17] Thefts were also most often of single pairs. Although this may be a factor of easy concealment and portability, it also invites the question whether these items of clothing, perhaps more than others, may have been stolen by a working community for personal use. But evidence we have of disposal tends to belie this. Caught stealing a 2 shilling pair of shoes in 1807, Charles Walker owned, 'I did it through distress; I left my wife at Chatham to seek for work;

15   Anne Buck, *Dress in Eighteenth-Century England* (London, 1979), p. 186.
16   Styles, *Dress of the People*, pp. 114–22.
17   Giorgio Riello, *A Foot in the Past: Consumers, Producers and Footwear in the Long Eighteenth Century* (Oxford, 2006), pp. 35, 41–2.

Table 21. Clothing thefts by type – London and Northern England, 1726–1829*

Type	London 1743–1807		North 1726–1829	
	No.	%	No.	%
Handkerchiefs/shawls/neckcloths	105	29	39	75
Stockings	82	22	2	4
Shoes/boots/gaiters/spatterdashes	59	16	2	4
Womenswear				
Cloak/spencer	25		0	
Gown	18		0	
Petticoat	9		0	
Apron	6		0	
Cap	4		0	
Underwear (Shift/stays/garters)	4		0	
Tippet/muff	2		1	
Subtotal	68	19	1	2
Menswear				
Coat/jacket	8		1	
Waistcoat	13		1	
Breeches/trousers/pantaloons	12		2	
Shirt	2		1	
Peruke	2		0	
Subtotal	37	10	5	9
Hats/gloves/mitts	16	4	3	6
Total	367	100	52	100

Source: Combined sample

* Trial records only intermittently indicate whether the handkerchiefs, stockings, shoes, hats and gloves stolen were menswear or womenswear, and these have consequently been categorised separately. The few items identified as children's wear have been included within the main gendered clothes categories.

Table 22. London clothing thefts by type of crime

Type	Housebreaking and burglary London 1750–1811*		Shoplifting London 1743–1807	
	No.	%	No.	%
Handkerchiefs/shawls	241	15	105	29
Stockings	144	9	82	22
Shoes/boots	68	4	59	16
Womenswear	619	37	68	19
Menswear	406	24	37	10
Hats/gloves	62	4	16	4
Other clothing and accessories	116	7		
Total	1656	100	367	100

Source: London sample; Horrell, Humphries and Sneath, 'Cupidity and Crime'

* Figures extrapolated from Horrell, Humphries and Sneath, 'Cupidity and Crime', p. 261, Table 10.3

I could get no work, I had nothing to eat'.[18] In fact there is no instance in the sample of a shoplifter explaining their theft in terms of an immediate clothing need. More typical was the defence of James Dunn who stole a pair of trousers from a sale shop: 'I saw the trowsers laying on the ground; no person owning them, I took them away: being short of money, I went to pledge them'.[19]

If we compare the profile of clothing stolen by shoplifters with those taken by housebreakers and burglars (Table 22), an interesting opposition emerges. Handkerchiefs, stockings and shoes, which comprise two-thirds of the items selected by shoplifters, count for hardly more than a quarter of the haul in the other crimes. If, as Horrell *et al.* assert, house thieves were selective in their 'systematic sifting of property for its attractiveness and value', this would suggest that the buying public preferred their handkerchiefs, stockings and shoes new – another incentive for shoplifters to target these items.[20]

Shoplifters were clearly responsive to market demand. Customarily, certain items within working wardrobes were replaced more frequently due to their greater use or limited durability. If we look at the overall pattern of clothing thefts we observe such items were correspondingly stolen in greater numbers.

18   *OBP*, July 1807, Charles Walker (t18070701-34).
19   *OBP*, September 1807, James Dunn (t18070916-76).
20   Horrell, Humphries and Sneath, 'Cupidity and Crime', p. 254 and p. 261, Table 10.3.

John Styles has analysed the clothing component of the income and expenditure studies of labouring families compiled by the Reverend David Davies
and Sir Frederick Eden at the end of the eighteenth century. These give an
indication of the rate of turnover of clothes in poorer families. Taken broadly
the budgets infer that, to maintain a minimum standard of dress, working
men, and often women, required at least two pairs of stockings and a pair
of shoes each year. Women would additionally expect to acquire a new
shift, handkerchief, cap and two aprons each year, a gown and petticoat
annually or biennially, a cloak and hat every two years and to replace their
stays every six years. Men needed two shirts a year, but their coats, jackets,
waistcoat and breeches were expected to last several years longer, albeit with
patching and repair.[21] These clothing life cycles are consistent with the higher
volume of handkerchief, stocking and shoe thefts, and even of womenswear
in contrast to menswear. The rare theft of women's stays becomes immediately understandable in this light. There are some inconsistencies: one would
expect thefts of aprons, caps and shirts to be more common, although an
explanation may be their greater likelihood of home manufacture. However,
though the correlation is imperfect, one cannot dismiss it. If shoplifters stole
to sell, it would make sense to steal a higher proportion of those items that
had the highest turnover in second-hand markets.

The frequency distribution of clothing thefts provides further pointers to
the correspondence of shoplifters' choice to deficiencies in labouring budgets.
Spending on wives' clothing was often subsumed to that of their husbands,
due both to men's common need for separate or more durable working
clothes and to male tailoring being generally more expensive.[22] Families'
clothing budgets were also most constrained when children were young, the
life-cycle stage of the majority of female shoplifters, as we have seen earlier.
Both factors would have created a climate in which the illicit acquisition
of items of women's clothing became an economic expedient, particularly
for higher-valued items such as cloaks. Yet the rarity of thefts of children's
clothing suggests that crime was not a standard response to all shortage and
that in the case of children, families were more likely to resort to the more
conventional recourse of adapting and handing on adult clothes.

Ribbon and lace were the dual targets of choice for haberdashery thefts
nationwide (Table 23). Although both items were widely used for dress
trimmings and decorative wear, the individual amounts stolen, averaging 27
yards for ribbon and 14 yards for lace, generally exceeded that which might
be taken for personal use. Two-thirds of the lace, where specified, was thread
and the remainder silk. Women were as likely to steal ribbon as lace, while
men were twice as likely to steal ribbon. Within the 'female' haberdashery shop

21   Styles, *Dress of the People*, pp. 222–3.
22   Styles, *Dress of the People*, pp. 218–19.

Table 23. Haberdashery thefts by type – London and Northern England, 1726–1829

Type	London 1743–1807		North 1726–1829	
	No.	%	No.	%
Ribbon	38	49	10	45
Lace	27	35	10	45
Other (sewing silk/bindings/ gartering/beads etc.)	12	16	2	10
Total	77	100	22	100

Source: Combined sample

environment, the traditional custom of men giving their sweethearts ribbons as gifts may have made it easier for them to ask to view drawers of ribbon at the counter. Thomas Wood, caught stealing 36 yards of pink and blue ribbon in such circumstances in 1787, had told the shopgirl that he wanted it for his wife.[23]

The influence of fashion

So just how significant was the impact of fashion? Having analysed thefts of cloth, clothing and haberdashery – three main components of fashionable wear – we might now examine the degree to which shoplifting was an enabler, or indeed instrumental in encouraging the introduction of new consumer fashions to plebeian communities. At its most rudimentary, the cases provide little evidence of a personal desire for a stylish item inspiring an individual to shoplift. There are rare instances, such as Elizabeth Wild's plea, when caught stealing silk gloves early in the century, that 'she long'd for them, and that she knew not why else she did it, not having any occasion as she knew of for them', or Elizabeth Murphy who stole 'a very fine straw bonnet' from James Maine's shop in 1801 and was seen wearing it three weeks later.[24] More commonly, the amounts stolen exceeded that appropriate for an individual lace or ribbon trimming for a petticoat or cap, or a single gown length. When Ann Cuthbert claimed the 9 yards of printed cotton she had stolen had been bought elsewhere for a gown, the shopkeeper retorted, 'how came you to buy nine yards, when six is a good pattern?'[25] Although we cannot entirely

23   Styles, *Dress of the People*, p. 315; OBP, September 1787, Thomas Wood (t17870912-7).
24   OBP, February 1716, Elizabeth Wild (t17160222-41); October 1801, Elizabeth Murphy (t18011028-68).
25   OBP, February 1748, Ann Cuthbert, Mary King (t17480224-8).

discount evidence that pairs of female shoplifters did sometimes steal a longer piece that was later divided into shorter lengths to be shared between the two.

There is also limited sign of emulative aspiration. As we have seen, fabrics and clothes stolen were not predominantly those of high fashion and it is very uncertain how engaged shoplifters were with the rapidly changing tastes of the elite. Bargaining exchanges reported in court by shop staff are generally mundane, rarely demonstrating a marked alertness to fashionable fabrics or styles. For instance, in 1788 a shopman described how Ann Gibson and her companion had asked to see the goods they subsequently stole: 'they went to the apprentice for half a yard of Irish, and he being busy, desired me to serve them, which I did; when I had served them, they desired to look at some muslins which were lying on the counter with some other goods'.[26] It contrasts with apparently higher-class Charlotte Power's articulate involvement in the style of the stockings she viewed at an Oxford Street hosiery:

> I asked him to let me see some black silk stockings, which he brought; I told him I did not like them, they were not so good as I wanted them, I wished to see others; he brought another parcel, they were not the clock that I wanted; I wanted to see open lace gores; these stockings lay on the counter; I then looked at the open lace ones, and they were striped down the gore; I told him I wanted them as good as I could get them, and as rich; I would thank him to let me have a pair of clear lace gores; he looked, and found a parcel of this description, he said; and when I examined them, I made him sensible that the description of stockings that I wanted, the gore ran broader at the bottom.

Power was acquitted after persuading the jury that the pair of embroidered silk stockings she was accused of stealing had only accidentally become entangled in the dress train of her gown.[27] In fact, items that were height of elite fashion were only very seldom stolen. Incongruous to wear and difficult to dispose of unremarked, the gold-laced hat, silk-velvet spencer or Hessian boots may have been the rare examples of thefts that fed an idiosyncratic private yearning.[28]

This does not mean that shoplifters were indifferent to fashion. Beverly Lemire has argued persuasively that working communities were as eager as those of higher ranks to adopt new fabrics, particularly cottons, and that by customising their dress and accessories the poor created their own distinctive styles for the purpose of self-definition and display.[29] It is clearly indicative

26 *OBP*, June 1788, Ann Gibson (t17880625-29).

27 *OBP*, September 1805, Charlotte Power (t18050918-98).

28 *OBP*, July 1753, Joseph Holdstop (t17530718-39); December 1806, Elizabeth Smith (t18061203-47); April 1806, John Williams (t18060416-79).

29 Beverly Lemire, *Fashion's Favourite*; Lemire, 'Second-hand Beaux', pp. 392–3, 407–8.

that the items of clothing she identifies as the vehicle of plebeian fashion, handkerchiefs, stockings, ribbons and prints, were those most commonly stolen. However, if fashion is to be accorded more meaning than simply conventional wear, then the information provided by the transcripts is too imprecise to confirm when goods were selected with style in mind or, indeed, that those stolen were the more fashionable of their type. In choosing what to steal, shoplifters were clearly also servicing a client market for whom maintaining a fashionable identity was less of a factor. When Agnes Boswell took 6 yards of check linen in 1747 it was not merely unfashionable, but in the shopkeeper's words, it 'happened to be a piece I have had a pretty while, that no body liked it'.[30] And if we look at the professional operation of Hannah Mumford and her fellow shoplifters, described in chapter 2, it is evident that they were only marginally responding to the demands of contemporary fashion. In the course of the twenty-six thefts in 1773 that Mumford admitted, her ring did steal 24 yards of printed cotton, 26 yards of lawn, 44 yards of muslin and 18 silk handkerchiefs, all potentially stylish. However, their main target was consistently the popular but more traditional printed linen of which they amassed and sold on lengths totalling 504 yards.[31]

Styles also sounds a note of caution, contending that rather than seeking fashionable show, working men and women were more often consumed by concern that their dress was sufficiently neat, modest and socially appropriate. He counters against generalising from small groups of the fashion-conscious to society as a whole.[32] More recently Styles has contested the established orthodoxy of viewing fashion simply as a means of bestowing image and identity. He argues for a more dynamic view of fashion as a process of change.[33] This is perhaps a more fruitful paradigm for interpreting the variances in goods stolen by shoplifters over time. New methods of production and advances in marketing, developing trade opportunities and periodic restrictions both diversified and constrained the products available to consumers as the century progressed. Tradition, cost and custom determined the speed and reach of these nationally, and to different levels of society. Fashion had its own impetus, but it would be stretching the evidence to claim that shoplifting was instrumental in pushing the boundaries and forcing the pace. So let us move on to the other goods that shoplifters stole and explore the incentives for their selection.

30   OBP, April 1747, Agnes Boswell (t17470429-22).
31   LMA, OB/SP/1773/12/006, Gaol Delivery Sessions, Hannah Mumford statement.
32   Styles, Dress of the People, pp. 210–11.
33   John Styles, 'Fashion and Innovation in Early-Modern Europe', in Fashioning the Early Modern: Creativity and Innovation in Europe, 1500–1800, ed. Evelyn Welch (Oxford, 2017), pp. 33–55.

Theft of food, jewellery, silverware, toys and household goods

Thieves periodically claimed in court that they had stolen joints of meat through hunger, but the type and quantity of food stolen suggests little was for personal consumption (Table 24). The bread, vegetables and cheaper groceries that largely made up the daily diet of working families hardly figure among the thefts. In part this is a factor of the court records interrogated here, the Old Bailey and assizes formally only hearing cases where the loss was valued at a shilling or more, but it may also signify that these foodstuffs were commonly purchased from street sellers, or that they were perishable. Stolen goods were regularly sequestered until trial, which would naturally make food retailers think twice about the benefit of prosecuting. When cheesemonger William Hudson brought John Whaley to court for stealing from his shop, the constable admitted he had had the cheese in his possession for four months.[34] However, different rules may have been applied to the more rapidly putrefying items. Explaining how his bird came to be stolen twice, poulterer Thomas Morris testified that, following its initial theft, 'the goose being an article that would not keep, the officer brought it back'.[35] The limited life of fresh meat reduced its worth for the shoplifter also, and perhaps for this reason around 40% of these thefts were of bacon or dried ham. Cheese, stolen in whole or half rounds, was also a better investment, although disposal was rarely a problem. William George stole half a cheese from an Oxford Street cheesemonger and sold it in St Giles before being caught on returning to the store for a second half round.[36]

Tea, together with sugar, commanded a ready market as this steadily became a staple drink of the poor. In the quantities of a pound or more which were generally stolen, tea became one of the more lucrative thefts before 1784 when tea duty was commuted. After this, thefts were rare. Tubs of butter accounted for some of the most expensive individual thefts. Weights, which amounted to 84 pounds for cheese and over 50 pounds for butter in some cases, and the difficulty of concealing raw food within clothing, may account for food theft being largely a male shoplifters' crime.

The degree to which working households aspired to own jewellery, toys and silver plate in this period remains in dispute, and the limited numbers of these in our sample mean our findings can only be indicative (Table 25).[37] Toys were stolen more frequently than either watches or jewellery. The majority of these thefts were of buckles, but shoplifters were also caught stealing twenty-five

---

34 *OBP*, February 1806, John Whaley (t18060219-73).
35 *OBP*, February 1805, Sarah Briggs (t18050220-68).
36 *OBP*, December 1774, William George (t17741207-25).
37 Common usage of the term 'toy' has changed over time. In the eighteenth century it denoted an adult ornament.

Table 24. Food thefts by type – London, 1743–1807 and Northern England, 1726–1829

Type	No.	%
Meat/Poultry	51	47
Cheese/Butter	35	33
Tea/Chocolate/Sugar	17	16
Other	4	4
Total	107	100

Source: Combined sample

Table 25. Jewellery, silverware and toys thefts – London and Northern England, 1726–1829

Type	London 1743–1807		North 1726–1829	
	No.	%	No.	%
Watches	13	17	5	28
Jewellery	16	21	1	5
Silverware	8	11	0	0
Toys	38	51	12	67
Total	75	100	18	100

Source: Combined sample

other varieties of toy, often in multiples. Plebeian shop thieves were clearly as much attracted by the abundance of novel trinkets and accessories that were being newly manufactured as the wealthier clientele to whom they were primarily marketed, although portability and disposal value would have had a bearing on their choice.[38] Items stolen included penknives, combs, snuff boxes, thread cases and a fish-skin smelling bottle. Unfortunately we have virtually no information on their disposal, so are unable to determine whether they were sold on, or retained as keepsakes. Buckles comprised around a third of thefts overall in this category. They were worn by all levels of society, although only a quarter of those stolen, and mainly in the north, were made of the cheaper white metals or silver plate that might be within a labourer's financial reach. They ceased to be stolen from the 1790s when they fell out of

38   Maxine Berg, *Luxury and Pleasure in Eighteenth-Century Britain* (Oxford, 2005), p. 158.

fashion as an elite shoe decoration.[39] Almost certainly this was a matter of supply rather than demand, their no longer being on sale to steal in shops, since many of the buckles were of silver and their metal content had value. William Corbyn stole a pair of silver buckles from a Liverpool silversmith in 1780, broke them in two and took them to a watchmaker in the town who later deposed, 'he said he had broken them by accident ... and he desired we would knock the anchor out of the whole buckle and weigh the silver which this informant did and ... gave him half a guinea for them'.[40]

Fewer watches were stolen than one might anticipate, given their growing popularity and ownership among working men. But this is certainly because there were other, easier means of illegally acquiring watches. Styles has documented the increase in the number of Old Bailey trials from mid-century that involved stolen watches.[41] Gold and silver watches were undoubtedly stolen for their high value, rather than use: only three of the eighteen watches shoplifted were of the base metal common to labourer's watches. Silver tableware and jewellery were other high-value targets. Twelve of the thefts were of gold rings, the intrinsic value of gold fetching a good return if sold or pawned. Jewellery was, of course, also a fashion item. One theft from a goldsmith was of three bunches of mock garnets and a mock-garnet necklace.[42] Garnet was a semi-precious stone popular with the middling sort, but this illustrates that they were not above wearing paste jewellery. And fish-seller Mary Dowle's theft of twelve strings of mock-garnet beads from a Cheapside haberdasher the following year stands out as an example of how an elite fashion could permeate to lower ranks. In her defence, Dowle protested, 'I saw a heap of garnets in the window; I took some, and put them about my neck, and said, how do these look'.[43]

A range of household goods were stolen by both sexes, but again too little information is given in the surviving court records of these cases to ascertain whether the goods were stolen for disposal, or to furnish the shoplifters' own homes. Certainly many of the goods stolen were simply the basic accompaniments to daily living for working people: flock-beds and blankets, earthenware pans and pewter plates, gridirons and flat irons, soap and starch. As these were only valued at a few pence there is cause to think that they might be have been taken to fulfil an immediate household need. But as the list of items stolen includes knives and forks, china, table linen, clocks and carpet, we might reflect whether these could have been objects of desire. By the early eighteenth century the more prosperous middling sort were

39 Riello, *A Foot in the Past*, p. 82.
40 TNA, PL 27/5, Lancaster, Crown Court, 12 August 1780, William Corbyn.
41 Styles, *Dress of the People*, pp. 98, 343.
42 OBP, May 1765, Elizabeth Arthur, Mary Kinnaston (t17650522-14).
43 OBP, October 1766, Mary Dowle, Anne Hinckley (t17661022-54).

already accumulating an increasing collection of domestic goods to ease and embellish their houses, from china to curtains, clocks, and looking glasses.[44] As workshop and industrial manufacture increased the supply and variety of such items, and versions in different materials brought them within the means of lesser pockets, it seems probable that such goods would have become increasingly attractive to poorer households. So can we draw any evidence from this category that thieves were seeking to acquire some of these new consumer goods by the most economical means available?

Only two of the thefts of household items took place in the north; it was almost entirely a London phenomenon. Lorna Weatherill, in measuring the distribution of these new domestic goods in early-century probate inventories, found a far higher proportion were owned in urban settings.[45] Such consumer goods were available new from shops, but also second-hand from brokers (Plate 4). Both were sources for theft, though we should acknowledge that the ubiquity of brokers in London as purchasers of second-hand household goods probably also fuelled such thefts. The individual items stolen in greatest numbers were looking glasses and books. The former brought light and decoration to a home but have also been associated with an increasing eighteenth-century interest in appearance and self-fashioning. Probate sources suggest they were already found in over a half of gentry and middling homes by 1725.[46] The most expensive looking glasses stolen were those with fine frames and transcripts suggest that resale may have been the main purpose for these thefts. Certainly one glass with a gilt frame was sold on to a broker by a shoplifter who was caught when he returned to the shop for a second mirror in a walnut frame.[47] However, to Mary Mannon who picked up a looking glass in passing from a cabinet-maker's stall, or Mary Ward who dashed into an Oxford Market shop to take one while the shopkeeper was at lunch, they may have had a more intrinsic worth.[48] For looking glasses, like china, were not an ideal shoplifting choice as they were so easily dropped and broken. Such was the fate of three of the ten looking glasses taken and also the white china teapot with a gilt edge snatched by Elizabeth Evans from the counter of a Ludgate Hill china shop: 'I heard the tea-pot fall from her', the shopkeeper ruefully testified.[49] Broken glass and ceramics had recycle value in eighteenth-century England but this was unlikely to have been the thieves' intention.

44   Lorna Weatherill, 'The Meaning of Consumer Behaviour in Late Seventeenth- and Early Eighteenth-Century England', in *Consumption and the World of Goods*, ed. J. Brewer and R. Porter (London, 1993), pp. 206–27 (pp. 210, 222).
45   Weatherill, *Consumer Behaviour*, p. 77.
46   Weatherill, 'The Meaning of Consumer Behaviour', pp. 212, 222.
47   *OBP*, October 1747, Thomas Bavin (t17471014-14).
48   *OBP*, April 1771, Mary Mannon, Mary Murphy (t17710410-18); April 1806, Mary Ward (t18060416-43).
49   *OBP*, December 1807, Elizabeth Evans (t18071202-18).

Plate 4   *A Connoisseur in Brokers Alley*, 1818: a range of domestic goods, including looking glasses, were sold by brokers

Styles has also identified looking glasses among the dozen items most frequently stolen from furnished lodgings by plebeian tenants in the 1750s and 1790s.[50] However, the items most commonly taken in lodging thefts – sheets, blankets, pillows and bed covers – were rarely stolen from shops, even though such contents of furnished rooms were often disposed of to brokers, who were in turn a regular source of these goods to landlords.[51] Bulk may have been an issue, but it is more likely that shoplifters simply had no incentive to fulfil a market already easily supplied through lodging thefts.

Books were invariably stolen by men. Only one of the eighteen book thefts is attributed to a woman and she had acquired them in a morning's sweep of Holborn that had also netted her twelve china plates and a bunch of turnips.[52] This is not simply an indication that women were uninterested in books.

50   John Styles, 'Lodging at the Old Bailey: Lodgings and their Furnishing in Eighteenth-Century London' in *Gender, Taste, and Material Culture in Britain and North America, 1700–1830*, ed. J. Styles and A. Vickery (New Haven, 2006), pp. 61–80 (pp. 72–3).
51   Styles, 'Lodging at the Old Bailey', p. 76.
52   *OBP*, February 1787, Ann Eldridge (t17870221-5).

Plate 5   *Lackington Allen & Co.: Temple of the Muses, Finsbury Square*, 1809: bookshop

Bookseller James Lackington wrote of his good fortune in his second marriage, as his wife's 'extreme love for books made her delight to be in the shop', thus serving to promote his trade, and prints of his bookshop prominently feature female customers (Plate 5).[53] But these are clearly elite women. The literacy levels of working women may have been lower than those of men, but literacy alone fails to account for the gender bias as the range and type of book stolen suggests they were not for personal consumption. A barber's apprentice stole ten books including *The History of the Families of the Irish Nobility* and *Belles Lettres* in four volumes.[54] In fact, only one of the shoplifters is known to have been a regular reader: a retired businessman in York who appears to have exploited his free run of many bookshops to use the contents for an occasional subsidy.[55] Given that the primary intention for most was unobtrusive theft, working women may simply have recognised that as less frequent browsers at bookstalls and shops, they were more likely to arouse attention and suspicion.

Beyond books and looking glasses, the sample rarely contains more than one or two thefts each of any other type of household goods. We might recollect

53   J. Lackington, *Memoirs of the First Forty-Five Years of the Life of James Lackington, the Present Bookseller in Chiswell Street, Moorfields, London* (London, 1791), p. 204.
54   *OBP*, January 1769, Hooper Bennit (t17690112-50).
55   TNA, ASSI 45/60, Criminal Depositions and Case Papers, 25 June–25 July 1827, William Baynes.

here from the discussion of the 'dark figure' of unreported crime in chapter 2 that the cases studied inevitably represent only a percentage of the shoplifting thefts perpetrated: those where the shoplifter was caught and prosecuted. So although we may have evidence of only small numbers of consumer thefts of decorative goods, actual numbers and therefore their acquisition by plebeian households may have been more significant. Regrettably, as few probate inventories survive from the period after 1725 we have too little information to assess the proportion of labourers' homes that were accumulating books, glasses, china and clocks by the end of the century.[56] However, such evidence as there is of the motivation for stealing the finer domestic goods does tend towards theft for immediate income rather than personal use. Illustratively, of the two clocks stolen, one was pawned and the other sold.

The disposal of stolen goods

The way shoplifters disposed of the goods they stole reinforces the impression that ease of exchange was a dominant concern. The means they adopted reflect a sensitivity to prevailing market demand, but it is also apparent that thieves constructively capitalised on the network of social relationships that characterised and underpinned the economy of their communities. Unless they intended to retain the goods for their own use, the practical options for the thief were to sell, pawn, gift, or exchange the goods. These were all transactions as familiar to the poor in their daily working lives as in any illicit dealings. Possessions acquired during a lifetime, and particularly clothing, were financial assets that could be sold or pawned at times of hardship.[57] Gifting and exchange served to oil and reinforce social relations with neighbours and friends. The dataset on disposal is predictably more limited than that of what was stolen. The vast majority of shoplifters prosecuted were 'caught in the act' before they had any opportunity to divest themselves of the goods. Though the numbers of incidents for which we have disposal information are too few to allow reliable statistical analysis, a qualitative study of these thefts is instructive: in nine out of ten cases the goods were either sold or pawned.

The cases show that shoplifters frequently worked with a receiver or had

---

56   Sara Horrell, 'Consumption, 1700–1870', in *The Cambridge Economic History of Modern Britain*, vol. 1: *1700–1870*, ed. R. Floud, J. Humphries and P. Johnson (Cambridge 2014), pp. 237–63 (pp. 239–43).
57   Beverly Lemire, 'Plebeian Commercial Circuits and Everyday Material Exchange in England, c. 1600–1900', in *Buyers and Sellers: Retail Circuits and Practices in Medieval and Early Modern Europe*, ed. B. Blondé, P. Stabel, J. Stobart and I. Van Damme (Turnhout, 2006), pp. 245–66 (pp. 247–8).

favoured purchasers who were willing to operate beyond the law. Of the twenty-six thefts that Hannah Mumford admitted in 1773, the proceeds of seventeen were sold to Thomas Wright who lived in Chick Lane, in one of London's most notorious criminal districts. Wright provided a market for the textiles that Mumford and her associates stole, particularly the printed linen. But when they stole handkerchiefs, they chose, or perhaps found it more profitable, to sell them directly to 'different persons at different prices'.[58] Receivers' preferences could therefore influence the choice of items stolen. Those living by crime had to be confident of easy disposal. As hawkers who were not averse to some dishonest dealing, John Carroll and his wife and sister-in-law encountered problems when they stole an unopened parcel of handkerchiefs in Fleet Street and then attempted to sell them to their regular customers among the second-hand retailers of Field Lane. One of these, Catherine Taylor, who identified herself as seller of linen handkerchiefs, checks and old clothes, refused their offer of some blue-bordered handkerchiefs: 'I said they were too fine for me ... I bought a dozen of handkerchiefs, fancy-grounds, or mosaic; my man came in, and bid them money for some damaged ones'. And the Carrolls' ill-judged acquisition had a further repercussion when they subsequently sold three handkerchiefs from the same parcel to clothes dealer Betty Hatton. These, it transpired, were of a new pattern, and therefore more easily identifiable by their original owner in court.[59] Ideally, thieves sought to maintain a range of outlets for fencing their goods. The Northern Circuit depositions are particularly revealing in this respect as a higher percentage of offenders were charged after they had divested themselves of the goods. Matt Neale, studying theft in Bristol, has argued that provincial cities did not foster the types of receiver network found in the metropolis.[60] Evidence from the Northern assizes suggests otherwise. In York, John Ullathorne and William Jennings, working with receiver Isabella Thirkill, disposed of stolen poultry and silk handkerchiefs to dealer Francis Spencer. In his evidence, Ullathorne related how they were able to sell the cotton handkerchiefs to a Mrs Gray and that the proceeds of further thefts were fenced variously to John Nelson, a Mr Hanson, and to 'one Beans in Feasegate'.[61]

This is not to deny that receivers also used more informal sale and pawning networks to convert their gains. Susannah Widdup, active in Hull in 1804, sold to local households the printed cottons that her daughter regularly shoplifted

---

58   LMA, OB/SP/1773/12/006, Gaol Delivery Sessions, Hannah Mumford statement; White, *London in the Eighteenth-Century*, p. 401.
59   *OBP*, February 1765, Mary Carroll, John Carroll, Mary Carroll (t17650227-23).
60   Matt Neale, 'Making Crime Pay in Late Eighteenth-Century Bristol: Stolen Goods, the Informal Economy and the Negotiation of Risk', *Continuity and Change* 26/3 (2011), 439–59 (p. 454).
61   TNA, ASSI 45/50, Criminal Depositions and Case Papers, 24 March 1817, John Ullathorne.

from linen drapers in the town. At her trial, four women gave evidence that she had sold them lengths of cloth, several of which had since been made into gowns. The description of the textiles she and her daughter were accused of stealing suggests they may have targeted bright patterns that would appeal to their market:

> These examinants being charged before me, upon oath with suspicion of feloniously stealing and taking away one piece of blue and yellow printed calico containing six yards, one other piece of the same kind of calico, one piece of brown calico, one piece of red and white cambrick muslin, one piece of green printed calico, one other piece of blue and yellow printed calico, seven yards of green and blue checked calico.[62]

Sale brought finality to a transaction and reduced the possibility of the goods being traced back to the offender. There was a far higher chance of acquittal where the goods the shopkeeper had observed being stolen could no longer be physically linked to the defendant.[63] Partly through expedience, but also to provide an additional layer of anonymity, receivers and thieves often sought assistance from hawkers and street sellers operating within existing local trading networks. Thomas Fidler, a Liverpool innkeeper, claimed in 1767 that he was unaware the roll of silk he had bought from Ann Jones and passed to Ann Gyllis to sell, had been stolen from Richard Williamson's shop. Fidler deposed that 'he seldom or ever deals in the buying of goods', but in her information Gyllis spun a rather different tale, relating that:

> having some India handkerchiefs to sell for the wife of some sailor as she makes a practice of selling and hawking goods for different people she called at the house of the said Fidler to expose those handkerchiefs to sale there but instead of purchasing any he then told this examinant that he had a couple of pieces of silk which he had bought reasonable which she should sell for him if she could. Whereupon he conducted her into his bed chamber up stairs and unlock'd a box or chest there and took out two pieces of silk one of them a pea green ground with colour'd flowers and the other a garnett ground with colour'd flowers ... Says she carried them away and sold part to Mrs Banner at the Fleece. And the remainder to Mrs Somerskill and received about fifteen pounds which she paid into the hands of said Fidler. Says that he returned her four shillings and sixpence for her trouble and say'd he expected more silks soon which she should have the disposal of.

---

62   TNA, ASSI 45/42, Criminal Depositions and Case Papers, 3 February 1804, Hannah Ellison, Mary Widdup, Susannah Widdup.
63   On the evidence of the combined sample, shoplifters were 30% more likely to be acquitted when the goods were not recovered.

Gyllis subsequently sold fabrics door-to-door for Fidler on three further occasions.[64]

Using the same dealers that customers bought from regularly to dispose of illicit goods gave the transaction a specious authenticity. We might wonder why these sellers, mainly women, took on a task so unquestioningly that might land them in court. Certainly it was not without recompense, as the case above demonstrates, and therefore attractive to those surviving on an irregular income. One shoplifter testified that having stolen a parcel of stockings from a hosier in the Strand, he and his accomplice could not initially find a buyer: 'we offered them to several people, none would buy them; then a woman said, she would sell them for us, if we would give her any thing'.[65] And such arrangements could operate to mutual advantage as Patrick Glynn's case demonstrates. He had frequently bought stockings from Abigail Ryley, who sold them around town, so she was predisposed to meet his request to find a buyer for the 21 yards of woollen cloth he had stolen from Peter Sarney's shop. On Ryley successfully returning to Glynn with the proceeds of the sale, he acknowledged his debt by purchasing some more stockings from her.[66] But financial gain is only a partial explanation. It can perhaps be better contextualised by understanding that these sellers operated in a milieu where the law against receiving was weak and the extensive public tolerance of certain quasi-legal dealings, including the sale of supposedly smuggled goods, spread reassurance.[67]

The streets of London reputedly abounded with duffers: 'cheats who ... pretend to deal in smuggled goods, stopping all country people, or such as they think they can impose on; which they frequently do, by selling them Spital-fields goods at double their current price'.[68] When Robert Foler was caught surreptitiously pocketing some green tea in 1774, the shopkeeper Peter Anstie testified, 'He used to buy a pound, or two, or three, and then carry it about to sell as smuggled tea; that is his trade, and many others that use our shop.'[69] So when soldiers' wives Thomasin Wild and Martha Chadwick stole a length of muslin from a milliner in Warrington, they adeptly employed both a compliant go-between and plausible excuse to broker the wares:

it was proposed between them that this examinant should take it to be disposed of, at the shop of Betty, the wife of John Whittle ... where this examinant a little while before had sold another parcel of muslin ... but

64   TNA, PL 27/4, Lancaster, Crown Court, 19 November 1767, Thomas Fidler.
65   *OBP*, January 1767, William Egan (t17670115-25).
66   *OBP*, September 1743, Patrick Glynn (t17430907-38).
67   Kathy Callahan, 'On the Receiving End: Women and Stolen Goods in London 1783–1815', *London Journal* 37/2 (2012), 106–21 (p. 108).
68   Francis Grose, *A Classical Dictionary of the Vulgar Tongue* (London, 1788).
69   *OBP*, January 1774, Robert Foler (t17740112-8).

this examinant thinking some suspicion might arise against her, afterwards declined going with the said Miss Clare's piece of muslin, but desired Mary Ainsworth of Warrington aforesaid singlewoman to take the same to the said Betty Whittle's in order to dispose of it upon the best terms she could, and she was to say it came from Liverpool and that she had bought it as run goods.[70]

Mary Ainsworth escaped charge, as was the case for most intermediaries, but others did not emerge completely unscathed. Mary Emmerson, who unwittingly negotiated the sale of a shoplifted medal for the brother of a friend, lost her place as a consequence.[71]

In spite of the potentially greater risk of discovery and exposure, accustomed thieves also pawned their takings. Witness John Egan explained to the court that he accompanied Ann Perkins and two other women to a linen draper's shop: 'We went on purpose to take what we could. Sometimes we looked at muslins, sometimes handkerchiefs, and sometimes we wanted neckcloths ... they made a common practice of it.' Later he went with Perkins to her regular pawnbroker, John Delafore, who was also called to give evidence:

> I am a pawnbroker, in Bishopsgate-street. (He produced thirteen pieces of muslins and lawns.) Mrs. Perkins pawned these with me at different times. The 28th of March next will be two years since she brought some of them: the last was about November was twelvemonths. She used to tell me she brought them for one Mr. Scott in Hoxton-market-place, a man that deals in drapery.[72]

This case illustrates that although some effort was taken to give the transaction plausibility and obscure the source of illicit goods, the pivotal role of pawnbroking in the period as a source of both personal and business credit afforded shoplifters considerable compass in this respect. Proficient thieves sought to make their dealings inconspicuous. Hannah Messiter, who stole 63 yards of black silk from a City mercer, cut it into pieces and distributed these to a number of pawnbrokers across London. A woman pawning a gown length of such valuable cloth would logically raise less suspicion than had she attempted to pawn the full roll, and particularly a working woman – when caught she offered to recompense the shopkeeper from the proceeds of her wet-nursing.[73] Indeed, servant Sarah Taylor was detained by a pawnbroker

70 TNA, PL 27/6, Lancaster, Crown Court, 26 February 1782, Thomasin Wild, Martha Chadwick.

71 *OBP*, September 1765, Edward Jones (t17650918-60).

72 *OBP*, December 1768, Margaret Kelly, Eleanor Morgan, Ann Perkins (t17681207-38).

73 *OBP*, February 1772, Hannah Messiter (t17720219-57).

because he considered the 25 yards of Irish linen valued at £5 that she offered him was 'a thing of too much consequence for her to be the owner of'.[74] Aliases were a ploy used frequently. Apart from their sale of stolen fabrics, mentioned above, Susannah Widdup, her daughter and associates pawned textiles with at least four Hull pawnbrokers under the assorted names of Mary Marshall, Mary Cooper, Mary Atkinson, Ann Johnson and Elizabeth Wilkinson.[75] Yet even this could be explained away in terms of custom. In 1745, Elizabeth Stavenaugh, a London shoplifter, attempted in her defence to give the practice of using others' names some legitimacy: 'I being a market woman, and an honest woman, people carry things in my name, and they will give more upon them than if they were not brought in my name'.[76]

It was obviously prudent to dispose of the goods before news of the theft had spread by advert or word of mouth to potential purchasers. The danger of recognition following such an alert might be especially acute in smaller communities. Shoplifter John Muers and his companions did not attempt to sell their handkerchiefs in Whitby from where they had been stolen, but walked 2 miles to the adjoining hamlet of Newholm.[77] The same tactic was adopted by Thomas Apler, John Hodgkinson, George Stocks and Samuel Barnsley of Sheffield who set off together to neighbouring Rotherham to steal in January 1790. Arriving there at dusk, they were back in Sheffield with their proceeds by seven the same evening and within two hours had successfully pawned them.[78] In a city the size of London there was even more opportunity for shoplifters to distance themselves from the scene of the crime. So the almost reckless speed with which some shoplifters sought to divest themselves of their goods while still within the near vicinity of the theft is striking, and perhaps reflects their financial desperation. Such, perhaps, as that of Mary Ann Matthews, her accomplice testifying, 'The prisoner came to me to go with her to the prosecutor's shop, she wanted money, and she should go to the gallows.'[79] Elizabeth Bates, who stole fourteen pairs of worsted stockings from Charles Forth's shop in Leather Lane, was captured within fifteen minutes having meanwhile unsuccessfully offered them for sale to a neighbouring shopkeeper only doors away in Baldwin's Gardens and then attempted to pawn them.[80] In a like manner, shopman Samuel Addington

74 OBP, April 1743, Sarah Taylor (t17430413-1).
75 TNA, ASSI 45/42, Criminal Depositions and Case Papers, 3 February 1804, Hannah Ellison, Mary Widdup, Susannah Widdup.
76 OBP, May 1745, Elizabeth Stavenaugh (t17450530-8).
77 TNA, ASSI 45/32/2/118–119, Criminal Depositions and Case Papers, 18 November 1775, John Muers.
78 TNA, ASSI 45/37/1/128–131, Criminal Depositions and Case Papers, 9 January 1790, Thomas Apler, John Hodgkinson, George Stocks, Samuel Barnsley.
79 OBP, December 1747, Mary Ann Matthews (t17471209-15).
80 OBP, October 1747, Elizabeth Bates (t17471014-22).

followed Mary Frickens out of the haberdashers where she had just stolen a piece of thread lace and spotted her trying to sell it to someone in the next street.[81]

Clothing stolen from individuals was often altered or remade to avoid recognition, as Lemire has identified, but there is little evidence of this in shoplifting cases.[82] Textiles were occasionally turned into clothing, but the primary motive for this was unlikely to be disguising its origin. Elizabeth Page, who sold six short lengths of Irish linen she had stolen from an Oxford Street store to a sale shop in Monmouth Street, did claim that after buying the cloth the shopkeeper had vouched that 'they should not be known, for she would put them in water, and wash them directly'.[83] However, this case perhaps tells us more about the extent to which some shopkeepers were complicit to a greater or lesser degree in the conversion of stolen goods, and draws attention to the fact that shoplifted items did not necessarily leave the retail chain, but were frequently re-commodified. Tailor Joseph Fisher stole some mohair twist from William Walker's shop and sold it to Thomas Davis, another shopkeeper. Receiving a tip-off, Walker reported, 'We went into Mr. Davis's shop, and Mrs. Davis said they had bought the twist two days before I sent; and that her husband bid her say she had not bought it'; in court Davis was 'severely reprimanded ... for his conduct in purchasing goods at half their value'.[84] Broker George Pain was not only a shop owner but also a constable when he purchased Irish linen that Mary Kynaston had shoplifted from linen draper James Webb. The unsuspecting Webb enjoined Pain in his policing role to pursue Kynaston, later telling the court, 'he took her in charge with great reluctance'.[85] Pawnbrokers were particularly suspect during the period, frequently accused by the press and commentators of dishonest dealing.[86] When servant Sarah Hirst stole 21 yards of black silk lace from a York haberdasher, Joseph Nollans, she sold an 8½ yard length to pawnbrokers Thomas and Frances Palmer, claiming in her deposition that she was an old customer of theirs and had been asked no questions regarding its provenance. Nollans had no hesitation in insinuating collusion. He related how he had gone to the pawnbroker's house to enquire about the lace, only

81   OBP, April 1773, Mary Frickens (t17730421-17).
82   Lemire, 'The Theft of Clothes', pp. 268–9; Beverly Lemire, Dress, Culture and Commerce: The English Clothing Trade before the Factory, 1660–1800 (Basingstoke 1997), p. 143; see also Miles Lambert, '"Cast-off Wearing Apparell": The Consumption and Distribution of Second-hand Clothing in Northern England during the Long Eighteenth Century', Textile History 35/1 (2004), 1–26 (pp. 10–11).
83   OBP, September 1769, Elizabeth Page (t17690906-6).
84   OBP, February 1772, Joseph Fisher (t17720219-2).
85   OBP, June 1769, Mary Kynaston (t17690628-40).
86   Alannah Tomkins, The Experience of Urban Poverty, 1723–82: Parish, Charity and Credit (Manchester, 2006), pp. 205–8.

to be peremptorily told by Palmer that he 'might punish the woman who had stolen it but that he would not deliver it up', at which Nollans had protested:

> that as the wife of the said Thomas Palmer had been brought up as a haberdasher and is well acquainted with the value of laces and as the said Sarah Hirst has as she says been frequently at the shop of the said Thomas Palmer this deponent apprehends she must have supposed that Sarah Hirst had stolen the piece of lace she sold her particularly as from her position in life it was not probable she should be able to purchase so valuable an article.[87]

This is not to discount the probability that some shopkeepers were unwitting purchasers of stolen goods. Miles Lambert has concluded that most retailers, including linen drapers, were willing to accept second-hand material, at the least in exchange.[88]

While much of the preceding discussion has suggested that criminal disposal can be clearly differentiated from legitimate dealing, this is in a strict sense misleading. We should recognise that to occasional thieves, for whom shoplifting was simply one of a raft of expedients in their daily struggle for survival, the conversion of stolen goods might be completely integrated into, and indistinguishable from, the routines of borrowing, exchange and pawning that defined their neighbourhood relations. Shoplifters belonged to local communities that collectively functioned in the fluid area between makeshift and crime. In her defence for receiving shoplifted material, Mary Brown described how she 'bought this silk of a woman … from Wapping, I had not money enough to pay for it, and I borrowed half a guinea, and pawned a sattin cloak, and then could not make the money up, without borrowing half a crown of my next door neighbour', an explanation which might be disingenuous, but almost certainly familiar to the courtroom audience.[89] Pawning was integral to the economy of the poor, irrespective of the provenance of the goods pawned. Lynn MacKay, in her study of women's theft in the Old Bailey records of the 1780s, found that unauthorised 'borrowing' of the goods of a landlord or a neighbour to obtain a short-term loan through pawning was far from uncommon.[90] And in *Moll Flanders*, Defoe uses the same term in describing how the eponymous heroine's mother was convicted of felony after taking 'an opportunity of borrowing three pieces of fine *Holland*, of a certain draper in *Cheapside*'.[91] Sarah Robinson, who stole three pieces of

---

87 TNA, ASSI 45/34/2/30, 34, Criminal Depositions and Case Papers, 23 July 1781, Sarah Hirst.
88 Lambert, 'Cast-off Wearing Apparell', p. 11.
89 *OBP*, February 1766, James Burnham, Mary Brown (t17660219-19).
90 Lynn MacKay, 'Why they Stole: Women in the Old Bailey, 1779–1789', *Journal of Social History* 32/3 (1999), 623–39 (pp. 631–2).
91 Daniel Defoe, *The Fortunes and Misfortunes of the Famous Moll Flanders &c.* (London, 1772; London, 1989), p. 44.

woollen cloth from the shop of a Yorkshire mercer over a three-month winter period in 1762, was able to return all three when charged with the crime some months later.[92] Theft might even be a response to the failure of this staple lender to meet a pressing need, as a pawnbroker's testimony in another case suggests: 'the prisoner came into my shop to pledge an article; she refused taking the money offered, she went out; presently a person came in and told me a woman had stole some handkerchiefs from the door'.[93] Clothing and textiles, the items most commonly stolen, were also the items most commonly pawned. They comprised 81% of the items taken in by the York pawnbroker George Fettes, whose Pledge book for the period 1777–78 survives as a rare witness.[94] A pawnbroker, Richard Grainger, giving evidence in 1745 to a Parliamentary Committee on the regulation of the trade, identified among the customers he served:

> the very poor sort of people, such as persons who cry fish, fruit or other wares, about the streets, and other people who may be reckoned in the lowest class of life, who, not having any personal credit, are obliged to have recourse to the pawnbrokers, and by the money borrowed from them, are enabled to purchase the several commodities they deal in[95]

It is feasible that street sellers Hannah Railton and Mary Daley, whose acquaintance reportedly arose from their both 'being in the habit of resorting to Covent Garden to purchase fruit', and who jointly stole and then pawned three silk handkerchiefs, were using shoplifting as business credit.[96] Thomas Conner, a dealer in old clothes found guilty of stealing five handkerchiefs from a shop in the Strand, specifically admitted, 'I pawned them for money to go on in my business'.[97] And the same pragmatism seems to have been applied to self-clothing. Where goods were stolen primarily to raise income, a part might be utilised for immediate needs. Susanna Kirby and her companion stole 13 yards of linen check from which both women made aprons before selling the remaining 8 yards.[98] Similarly, Sarah Chapman and Ann Johnson stole twenty red and ten blue linen handkerchiefs from a Soho linen drapers and were each wearing one of the blue when they were caught pawning the red.[99]

92   TNA, ASSI 45/27/1/73, 74A, Criminal Depositions and Case Papers, 13 December 1762, Sarah Robinson.
93   OBP, February 1806, Ann Broughton (t18060219-32).
94   Beverly Lemire, *The Business of Everyday Life: Gender, Practice and Social Politics in England, c. 1600–1900* (Manchester, 2005), p. 94.
95   JHC, vol. 25, p. 46 (31 January 1745).
96   OBP, October 1806, Hannah Railton, Mary Daley (t18061029-21).
97   OBP, June 1767, Thomas Conner (t17670603-34).
98   OBP, February 1748, Susanna Kirby (t17480224-9).
99   OBP, September 1752, Sarah Chapman, Ann Johnson (t17520914-75).

The ability of communities to extend moral licence to illicit dealing in circumstances of hardship has been described by Stuart Henry, in his classic criminological study of the 'hidden economy'. He observed how illegal transactions, particularly those resulting from employee theft, were represented in the innocuous language of the market economy and frequently connected with the desire to do friends a favour. Reciprocity and co-dependency were necessary to retain one's membership of the community and preserve loyalty.[100] Such relationships are clearly visible in shoplifting cases. In 1789 Ann Blackburn stole 28 yards of dark-coloured calico chintz from George Johnson's linen draper's shop in Lancaster and systematically set about making her prize work to its maximum benefit. Prevailed upon to give a full confession, she described how she had cut the length into five pieces, one of which she had made into a gown for herself and a second that she had sent a young girl to pawn for her. She then made a remnant into a cradle cloth before approaching neighbours Mary Standen and her sisters Jane Standen and Betty Batty, with a view to selling them the three remaining pieces. Jane and Betty agreed to buy the lengths of cloth for a guinea, and Betty, the only married sister, was further enticed into taking the cradle cloth for a shilling. Ann was paid 15 shillings and Betty agreed to wash for her to the value of 3 shillings. So far this exchange illustrates the classic features of a transaction in the hidden economy: the element of low price, reciprocity as represented by the agreement to provide washing services, and crucially, a remaining 4 shillings owed from the agreed sale price, locking the purchaser into an ongoing obligation and complicity in such illicit dealing. It also illustrates the latent subsistence value of textiles and clothing in the eighteenth-century plebeian community. Within a week of the theft, three pieces of the chintz were found in the possession of local pawnbroker, James Murray. The Standen sisters had obviously taken the first opportunity to convert two of their purchases into an immediate subsidy.[101]

This brings us ultimately to the question of how much shoplifters gained financially from their thefts. Were goods stolen with specific proceeds in mind, and how easily were they able to realise this? It is probable that in communities so reliant economically on pawning and occasional sale, there would be a working knowledge of what an item of clothing or length of cloth should fetch. In fact the ability to predictably target a specific, easily convertible item with a known financial return is said to be one of the attractions of shoplifting over other crimes, such as housebreaking. It is notable from the study of Horrell *et al.* that in the early 1800s housebreakers were still finding and taking in their haul certain items, such as stockings, that shoplifters were largely eschewing, presumably because demand or value no longer

---

100   Stuart Henry, *The Hidden Economy: The Context and Control of Borderline Crime* (London, 1978), pp. 84, 101, 118–19.
101   TNA, PL 27/6, Lancaster, Crown Court, 29–30 December 1789, Ann Blackburn.

made them a worthwhile target.[102] Jacqueline Schneider, in work arising out of her extensive modern-day study of the disposal of stolen goods, found that 88% of the burglars that she profiled also shoplifted.[103] Nevertheless, it appears that some thieves struggled to recognise differences in the quality of textiles they stole. Mary Kynaston and Mary Crosier shoplifted 23 yards of a particularly fine Irish linen, valued at £3, which they sold for sixpence a yard, an 80% markdown. Hearing on the grapevine the true value of the cloth, they returned to the purchaser to try to negotiate a higher sum, but without success.[104]

It is difficult to generalise on the average markdown that shoplifters might have anticipated accepting on their goods because of the sparsity of cases where there is reliable information on both the retail valuation and the proceeds of sale or pawning of specific items. The few cases where comparative figures are available suggest that shoplifters might realise between half and two-thirds of the stock value. However, this calculation was subject to their reputation and the degree to which they could authenticate the exchange. Shoplifters' bargaining power was inevitably reduced where the illicit nature of the goods was known or suspected. John Muers and his associates managed to sell handkerchiefs valued at 16 pence for 10 pence to the wife of a Newholm joiner, but only after they convinced her they were seamen who had bought the goods cheaply abroad.[105] John Downs, a member of a criminal gang and notorious as an informer in a previous Old Bailey trial, could only raise 2 shillings from a 20 shilling silver fruit basket he had stolen.[106]

This introduction and circulation within working communities of newly merchandised goods at cheaper prices would have inevitably extended the reach and affordability of eighteenth-century textiles and consumer goods. In a society where goods were regularly acquired from alternative channels to shops, the provenance of those which were illicitly sourced may have been little questioned. Alison Toplis, examining cases of provincial clothing theft in the early nineteenth century, was struck by how apparently incurious buyers were in informal exchanges in contrast to their concern over the origin of shop-bought goods, suggesting that participants in such transactions may have little cared whether goods were stolen or not.[107] However, the ready accessibility of quality fabrics, stylish clothes and decorative household goods

102 Horrell, Humphries and Sneath, 'Cupidity and Crime', p. 261, Table 10.3.
103 Jacqueline L. Schneider, 'The Link between Shoplifting and Burglary: the Booster Burglar', *British Journal of Criminology*, 45 (2005), 395–401 (p. 396).
104 *OBP*, June 1769, Mary Kynaston (t17690628-40).
105 TNA, ASSI 45/32/2/119, Criminal Depositions and Case Papers, 18 November 1775, John Muers.
106 *OBP*, May 1766, John Smith, John Downs (t17660514-30).
107 Alison Toplis, 'The Illicit Trade in Clothing, Worcestershire and Herefordshire, 1800–1850', *Journal of Historical Research in Marketing* 2/3 (2010), 314–26 (pp. 316–17).

does not necessarily imply that these became a staple of plebeian fashion or domestic arrangement during the century. Emulating elite fashion in working communities would have been impractical and ran the risk of being labelled or denounced for ostentation. Plebeian style was less ambitious and those aspiring to it were not reliant on theft. Cheaper-end cotton prints were affordable to working budgets; a silk handkerchief or ribbon would customarily enter a wardrobe at times of favourable earning. And in an age when personal goods were constantly hostage to the vagaries of financial fortune, it is debatable whether the poor could develop the affective attachment to possessions of later centuries. Decorative figurines, first mass-produced in the eighteenth century, increasingly became objects of desire for middling homes, and indeed one 1787 shop theft was of two china figures.[108] Yet it is only from the following century that literary and archaeological evidence places such cherished 'chimney ornaments' in any volume in labourers' homes.[109]

Through examining what shoplifters stole and how they disposed of their proceeds, this chapter has sought answers to some pertinent questions. It has explored whether and to what extent shoplifting enabled the spread of new fashions and consumer goods to those lower in the social scale, concluding that it was contributory, but not necessary, to the rate of appropriation of such goods by the poor. Overwhelmingly from working communities, the shoplifters portrayed here remained largely marginalised from the new consumer culture so enthusiastically adopted by wealthier households. While textiles, clothing and haberdashery were prime targets, the types and amounts stolen suggest this was rarely to satisfy a personal desire, or to emulate elite fashions. And while those in working communities were increasingly embracing self-styled popular fashions of dress, shoplifters' choice of items taken was consistent with supply-side availability and often demonstrated a more conservative taste. Although clearly not immune to fashion trends, or the lure of certain consumer goods, their thieving was principally an expedient, a source of the means necessary to sustain a living. And this should not simply be seen in terms of cash; the study also uncovers the complexity of their economy. While for some, shoplifting might represent food to eat, or essential clothing, for others it provided discounted stock or business credit to support their livelihood, or the means to assist and subsidise neighbours, binding them in mutual obligation and future insurance of their goodwill and support. Friends' future co-operation and skills might be crucial to the safe disposal of stolen goods or obtaining the best price, and needed nurturing in local communities where universal approval of such makeshift was by no means assured.

108   OBP, September 1787, William Smith (t17870912-58).
109   Paul R. Mullins and Nigel Jefferies, 'The Banality of Gilding: Innocuous Materiality and Transatlantic Consumption in the Gilded Age', International Journal of Historical Archaeology 16/4 (2012), 745–60 (pp. 749–50).

5

The Impact on Retailers

On Saturday, 24 April 1784, William Mawhood, a London woollen draper with a shop in West Smithfield, recorded an eventful day in his diary:

> Call'd on Sargeaunt. His clerk says they'll pay Bunting dividend of 10s. More next week. Lukin nor Rackett at home. See Mr Lamb and came to the Bank in his chariot. ... Was meet by Mr Webb and others and told I had been robb'd. On arriving at my house found the[y] had taken the thief by the assistance of 2 blacksmiths, & likewise Mr Sargeaunts lad as an accomplice the witnesses having seen the lad come out of the shop and say to the two lurking fellows. viz I will do presently. The neighbours persuaded son Charles to let the Constable and Mr Brocklebank go with the 2 before a Magistrate, it happen'd to be Mr Aldm Hart who committed them both to Newgate. Self went to Mr Sargeaunt but he was from home but the clerk and a Mr Fawkes went to Newgate to see the lad and they think in Tuesday. The father and mother of the lad came, they say their son was always good till about a fortnight since[1]

This is the only surviving example we have of an eighteenth-century shopkeeper's unmediated, contemporaneous reaction to a shoplifting incident which was subsequently tried at the Old Bailey.[2] Perhaps surprisingly, there is no dwelling on the items stolen, or their value – later declared in court to be £5. The episode is portrayed as a minor neighbourhood drama; Mawhood's diary entry implies some regret that his son was persuaded to charge the perpetrators, some concern to keep on terms with a local business associate, and even some sympathy for a fellow parent. In financial terms, he is clearly more exercised by his earlier visit to the bank and the uncertainty of the forthcoming dividend.

William Mawhood may have been among London's wealthier traders. Joseph Collyer in 1761 estimated start-up costs for woollen drapers to be

---

1   LMA, CLC/477/MS09939/037, William Mawhood collection, Diary, 15 November 1783–23 July 1784 (24 April 1784).
2   *OBP*, April 1784, Edward Goodwin, Thomas Wilkin (t17840421-73).

£1,000 to £5,000, the highest for any London retail trade.[3] While he left no accounts for this period, a cash notebook for 1771 lists stock in trade and book debts of £15,000, and the business remained healthy enough to be passed on to his son Charles in 1797.[4] Preceding chapters have dwelt at length on the scale of the crime and the range and volume of goods shoplifters stole. This may have served to build an impression that constant anxiety at the financial depredations of shoplifters characterised the English shopkeeper. But, how accurate is this representation, and how common was William Mawhood's apparent indifference to his potential loss? In this chapter we address the economic impact of shoplifting, first analysing its financial toll on retailers and their attempts to mitigate this. We shall then examine the degree to which the crime's relative impact on business solvency was reflected in shopkeepers' attitudes, and the severity of their action against offenders.

Retailers' finances

While disclosing losses in individual incidents, transcripts and depositions offer almost no precise information on overall shrinkage rates for shoplifting.[5] As so much of the crime was undetected, this could only be assessed from stock depletion. We have no specific reason to distrust the linen draper who declared in 1733 that he had lost 'above ten pounds by them since last month', or the one who allegedly told the defendant in 1805 that 'he had lost about twenty or thirty pounds that week', but this may have been hyperbole, and in any case these are random claims.[6] Similarly, there may be little objective basis to the following press report, published in October 1783, which provides an alternative estimate of retail loss:

> Shoplifting is now so common, (though a capital offence) that it is asserted, that upon a fair calculation, the inhabitants of St Paul's, Covent-Garden, have for some time past been defrauded of upwards of a thousand pounds worth of goods per annum.[7]

---

3   Joseph Collyer, *The Parent's and Guardian's Directory and the Youth's Guide in a Choice of a Profession or Trade* (London, 1761), p. 301.
4   LMA, CLC/477/MS09940, William Mawhood collection, Cash account and note book; William Mawhood, *The Mawhood Diary: Selections from the Diary Notebook of William Mawhood, Woollen-Draper of London, for the Years 1764–1790*, ed. E. E. Reynolds (London, 1956), p. 12.
5   Shrinkage is defined in accounting terms as inventory loss, most commonly the result of employee theft, shoplifting, administrative error or waste.
6   *OBP*, February 1733, Elizabeth Coney (t17330221-7); May 1805, George Beals, Esther Merryman (t18050529-11).
7   *The General Evening Post*, 16–18 October 1783, p. 4.

In fact there may be little to be gained by trying to resolve such discrepant claims. Ultimately, attempts to reach a discrete figure for shoplifting losses are thwarted by the inability of many shopkeepers to distinguish these from other stock shrinkage. Linen draper Peregrine Hogg recalled in court that when he was asked by a fellow retailer in 1774 whether he had suspected the honesty of an employee who had worked for both: 'I said no, in a large shop like mine it is impossible to miss little things'; an admission echoed in 1795 when a shopman, questioned whether missing a piece of his muslin had caused him to suspect the shoplifter in the dock, responded 'It is impossible, the quantity is so great, to miss a piece.'[8]

An alternative approach to the question of the relative financial impact of shoplifting is to look at the overall economic model of an eighteenth-century retailer and to examine some of the known causal factors of business failure. Within these parameters we can assess the degree to which shoplifting may have been a contributory factor. The eighteenth-century trader operated at the centre of a web of mutual financial obligation. His yearly outgoings would include loan repayments on capital raised to fund the business initially; payments for stock to suppliers, factors, carriers, and possibly customs and excise; fixed property expenses of shop rent, local taxes, insurance, staff wages and other household outgoings; and sales expenses of marketing, customer hospitality and goods delivery. To meet these expenses and make a living, retailers relied on sales income from their customers, sometimes supplemented by rent from lodgers, shop apprentice premiums and, for the wealthier, rent from property holdings and dividends from the investment of any surplus income.[9] As costs were inevitably incurred prior to any receipt of income, eighteenth-century merchandising was sustained by credit. Retailers were reliant on credit from their suppliers, and were themselves routinely expected to extend credit to their customers. Such arrangements were largely based on personal trust, and dependent on maintaining lender confidence; the crucial nature of this being underlined by Defoe who devoted no less than half the chapters in his retailer's manual, *The Complete English Tradesman*, entirely or in part to the issue of managing credit relations. Readers of the guide would be left in no doubt that:

> Credit is so much a tradesman's blessing, that 'tis the choicest ware he deals in, and he cannot be too chary of it when he has it, or buy it too dear when he wants it; ... In a word 'tis the life and soul of his trade, and it requires his utmost vigilance to preserve it.[10]

8 *OBP*, May 1774, William Jones (t17740518-70); December 1795, Frances Johnson (t17951202-20).
9 Peter Earle, *The Making of the English Middle Class: Business, Society and Family Life in London, 1660–1730* (London, 1989), p. 113.
10 Defoe, *The Complete English Tradesman*, p. 185.

Business failure was frequently the result of mismanaging credit. Julian Hoppit has identified three key risks to traders as overtrading, synchronisation and interdependency.[11] Overtrading was buying more stock on credit than could be supported by sales or underlying capital; synchronisation was the failure to effectively manage credit periods, allowing creditors' payment deadlines to fall due before debtors'; finally, interdependency reflected the vulnerability of a business sector largely reliant on interpersonal lending, the failure of one business pulling down others. This danger was exacerbated by the common use of bills of exchange and other credit instruments drawn on trading partners. Circulating among tradesmen as a form of currency and often multiply endorsed, fraud or even loss of confidence in one of the parties could affect all signatories. For all his strictures on shoplifting, Defoe had no illusions as to the relative significance of theft or loss of credit to a retailer:

> the loss of his money or goods is easily made up, and may be sometimes repaired with advantage; but the loss of credit is never repair'd; the one is breaking open his house, but the other is burning it down; the one carries away some goods, but the other shuts out goods from coming in; one is hurting the tradesman, but the other is undoing him.[12]

In the febrile economy of the eighteenth century, with a succession of wars and financial crises repeatedly dislocating production and trade, businesses were highly sensitive to credit risk. With their business competency and degree of custom on daily display to the world, retailers had to protect their credit reputation. The mere suspicion that they might be susceptible in this respect could have serious implications for their access to, or terms of, credit.

Certainly, sudden credit failure could destroy a business virtually overnight. Mary Holl, a *feme sole* trader with a milliner's shop in the Strand, lost her own business in 1778 when that of her husband foundered. Loss of confidence led to her wholesalers reclaiming some of her stock, and more was sequestered by her husband's creditors. In a letter to one of her husband's assignees, written 'soon after my lace was taken from me', she identifies this as the crucial destabilising action:

> I was upon ground of getting more than three hund'd a year till you and Mr Greenwollers partner to Mr Holl's affairs involv'd me as they have done ... my poor laces, which has so sadly undone me, I can prove cost me, if Messrs Neville and Benezick had been paid, £470 ... and if it had been left

11   Julian Hoppit, 'The Use and Abuse of Credit in Eighteenth-Century England', in *Business Life and Public Policy: Essays in Honour of D. C. Coleman*, ed. N. McKendrick and R. B. Outhwaite (Cambridge, 1986), pp. 64–78 (pp. 66–7).
12   Defoe, *The Complete English Tradesman*, p. 193.

with me wou'd have served the creditors much more than I doubt it will now.[13]

It is uncertain how frequent such catastrophic income loss may have been. In 1797, the request by William Pitt for London tax collectors to assess the likely income of shopkeepers in their collection districts, received a robust response from some:

> It is impossible to answer to the proposition relative to the income of the 5 classes on each side of this paper with any degree of accuracy ... with respect to the profits of tradesmen, NO judgement can be formed, for the man who may settle his accounts this day & lay by £500 may in the course of a month thro' losses in trade become a bankrupt.[14]

Casual shoplifting losses were hardly likely to reduce a tradesman to bankruptcy so rapidly. But for most retailers it would be the drip-feed of smaller losses, eroding margins, that was more insidious in undermining their business. The *Great Grievance* petition in 1699 explicitly described shopkeepers as being 'insensibly ruined' by customer theft.[15] Competition between shops, and particularly those dealing in textiles, could be fierce with consequent pressure on profit margins. In one northern town, Sheffield, fifteen drapery shops were vying to make a living in the late 1780s, all situated within a hundred yards of the central Market Place.[16] Drapers trumpeted the cheapness of their goods compared with those of their competitors. In a typical newspaper advert, Whiteside and Brennand announced in July 1788 that they were shortly to take Robert Hincksman's linen draper's shop at 316 Holborn, where 'they are determined to sell at the most reduced prices ... on average every article is more than 20 per cent lower than ever remembered'.[17] Hincksman's bankruptcy had been announced in the *London Gazette* two months earlier.[18]

Increases in local taxes were also reported as being damaging to business solvency. In London the tax collectors, familiar with their districts and the existing problems of tax collection, were sceptical of local shopkeepers'

---

13 TNA, C105/30, Chancery, Master Lynch's Exhibits, Willan v. Clement, Valuation of lace and millinery, Strand, Westminster, fol. 15. This case is described in greater detail in Margaret Hunt, *The Middling Sort: Commerce, Gender and the Family, 1680–1780* (London, 1996), pp. 140–1.

14 TNA, PRO 30/8/280, William Pitt, Papers, fols 45–6 (Collector, St Benet Finch Division, Broad Street Ward). See p. 53 above.

15 *The Great Grievance of Traders and Shopkeepers.*

16 Gales & Martin, *A Directory of Sheffield* (Sheffield, 1787).

17 *Morning Chronicle and London Advertiser*, 18 July 1788, p. 2.

18 *London Gazette*, 24–27 May 1788, Issue 12993, p. 253.

ability to weather the proposed additional levy in 1797. A collector in Farringdon Without, the City ward with the highest incidence of shoplifting prosecutions in the 1785–89 sample, commented, 'I am sorry to say that if this passes into a law that 71 industrious men declare they must shut up their shops'.[19] And, perhaps surprisingly, similar concerns were expressed in richer areas, one of the collectors for St George Hanover Square, reporting:

> those from £10 to £20 are most of those shopkeepers who from their situation particularly Bond Street/St James Street/and Piccadilly are compelled to pay heavy rents and of course their taxes must increase accordingly. I am of the opinion that if much increase is laid on those classes it will be attended with great difficulty for the Collectors to do their duty inasmuch that two parts out of three will not be possessed of means to answer their demands.[20]

Patrick Colquhoun estimated the average annual income of English shopkeepers in 1803 to be £150, although the basis for this has been questioned by Mui and Mui.[21] However, such generalisation is unhelpful given the disparities between provincial and London shops, and even between larger and smaller stores within the capital. In 1797 some collectors returned more detailed reports on the tax liabilities and income of selected shopkeepers in their areas.[22] In London these span both poorer and wealthier parishes. While their choice of streets and trades seems random, and their income assessments were subjective, with a consequent potential variance in reliability, they do give some indication of the income range in those shop trades most commonly the target of shoplifters (Table 26). A return from the Collector for York confirms similar disparities of income within shop trades in the north of England.[23] While we have no evidence that shoplifting, in the absence of other debts, drove any retailer to bankruptcy, it was more likely to be significant as a contributing factor for a trader in a lower income band.

What other factors might increase the financial significance of shoplifting to a retailer? For a short period during the century, many shopkeepers bore an additional excise charge. In 1785 Pitt imposed a Shop Tax on all retailers paying an annual rent of £5 or above. This levy was bitterly contested, above all by London retailers whose rents were consistently higher than their provincial counterparts, until repeal was forced in 1789 (Plate 6). In a 1788

19   TNA, PRO 30/8/280, William Pitt, Papers, fols 93–4 (Collector, St Brides, New Street Precinct, Farringdon Without Ward).
20   TNA, PRO 30/8/280, William Pitt, Papers, fol. 212 (Collector, Dover Street Ward, St George, Hanover Square).
21   Patrick Colquhoun, A Treatise on Indigence (London, 1806), p. 23; Mui and Mui, Shops and Shopkeeping, pp. 143–5.
22   TNA, PRO 30/8/281, William Pitt, Papers, fols 19–65.
23   TNA, PRO 30/8/281, William Pitt, Papers, fols 76–80.

Table 26. Income range of London shopkeepers (as extracted from London Tax Collectors' Reports, 1797)

Type of shop	No. of shops listed	Lowest assessed income	Highest assessed income	Median annual income
Linen draper/mercer	6	£150	£1,000	£375
Haberdasher	12	£50	£1,000	£250
Hosier	5	£100	£600–£700	£500
Shoemaker	13	£60	£300–£400	£150
Cheesemonger	5	£70	£400	£200
Silversmith	5	£250	£1,000	£400

Source: TNA, PRO 30/8/281, William Pitt, Papers, fols 19–65

petition to Parliament, the City of London Retail Shopkeepers Committee refuted the implication that raising prices to customers would negate the effect of the tax:

> In the case stated of the two persons in the same trade, one who pays scarcely any tax has no motive to raise his prices; and the other must pay the amount of the tax out of his profits or be undersold by his more fortunate neighbour.[24]

While none of the retailers bringing shoplifting prosecutions during this period commented in court on the extra burden of the tax, the prosecutor in a lodgings theft case of 1785, presumably a shopkeeper, invoked it in justifying why he had evicted the accused: 'for they owed me a great deal of rent, the taxes were so high, and now the shop-tax, that people find it difficult to live'.[25]

Perhaps most demanding, though, were daily trading pressures. Keeping credit and cash flow in equilibrium required astute management, particularly for concerns founded on limited capital. Smaller shops wanted sufficient stock to trade but could have low turnover, and activity was often seasonal, at its highest in summer.[26] No shop could risk being left with dated stock – a mercer 'derives no credit at all from a throng of old shopkeepers, as they

---

24 Guildhall Library, City of London, Broadside 7.143 (Case of the Retail Shopkeeper – March 8 1788).

25 *OBP*, September 1785, Elizabeth Henley (t17850914-68).

26 Earle, *The Making of the English Middle Class*, p. 119; Julian Hoppit, *Risk and Failure in English Business, 1700–1800* (Cambridge, 1987), p. 109.

Plate 6   *Paddy O Pitts Triumphal Exit*, 1785: satirical print of shopkeepers protesting at Pitt's shop tax, with shuttered shops inscribed 'to Lett' in the background

call them, (viz.) out-of-fashion things', chided Defoe.[27] In court, retailers hastened to assure the jury that stolen goods were not old shopkeepers, and fully of the value they claimed. Shops that sought to retain the loyalty of more affluent customers by offering generous credit terms needed to synchronise their receipts with commitments to creditors. Defoe writes in the 1720s of suppliers offering six to eight months credit for goods which were sold on to customers at three to four months credit, although Mui and Mui suggest that credit periods shortened as the century progressed.[28] However, customers rarely met their outstanding bills in full with periodic payments on account being more common, and the situation was further complicated by a tradition of customary repayment dates for debts, the upper and middling classes expecting to have bills presented annually at Christmas.[29] Thus solvency was contingent on how judiciously credit was afforded to customers. Court transcripts reveal that shop staff were constantly making small prudential judgements on the status and trustworthiness of their customers, though not always effectively. There is the linen draper who saw a defendant looking at some lawn 'and apprehended, by her appearance, she could not have occasion

27   Defoe, *The Complete English Tradesman*, p. 62.
28   Defoe, *The Complete English Tradesman*, p. 65; Mui and Mui, *Shops and Shopkeeping*, pp. 24–5.
29   Finn, *The Character of Credit*, pp. 95–6.

for such a thing', or the shopman who related how the defendant had stood next to another lady customer: 'The lady wanted change for a guinea; I could not change it: I said it was the same, she might pay another time.'[30] Where recommendation and connections counted, no retailer wanted to risk offending existing customers or missing the opportunity of attracting their friends through good reputation. A shoemaker explained such thinking:

> the prisoner came into my shop, he said he had burst the upper leather of his shoe, and asked my man to give him credit for a pair of shoes, I bid my man tell him I would do no such thing, then he came through the shop to me, and said he lived in credit, that he knew several people in the neigh-bourhood, whose names he mentioned; I thought he might be distressed and agreed to let him have a pair.[31]

The defendant nevertheless failed to capitalise on this change of heart; he was caught when he attempted to shoplift a second pair.

Interestingly, almost none of shoplifters prosecuted seem to have been credit customers. There is some presumption of class exclusion, as implied by the justice's comment to a shoplifter in 1746: 'are you not a fine lady to go into a tradesman's shop without money'.[32] Yet research has found that even small shopkeepers with a poorer clientele were obliged to extend credit, a practical response to both the intermittent income stream of their customers and the chronic shortage of coinage in eighteenth-century England.[33] Naturally a shopkeeper would only afford credit to those he knew and trusted, but even regular customers were described in evidence as paying cash for goods at the time of the theft. Ann Austin had shopped at John Hunt's shop for some years, but he was not prepared to release the cloak for which she had given a down payment of sixpence until she returned with the balance.[34] This immediately suggests that retailers were generally less magnanimous towards their poorer customers than previously thought; but it is more probable that the rare appearance of their credit customers in court reflects both the ease of compounding – simply adding the cost to their account in the day book – and the potential difficulties inherent in prosecution. In September 1789, City linen drapers, Joseph King and Richard Cotton prosecuted Mary Wilks. An old customer, she was regularly allowed to buy goods on account, but on the day in question had been caught secretly smuggling 14 yards of cotton fabric out of the shop beneath her cloak.

30 *OBP*, October 1751, Elizabeth Medows (t17511016-24); January 1770, Mary Steel (t17700117-19).
31 *OBP*, December 1774, Lewis Sharkey (t17741207-3).
32 *OBP*, September 1746, Mary Smith (t17460903-19).
33 Cox, *The Complete Tradesman*, pp. 160–1; Styles, *Dress of the People*, pp. 147, 173; Mui and Mui, *Shops and Shopkeeping*, pp. 215–16.
34 *OBP*, September 1773, Ann Austin (t17730908-47).

Unprepared in court and outmanoeuvred by William Garrow defending, King and Cotton's shopman listened dejectedly as the judge directed the jury: 'this woman must be acquitted; she is in conversation with a man, bargaining and dealing with him, from whom it is possible, she had the goods; and this very cotton might be in that very bill, and on credit'.[35]

Of course, some petty shopkeepers may have operated on such small margins that they were unable to offer credit. Before Elizabeth Hollinby stole some fustian from Edward Jones' shop on Old Gravel Lane off Ratcliff Highway, she sounded out the possibility of credit: 'she said her daughter had bought some linen to be paid for at so much a week; I told her there was no such a thing in our shop'.[36] And in practice such shopkeepers were not alone, as an increasing number of retailers were recognising the advantage of cash-only selling. The bookseller James Lackington, one of its keenest advocates, wrote in his memoir of how his saving on accounting and debt-chasing, and the ready availability of cash to 'lay out in trade to best advantage', enabled him to sell his books more cheaply.[37] At the same time he acknowledged, 'I was obliged to put my goods cheaper in my catalogue than others, or I should have lost my customers, as the trade and the public would go where they could have credit, if they were to pay the same price.[38] But this introduced new risks. Profit margins of ready-money retailers were conventionally lower.[39] Lackington compensated by increasing his turnover, but other retailers could struggle. And cash selling may have made it more difficult for retailers to exert tight accounting controls as cash sales were not customarily recorded individually. When Oxford Street haberdasher Francis Thompson was asked, during a 1788 forgery trial, 'Was it in the course of your dealings to make any entries of such goods as you sold for ready money?', he expostulated, 'Oh dear! no; it is impossible; it is too trifling; we never book any thing we sell for ready money.'[40] If many shopkeepers were operating on bare margins then shoplifting losses could have tipped the balance.

Trade protection societies

Although the economic situation of some retailers suffering customer theft might be grave, limited financial support to help deal with shoplifters was potentially available from another quarter: the trade protection society. It is

35 OBP, September 1789, Mary Wilks (t17890909-30).
36 OBP, January 1800, Elizabeth Hollinby (t18000115-15).
37 Lackington, Memoirs of the First Forty-Five Years, p. 213.
38 J. Lackington, To the Booksellers of London and Westminster (London, 1788).
39 Cox, The Complete Tradesman, p. 105.
40 OBP, May 1788, Joseph Slack (t17880507-57).

worth examining the role they played. On 17 April 1798, the London-based Society for Prosecuting Felons, Forgers, Cheats &c placed an advertisement in *The Times* for their anniversary dinner, recording proudly that 'The Society congratulates themselves on finding in the course of 30 years experience, that the principles on which it was established have been illustrated by the completest success in preventing the perpetration of many crimes, and the punishment of such offenders as are too profligate to be deterred.'[41] A year later, in a similar advert, they announced, 'This Society have in the course of last year, as well as in preceding years, brought to conviction a number of offenders, particularly SHOP-LIFTERS, who are the greatest pest to the trading part of the community.'[42] The Society was, however, exceptional among its peers in affording such prominence to the crime.

Local trade protection and prosecution societies had been formed throughout England in increasing numbers from the mid eighteenth century, to the extent that by 1839 there were over five hundred in existence.[43] While the primary business rationale for trade protection societies was credit management and for prosecution societies, crime prevention, those in urban areas tended to perform both roles to some extent. The earliest, the London Society of Tradesman and Shopkeepers &c for the Protection of their Property against the Inroads of Felons, Cheats &c, was founded in March 1767 as a later member recorded, 'under the sanction, and by the advice of the late Sir John Fielding'.[44] Fielding had in fact been promoting such an initiative for some time.[45] As mutual aid societies, they were a response to the business handicaps manufacturers, tradesmen and shopkeepers then operated under. Where dealing was conducted on trust, members could assist each other by sharing intelligence on the reliability or creditworthiness of traders and customers; additionally they could issue alerts on potential deceptions or the circulation of fraudulent credit instruments. In the absence of state prosecution, societies provided mutual insurance for a membership fee, covering the costs of detection, arrest and subsequent prosecution of offenders.[46] Other

41 *The Times*, 17 April 1798, p. 1.

42 *The Oracle and Daily Advertiser*, 1 April 1799, p. 1.

43 Robert J. Bennett, 'Supporting Trust: Credit Assessment and Debt Recovery Through Trade Protection Societies in Britain and Ireland, 1776–1992', *Journal of Historical Geography*, 38 (2012), 123–42 (p. 126).

44 *Public Advertiser*, 2 December 1767, p. 3; *The Times*, 7 September 1795, p. 3. The title was shortened within a year in the press to the Society of Tradesmen &c.

45 John Fielding, 'Plan for the Further Prevention of Frauds and Felonies committed on Tradesmen and Shopkeepers', in *Extracts From Such of the Penal Laws as Particularly Relate to the Peace and Good Order of this Metropolis* (London, 1761), pp. 238–42.

46 David Philips, 'Good Men to Associate and Bad Men to Conspire: Associations for the Prosecution of Felons in England 1760–1860', in *Policing and Prosecution in Britain, 1750–1850*, ed. D. Hay and F. Snyder (Oxford, 1989), pp. 113–70 (p. 121).

benefits were financial assistance with advertising stolen goods, which was an increasingly popular recourse from mid-century, and the payment of rewards or gratuities to individuals, constables or watch officers whose actions had assisted members in bringing offenders to justice.[47] Societies also offered a degree of advice and moral support in negotiating the eighteenth-century legal system. When two linen drapers approached a society in 1796 regarding the theft of goods from their shop by a maidservant, three of its Committee members agreed to accompany them to the police office.[48] Attorneys, who took on the arrangement of prosecutions and appointed counsel as required, were generally prominent among the membership.

A second society, the Guardians or Society for the Protection of Trade against Swindlers and Sharpers, was established in London in March 1776.[49] A membership roll from 1799 records 249 members of whom 40% were retailers.[50] A Bye-Law from 9 February 1791 attached to this list stated:

> THAT, whenever any Member shall have suffered by robbery of any kind, or by shoplifting, and shall have prosecuted the offender or offenders to conviction, he shall be at liberty, after such conviction, to lay a state of the facts, in writing, before the Committee for the time being accompanied by an account also in writing of the expences to which he may have been put in carrying on such prosecution, which expences the Committee shall have power to order the payment of to such Member, provided the same, in cases of robbery, do not exceed the sum of fifty shillings; and in cases of shoplifting the sum of forty shillings.[51]

However, there is little evidence that shoplifting was a leading concern to this society, whose membership list suggests tended towards larger and more elite traders. In a series of press advertisements between 1776 and 1798 they warned members of a number of individual fraudsters, false bills or bank notes in circulation, of treating all credit instruments with caution, and on some occasions offering rewards for further information.[52] The fashionable 'West End' London newspapers in which these adverts were invariably placed further pointed towards wealthier dealers and a primary interest in larger-scale transactions than those involved in shoplifting.

47   John Styles, 'Print and Policing: Crime Advertising in Eighteenth-Century Provincial England', in *Policing and Prosecution in Britain*, ed. Hay and Snyder, pp. 55–112 (pp. 63–5).
48   LMA, CLA/074/03/012, Clubs and Societies collection, Proceedings of Society for Prosecuting Felons etc. Rough Minute Book, April 1795–April 1800 (18 March 1796).
49   Bennett, 'Supporting Trust', p. 127.
50   *A List of Members of the Guardians; or Society for the Protection of Trade against Swindlers and Sharpers* (London, 1799).
51   *A List of Members of the Guardians*, p. 35.
52   For example, *The World*, 7 February 1787, p. 1; *St James's Chronicle*, 22–24 December 1789, p. 1; *Morning Chronicle*, 12 January 1791, p. 1.

In northern towns, where the incidence of the crime was significantly lower than in London, shoplifting also appears to have been a less important focus for trade and prosecution societies. An advert publicising the December 1788 meeting of Sheffield's Association for Prosecuting Felons carried the postscript, 'the daring depredations that have lately been committed in this town will certainly convince tradesmen of the utility of Associations of this kind'.[53] Yet the list of subscribers to a subsequent advertisement included no drapers, and when in December 1790 the Association advertised a series of monetary rewards on conviction for various property crimes, theft from a shop was conspicuous by its absence.[54]

Fielding's Society of Tradesman and Shopkeepers &c continued to advertise its monthly meetings until the 1790s when it reinvented itself as The Society for Prosecuting Felons, Forgers, Cheats &c. A Minute Book for the period 1795 to 1800, recording the business conducted at each monthly committee meeting, provides a more detailed picture of how London shopkeepers interacted with the Society.[55] The membership appears to have been smaller than that of the Guardians. Annual subscriptions had been increased from 5 shillings at inception to a guinea by 1795 with an audit that year listing the amount of subscriptions received as £87.14s. A similar record in 1799 has a total of only £73.17s.6d, which implies a declining membership of between seventy and eighty. Subscriptions were supplemented by ticket sales to the Society's annual dinner, the total receipts against expenditure being nevertheless sufficient for them to invest a surplus in South Sea stock.[56] The size of the Society is consonant with the relatively few tradesmen who approached it for assistance with prosecution, an average of five a year. The Society did issue warnings to its members on potential frauds, but these were generally by notices sent to members rather than public advert.

Over the five-year period of the Minute Book, the Society assisted with seven prosecutions for shoplifting. The first, in May 1795, was entered as 'Mr Atkinson presented a bill for prosecuting Mary Ann Nevitt for robbing him, being his servant and Ann Morton and Sarah Field for shoplifting amounting to £2.2s.6d'.[57] There is no evidence of the first case being heard at the Old Bailey, but the shoplifting trial of Ann Morton the previous September was notable for the rancorous cross-examination of linen draper John Atkinson. Forced into an admission that he had previously prosecuted twenty individuals in lower courts, Atkinson continued to be hounded, 'How

53 *Sheffield Register*, 27 December 1788, p. 3.
54 *Sheffield Register*, 2 December 1790, p. 2.
55 LMA, CLA/074/03/012, Rough Minute Book.
56 LMA, CLA/074/03/012, Rough Minute Book, 17 April 1795, 18 September 1795, 13 November 1799.
57 LMA, CLA/074/03/012, Rough Minute Book, 15 May 1795.

many persons have you charged with different things, and received money in order to drop the prosecution?', before suffering the defendant's acquittal.[58] We cannot assume from this one example that the combative attitude to prosecution visible in the actions of such retailers was characteristic of the members of prosecution associations, but it is suggestive. Where the costs reimbursed in the remaining shoplifting prosecutions are recorded, these ranged from 18 shillings to £3.13s.6d; useful amounts to recover and potentially more generous than the 40 shillings offered by the Guardians, but perhaps not overly significant in relation to annual membership contributions.[59]

In fact, much of the attraction of Society membership may have been the sense of common cause in a wider battle against crime. In 1796 the Society was consulted by Patrick Colquhoun. The minute of 17 June recorded:

> Mr Colquhoun, Police Magistrate of Worship Street, attended and conferr'd with the Committee on the very desirable end of amending the penal laws of the country. Several parts of Mr Colquhoun's treatise were read and which he kindly elucidated much to the satisfaction of members present, and which tended principally to prevent crimes rather than punishing them.[60]

It was agreed that members would get hold of copies of the Treatise for consideration at the next meeting.[61] But while prevention might be expedient, this did not preclude an inflexible attitude towards offenders. Two years later the minutes dispassionately note that 'The sub-treasurer reported that Susannah Skelton and William her son aged 10 years had been prosecuted at the expense of the Society for privately stealing in the shop of Mr Henry Wright of the Minories and were both capitally convicted.'[62] And when the Society was requested to intercede on behalf of Elizabeth Smith, a shopwoman convicted of stealing from one of their members, the minutes report: 'Resolved that this Society will by no means countenance any application to His Majesty for a pardon for any person who has been prosecuted by them as it would be incompatible with the duty that they owe to the public and their institution.'[63]

58   *OBP*, September 1794, Ann Morton (t17940917-92).
59   LMA, CLA/074/03/012, Rough Minute Book, 20 July 1798, 19 October 1798, 15 March 1799, 3 April 1799, 19 July 1799.
60   LMA, CLA/074/03/012, Rough Minute Book, 17 June 1796.
61   Patrick Colquhoun, *A Treatise on the Police of the Metropolis* (London 1796).
62   LMA, CLA/074/03/012, Rough Minute Book, 20 July 1798.
63   LMA, CLA/074/03/012, Rough Minute Book, 21 February 1800.

Business temperament

If trade societies could be belligerent in their attitudes, was this unique to their membership? Having recognised that shoplifting did have the capacity to financially undermine some traders, it is pertinent to ask whether there was any correlation between financial vulnerability and the propensity to prosecute. Unfortunately that question is unanswerable given our limited knowledge of prosecutors' financial circumstances. And even where we have data, it fails to support such a simplified premise. Let us take the example of two neighbouring London haberdashers: Major Blundell and Thomas Living. A successful retail and wholesale haberdasher, Major Blundell leased two shops on Holborn Bridge with warehousing behind.[64] His family and business papers exhibit his model accounting practices.[65] Taking a former employee into partnership in 1784, Blundell minutely recorded expenditure on servants' board, customer hospitality, and the sums including interest owed to him from profits 'to be equivalent with the cash Mr Strafford has taken'. Blundell's share of profits, averaging £514 a year, in fact doubled over the course of the partnership. A series of receipts attest to his regular payment of rent, taxes and insurance and he kept careful records of wages due, and payments to, his employees. Stock was reviewed and discounted to reflect decreasing value. There is no evidence that Major Blundell prosecuted a shoplifter, but we cannot safely assign this to complacency arising from his secure financial status. It seems that Blundell had no compunction in setting off losses against staff wages. In July 1780, John Hall had £9.6s.3d deducted for 'Goods lost/ missed Twights & Co'; in October 1795 another servant forwent £1.1s from his pay for 'cash from till unaccounted for'.[66] While it is difficult to know how common or widespread this practice was among retailers, the prospect of being held responsible for shoplifting losses would certainly have concentrated the mind and ensured extra staff vigilance. The second haberdasher, Thomas Living, ran a shop a little further up Holborn Hill and had at one time been an employee of Blundell. Although we have less to go on, we know that his business foundered in 1787 and that he was declared bankrupt.[67] Living did indeed prosecute a shoplifter for stealing a 10 shilling length of ribbon but, once again, we cannot easily associate this with financial insecurity.[68] The case came to court less than a month before his bankruptcy was

---

64   LMA, CLC/B/025/MS10033/001, Major Blundell collection, Deeds of property in Shoe Lane, Holborn Hill, Plumbtree Court and Stockwell Place, Lambeth.
65   LMA, CLC/B/025/MS10033A, Major Blundell collection, Business papers; MS10033/002, Ledger (private expenses).
66   LMA, CLC/B/025/MS10033/002, 003, Ledger (private expenses).
67   *London Gazette*, 9–13 October 1787, Issue 12928, p. 479.
68   *OBP*, September 1787, Thomas Wood (t17870912-7).

announced, when he must already have been aware of his desperate situation. If financial prudency was a key motivation, one doubts that Living would have embarked on proceedings generating costs in excess of his loss. In fact, to the financially straitened, alternative responses such as compounding or even simple goods recovery would have added inducement.

From elite London stores to small rural shops, most retailers who prosecuted shoplifters at the Old Bailey or assizes only did so once. The evidence from the sample suggests that at least three-quarters did not repeat their experience. Indeed some of these may, through the involvement of parish law officers in apprehending the thief, have been drawn into the process unwillingly. Others could have recognised the futility of its deterrent effect and chosen thereafter to concentrate on situational prevention. However, there did remain a minority who prosecuted repeatedly and by examining these we may gain a fuller understanding of eighteenth-century shopkeepers' behavioural drivers. There has been a tendency to treat shopkeepers as a unified interest group with a common attitude and agenda. But this simple stereotyping is misleading as an explanatory paradigm. Shopkeepers were individuals whose background, trade experience, and reaction to the social and cultural influences of society all moulded their business attitudes. It is true some shopkeepers suffered more than others, but equally so that, irrespective of loss, some felt the imposition more keenly. While the majority of trial transcripts and depositions give us no insight on the prosecutor's state of mind or motivations, those few that do, reveal often strong emotive reactions. In 1805 linen draper Thomas Powdich prosecuted two shoplifters for stealing from his Holborn shop, the second of four cases he presented at the Old Bailey that year. We can detect the sentiment within his shop from the testimony of his shop assistant who stated bluntly that he had not attempted to pre-empt the theft when the offenders were still in the shop 'Because I wanted to make it a capital offence.' When reproached for this by counsel for the defence, he was unrepentant:

Q. You had suspicions of these girls when they came into the shop?
A. I had.

Q. Your Christian charity did not prompt you to tell them you wanted them to commit a felony, that you might have the pleasure of prosecuting?
A. Exactly.[69]

Similarly strongly expressed was the spontaneous reaction of haberdasher John Walford to an incident in his shop. Told by his staff that they were suspicious of customer Sarah Lyons, the court heard how he 'desired that they

---

69   OBP, April 1805, Margaret Berry, Jane Scott (t18050424-70).

would not touch her, unless they were positive, as it was a delicate matter, and in fact would be cruel to take her into custody on slight suspicions'. But upon his shopman reporting that Lyons had been seen to drop a silk handkerchief from beneath her petticoat, Walford replied 'this is what we want; we will make an example of her'.[70]

A closer examination of one retailer, Joseph Craig, with a militant attitude to shoplifting, suggests that such attitudes and behaviours may have been inculcated and transmitted through the shop apprenticeship system. A prosperous linen draper, Craig opened his first shop in Holborn in 1792 and within five years had expanded into a second shop in more fashionable Oxford Street at an annual rent of £130, while still achieving an assessed income of £500 a year.[71] Between 1793 and 1810 he prosecuted shoplifters at the Old Bailey on sixteen occasions. His highest single loss was £2.12s, but in five of the cases the goods stolen were valued at less than 5 shillings. Craig's relentless determination to prosecute could hardly have been founded on a belief in its deterrent effect. In fact it seems that his attitude predated his shop ownership. Prior to setting up his business, Craig had been employed as a shopman by John Thwaites, a neighbouring Holborn linen draper. Appearing for Thwaites in a shoplifting case in February 1791, the court reporter found fit to include Craig's protestation, 'I have not sworn from any motives of resentment'.[72] It will be no surprise to learn that Thwaites was also a serial prosecutor, bringing twelve cases to the Old Bailey between 1788 and 1809. Testifying in one of these in 1788, his shopman recalled, 'I told my master I thought that woman had something with her; he told me to follow her; I rather refused, I was not sure; I did not like to go; he was angry, and I was obliged to go'.[73] And in a deposition attached to a second case we read that 'John Thwaites told his apprentice to follow the prisoners and see if they had not got something more than they had bought but the young man being unwilling to observe his directions the said John Thwaites followed the prisoners himself'.[74] We know that John Thwaites's personality was naturally combative from two advertisements he placed in the press in early 1787 to guard his business reputation:

WHEREAS some malicious and evil-disposed person or persons, from motives of envy did ... stick up, or cause to be stuck up in divers parts of Holborn, Chancery Lane and Lincoln's-inn-fields, and the adjacent streets &c an infamous, scandalous, lying and illiberal printed paper, tending

70   *OBP*, June 1788, Sarah Lyons (t17880625-4).
71   TNA, PRO 30/8/281, William Pitt, Papers, fol. 31.
72   *OBP*, February 1791, James Crawley (t17910216-4).
73   *OBP*, December 1788, Mary Dowling (t17881210-47).
74   LMA, OB/SP/1789/04/048, Gaol Delivery Sessions, Information of John Thwaites v. Thomas Stevenson and John Dudley.

to hurt the reputation and credit of Mr John Thwaites at the Bee-Hive, No. 306 High-Holborn and to injure him in his trade of a linen-draper, mercer and hosier ... The above Mr John Thwaites doth hereby offer a reward of one hundred guineas, to be paid to any person or persons, who will discover the author or authors of the aforesaid scandalous paper ...[75]

This challenge, appearing in a January edition of *The World*, was followed a month later by:

JOHN THWAITES ... RETURNS Thanks to the nobility, gentry and public in general, for their kind support, and begs them to beware of being misled by a shop lately fitted out by an envious neighbour, in the same street, in imitation of the said John THWAITES's shop front, and sign.[76]

In such context one can speculate that William Mawhood's apparent indifference to his shoplifting loss at the opening of this chapter was more a reflection of his generally sanguine business temperament than of any relative financial sufficiency.

As Margaret Hunt has written, eighteenth-century traders had little awareness of the wider economic forces affecting their trade, and persistently attributed any failure to the moral weakness or dishonesty of their creditors or debtors.[77] Sussex retailer Thomas Turner rails repeatedly in these terms in his diary. In February 1764 he typically complains that he has

just heard of a book debt of £40 I am likely to lose-and that in a measure through the knavery of the man and my own too great indulgence ... For what by our extravagant living and an indolent way of life ... rather than retrench our expenses, we too often see people run out of their estates and defraud their creditors.[78]

But even within this tendency, we can see a range of attitudes from passive acceptance to virulent rage. For some, bankruptcy was simply the contingency of fortune. City shopkeeper Holloway Brecknock, who prosecuted a shoplifter in 1748, later accounted for his business failure in such a manner: 'I am a poor unfortunate mortal, I have been so my whole life, tho I was in trade many years in credit and respect, but fate so order'd it at last I was oblidg'd to submit to crosses and losses'.[79] Others were keener to apportion blame. And

75   *The World*, 5 January 1787, p. 4.
76   *The World*, 9 February 1787, p. 1.
77   Hunt, *The Middling Sort*, pp. 35–7.
78   D. Vaizey (ed.), *The Diary of Thomas Turner 1754–1765* (Oxford, 1984), pp. 286–7.
79   *OBP*, May 1748, Elizabeth Philipson (t17480526-44); LMA, COL/CC/GPC/05/003, Corporation of London collection, Miscellaneous Papers and Rough Minutes in Relation to the Court of Requests, Letter, 19 April 1792.

their actual injury may have differed from that emotionally experienced. Even where shoplifting was marginal to a retailer's financial failure, he may have felt more resentment against its tangible perpetrators than more culpable, but distant, creditors. Frequency and immediacy of contact might subconsciously magnify shopkeepers' perception of the financial damage shoplifters inflicted. London haberdasher Joseph Slack opened his first shop in 1786 at the age of twenty, but within a year was disastrously embroiled in a prosecution for fraudulently altering a payment draft, causing substantial alarm to his creditors.[80] Although acquitted, the memory of this case, with its implication for his credit reputation, remained in the public realm, to the extent that a shoplifter he prosecuted two years later seized the opportunity to retaliate in court: 'The gentleman has been tried here himself, by all account.'[81] A further shoplifting prosecution followed in 1792, but at the end of that year Slack's business troubles overtook him and he was declared bankrupt on 18 December.[82] In a third shoplifting prosecution three days earlier, conducted it seems, like Thomas Living's, in defiance of his financial situation, the defendant recalled how he had been berated on capture: 'if it was in my power I would hang you, and if you are not heavy enough, if I could have my will, I would pull your legs'.[83]

This chapter has examined the potential financial impact of shoplifting on retailers and the role of trade protection societies in supporting shopkeepers to combat the crime. It contends that in the absence of reliable statistical data, we are reliant on gauging the likely effect on commercial solvency of shoplifting losses, taking into account the range of contemporary business models, retailer's customary reliance on credit and the impact of shop tax. It demonstrates how the crime would be more significant to small-scale traders and those in competitive situations, perhaps experimenting with cash-only selling. And while trade protection and prosecution societies were a resource for some traders, they appear ultimately to have provided greater social than financial benefits. The chapter concludes by arguing from shopkeepers' testimony and history of prosecution that prosecution rates were more reflective of retailers' attitude to the crime than any marginal financial vulnerability.

---

80 *OBP*, May 1788, Joseph Slack (t17880507-57).
81 *OBP*, January 1791, Jane Burn, Mary Vallens (t17910112-41).
82 *London Gazette*, 18–22 December 1792, Issue 13486, p. 959.
83 *OBP*, December 1792, Richard Goodall, Edward Marshall (t17921215-117). In fact Slack may have had less discretion than Living. One of the accused was apprehended by two constables and would therefore have been brought before a magistrate as a matter of routine. Once bound by recognisance, Slack could little afford to have this forfeited. He knew the risk more personally than most, having being called to account by the court for non-appearance in another case some years earlier (see ch. 2, pp. 45–6).

6

Retailers' Recourse to Law

England's law and criminal justice system were commonly accepted to be the primary means by which retailers could discourage theft of their stock, protect it from depredation and obtain a measure of legal redress for losses suffered. But prior to 1699 there was no specific law on shoplifting. It was the accession of William III and Mary II in February 1689 that heralded a period of more active parliamentary government and the fresh possibility of tackling perceived criminal ills legislatively. Beattie asserts that the ensuing momentum to extend the law was driven not by any formal programme or campaign, but by a pervasive national anxiety. In the wake of the Glorious Revolution England had entered a period of war and financial instability, intensifying a public suspicion that society was becoming increasingly immoral; crime, particularly that committed by women, was viewed with new alarm as a serious and growing problem.[1] The institution of regular parliamentary sessions provided back-bench MPs with an unprecedented opportunity to confront these fears by lobbying for change. They, rather than the state, were the proposers of repeated Bills over the following two decades designed to address what was conceived to be the threat to life and property presented by an increasingly vicious working populace. The overall intention of these parliamentarians and their supporters was to strengthen the punitive impact of the criminal law. However, one of their first Acts, passed in 1691, carried a clause that sought to remedy an apparent unfairness by extending 'benefit of clergy' to women on the same terms as men.[2] As a result, women were no longer subject to the death penalty for the theft of goods over 10 shillings.[3] It was in part the adverse impact of this on London retailing that culminated in

---

1 Beattie, *Policing and Punishment*, pp. 315, 322.
2 Benefit of clergy was a legal device originating in mediaeval times that enabled the clergy to escape capital punishment in secular courts on passing a literacy test. By this period it was applied generally to commute the death sentence on crimes designated as 'clergyable'. Although the privilege still required proof of literacy and applied only to a first offence, these provisos were largely disregarded.
3 3 & 4 Wm & Mary, c. 9. s. 6 (1691).

the passing of the discrete Shoplifting Act in 1699 by which the theft of goods with a value exceeding 5 shillings became a capital offence.[4]

In this chapter we explore retailers' engagement with the law on shoplifting, from their formative role in the genesis of the Shoplifting Act to their more equivocal part in its repeal some 120 years later. It examines in some detail the evolution of the Act and how traders as a sector were actively courted by the magistrates Henry and John Fielding in their crusade to make the criminal justice system more effective. Retailers readily co-operated with such initiatives where these were seen to bring results and found practical ways of manipulating the laws to their advantage. But their initial enthusiasm for stronger penal measures disguised a more pragmatic outlook. The thinking of the majority was 'risk-based', weighing prevention costs against other factors, rather than 'crime-based', privileging the importance of detecting and punishing offenders.[5]

The making of the Shoplifting Act

Shoplifting was not a new crime, so we should first trace how and why it became the subject of such draconian and wide-reaching legislation.[6] In their *Great Grievance* petition to Parliament, London shopkeepers complained in 1699 of the increase in shoplifting, the excessive losses sustained by traders which 'very much exceed in value all other robberies within this Kingdom', and of their difficulties in controlling it given the lightness of punishment:

> for if the facts be not notorious, and the goods secured, the criminals escape with a *Bridewell*-whipping, and soon return to their trade, and this very often before they reach *Newgate*. But if convicted of felony, burnt in the hand for the first offence; and when indicted a second, third, or fourth time, escape with the same punishment, by reason of the difficulty in proving the record, they being usually indicted and convicted every time by several names, so escape death, and are sometimes burnt in the hand six or seven times.[7]

---

4   10 & 11 Wm III, c. 23 (1699).
5   Joanna Shapland, 'Preventing Retail Sector Crime', in *Building a Safer Society: Strategic Approaches to Crime Prevention*, ed. M. Tonry and D. P. Farrington (London, 1995), pp. 263–342 (p. 276).
6   The word 'shop-lifter' was in common usage in the 1660s and is likely to have predated this. It appears, for example, in, Pietro Aretino, *The Wandering Whore Continued* (London 1660), pp. 11–12, among a list of criminal types. Shoplifting cases are recorded in the *Proceedings* of the Old Bailey from 1676.
7   *The Great Grievance of Traders and Shopkeepers.*

Table 27. Comparison of value of stolen goods at Old Bailey shoplifting trials in 1689–99 and 1745–54

Value of Stolen Goods	1689–99		1743–54	
	No of Cases	%	No of cases	%
Under £1	44	36	133	74
£1 up to £3	37	30	33	18
£3 up to £5	19	16	5	3
£5 and over	22	18	9	5
Subtotal	122	100	180	100
No value given	16		21	
Total	138		201	

Source: OBP, London sample

A comparison of shoplifting cases brought to the Old Bailey in the decade before the Act with those of the early eighteenth century lends credence to their claims, and helps explain why heightened alarm served to propel the Act through its political hurdles. Two factors which clearly differentiate cases in the late seventeenth century from those in the earliest London sample of 1743 to 1754 are the proportion of women offenders and the value of the goods stolen. Transcripts of shoplifting cases in the *Proceedings* prior to 1700 are frequently confined to a few lines, so there are difficulties with categorising these safely. However, it has been possible to identify 138 cases for the period 1689–99 with certainty, and some seventy-two others where there is a high probability that they were shop theft. The number of female defendants in these trials was 213, or 77% of those indicted, in comparison with 52% in the 1743–54 sample. Certainly, one of the likely motives in reducing the threat of the death penalty to women in 1691 had been to encourage more victims to prosecute property offences, but from the female offender's perspective it had also made shoplifting one of the most accessible, remunerative and least-rigorously punished crimes.[8] A comparison of the value of goods stolen is even more striking (Table 27). If we take only those cases securely identified as shoplifting we see that, where a value is given, 64% of thefts in the period 1689–99 were of over £1 with 18% exceeding £5, compared with 26% and 5% respectively in the period 1743–54.[9]

The most plausible explanation for this differential was the greater value

8 Beattie, *Policing and Punishment*, p. 318.
9 Early editions of the *Proceedings* did not report every trial, but the contrast in value between the two periods is too marked for this to account for the anomaly.

of the more marketable textiles in the earlier period, a high percentage of stolen goods being silk and bone lace. It was uncustomary to direct lesser-value thefts to lower courts in the 1690s, so these were not simply the higher-priced end of a broader spectrum. In contrast with the rest of England, larceny offences were rarely heard at London quarter sessions in the late seventeenth century for, as the petitioners complained, magistrates routinely committed petty offenders directly to the City Bridewell or other Houses of Correction.[10] And although perhaps no more than a third of committals are registered in the Minutes of the Bridewell Court of Governers, an examination of these shows shoplifting to be relatively rare among the hundreds of property thefts recorded.[11] Neither is the impact of the later Shoplifting Act a sufficient explanation. While we might expect the capital penalty for thefts exceeding 5 shillings to have a deflationary effect on the value of goods stolen, there is little evidence that high value was a significant factor to the courts in sentencing. Only three of the 47 convictions for stealing goods valued over £1 in the 1743–54 sample resulted in a death penalty, and Palk has estimated that the high value of goods stolen was an influencing factor in awarding the death sentence for only 3% of female defendants in her later century sample.[12]

A further observation that supports the petitioners' claim is the number of repeat offenders indicted in successive sessions. Those receiving the standard sentence of branding on the thumb were at liberty to leave the court and reoffend. Elizabeth Askew, responsible for thefts amounting to £11.15s, was branded on each of the three occasions she appeared in court between 1691 and 1696.[13] Jane Brown, alias Jenkins, received a similar sentence on her first two court appearances in 1695, only on the third occasion in December that same year being ordered for transportation, a punishment that was becoming increasingly difficult to enforce.[14] The extension of benefit of clergy to women in 1691 normalised this revolving door. Sarah Hill, alias Burrows, recognised in court as an old offender, was sentenced to death in October 1689 after twice being found guilty of shoplifting offences; this was immediately respited for

10 Beattie, *Policing and Punishment*, pp. 313–14.

11 Faramerz Dabhoiwala, 'Summary Justice in Early Modern London', *English Historical Review* 121/492 (2006), 796–822 (p. 806); Tim Hitchcock, Robert Shoemaker, Sharon Howard and Jamie McLaughlin, *et al.*, *London Lives, 1690–1800*, Bridewell Royal Hospital, Minutes of the Court of Governors, February 1689–February 1699 (http://www.londonlives.org, accessed 19 April 2018): yearly totals for shoplifting fluctuate between four and fifteen cases, averaging ten cases.

12 Palk, *Gender, Crime and Judicial Discretion*, p. 51, Table 4.

13 *OBP*, April 1691, Elisabeth Hale, Elizabeth Askew (t16910422-11); October 1692, Elizabeth Askue (t16921012-2); February 1696, Elizabeth Askew, Elizabeth Grimes (t16960227-26).

14 *OBP*, February 1695, Jane Brown, Elizabeth Belwood (t16950220-26); August 1695, Jane Brown, Elizabeth Hutton (t16950828-4); December 1695, Jane Jenkins, Anne Jones (t16951203-28). Beattie, *Crime and the Courts*, pp. 480–2.

pregnancy and the sentence not subsequently enforced.[15] Burrows continued to steal, receiving no more than the customary branding when caught a further two times.[16]

Such were the impelling retail trading and judicial concerns in February 1699 when three members of the Commons, Richard Dyott, William Lowndes and Robert Byerly were given leave to bring in a Bill for 'the encouraging the Apprehending of House-breakers, Horse-stealers, and other Felons'.[17] Although the exact influence for its redirection is unknown, by the time the Bill was given its first reading in the Commons a fortnight later it had been renamed, 'for the better Apprehending, Prosecuting and Punishing of Felons that commit Burglary or House-breaking or Robbery in Shops and Warehouses'.[18] Beattie has attributed the insertion of the shoplifting clause into this Bill to the City retailers' *Great Grievance* petition, though it is uncertain whether the title on the cover of the printed broadsheet, 'The Case of Traders, relating to Shop-lifters, for the Bill against House-breakers, Shop-lifters etc. now depending in the Honourable House of Commons', confirms this, or suggests that the petition was presented after the decision to refocus the Bill on shop crime had been made.[19] The Bill was swiftly given a second reading and referred to Committee. A day later on 3 March it was ordered that further members be added to the Committee, including Thomas Brotherton who would thereafter steer the Bill through to enactment.[20] It is apparent, given the background of many of the newly added Committee members, who represented both Whig and Tory interests, that they would have raised the Committee's awareness of the issues at stake. Sir William Ashurst was a City MP and alderman, and a past lord mayor who had been the presiding judge at the Old Bailey during the 1693–94 session. Sir Robert Clayton was also a former London MP and mayor, and Governor of Bridewell Hospital. Sir Bartholomew Shower was a former Recorder of London and Chairman of Middlesex Quarter Sessions. Sir Michael Biddulph and Walter Kent were from City merchant families and Sir Richard Cocks also had commercial interests. Thomas Blofield had been selected to present a Bill that had failed in the previous session which had considered methods for preventing felonies and robberies.[21]

15   OBP, October 1689, Ann Dye, Sarah Hill (t16891009-6); October 1689, Sarah Burrows, Ann Dye (t16891009-32).
16   OBP, June 1692, Mary Mullinax, Sarah Burrows (t16920629-21); October 1693, Sarah Burrows (t16931012-29).
17   JHC, vol. 12, p. 497.
18   JHC, vol. 12, p. 525.
19   Beattie, *Policing and Punishment*, p. 328; *The Great Grievance of Traders and Shopkeepers*.
20   JHC, vol. 12, pp. 540, 541.
21   Biographies from http://www.historyofparliamentonline.org/research/members/members-1690-1715 (accessed 14 March 2013).

During the succeeding two months that the Bill was with the Commons Committee, and on the three occasions it was brought back to the full House, it was amended several times with some attempted changes simply playing out long-standing disagreements on how legislation could best serve criminal prevention.[22] Nevertheless, the final version was drafted to satisfy broadly most of the issues raised in the shopkeepers' petition. Their complaint that current punishments were ineffectively deterrent was met by the withdrawal of benefit of clergy for 'private' shop thefts of over 5 shillings in value, and branding on the thumb replaced by branding on the cheek. Their suggestion that retailers were discouraged from prosecuting and tempted to compound was addressed by a reward for successful prosecutors in the form of a certificate (later commonly known as a 'Tyburn ticket'), releasing them from the obligation to serve as parish officers. And their contention that shoplifters were organised criminals having 'their several Societies and Walks, their Cabals, Receivers, Solicitors and even their Bullies to rescue them if taken', accounted for the addition of a clause pardoning any defendant that gave evidence that convicted two associates.[23] The Bill received its third reading in the Commons on 28 April 1699, passed swiftly through the Lords, and received Royal Assent on 4 May. The newly passed 'Act for the better apprehending, prosecuting and punishing of felons that commit burglary, housebreaking, or robbery in shops, warehouses, coach-houses or stables; or that steal horses' came into effect on 20 May 1699.[24]

The immediate impact of the Act is difficult to judge as relatively few copies of the *Proceedings* survive for the five years after it was passed. The effect of making higher value shoplifting a capital offence was almost certainly mitigated by the practice of allowing juries to give partial verdicts, reducing the value of goods stolen or stating the theft was not accomplished privately: that is, unobserved.[25] Such discretion had a long history and it was probable that shopkeepers, who regularly served on London juries, conformed to the view that the Act was primarily deterrent in purpose.[26] However, they soon

---

22 A clause that would require witnesses to give evidence under oath was added at the request of the Commons, but later rejected by the House of Lords.

23 *The Great Grievance of Traders and Shopkeepers.*

24 *JHC*, vol. 12, pp. 556, 607, 625, 659, 669, 671, 675, 681; *Journal of the House of Lords*, vol. 16, pp. 455, 456, 460, 464–5; 10 & 11 Wm III, c. 23 (1699).

25 From a study of indictments, John Beattie has calculated that in the three years from May 1699, thirty-eight shoplifters were prosecuted under the Act in the City of London, five of whom were acquitted and two-thirds awarded partial verdicts. See J. M. Beattie, 'London Crime and the Making of the "Bloody Code", 1689–1718', in *Stilling the Grumbling Hive: The Response to Social and Economic Problems in England, 1689–1750*, ed. L. Davison, T. Hitchcock, T. Kiern and R. Shoemaker (Stroud, 1992), pp. 49–76 (p. 67).

26 Beattie, *Crime and the Courts*, pp. 420–1; J. M. Beattie, 'London Juries in the 1690s', in *Twelve Good Men and True: The Criminal Trial Jury in England, 1220–1800*, ed. J. S. Cockburn and T. A. Green (Princeton, 1988), pp. 214–53 (pp. 239, 243).

realised that branding on the face for shop larceny was counter-productive. A 'Petition of the Grand Jury, Citizens and Shop-keepers, of the City of London', presented to the House of Commons in December 1704, stated that it 'hath been found by experience not to have the intended effect, such punishment having not only made them incapable of being admitted into any service or employment, but has hardened them, and made them desperate'.[27] An Act returning branding to the hand was passed into law in 1706.[28] The incentive of the Tyburn ticket appears to have remained popular with shopkeepers who were among the most eligible for parish offices, and perhaps more so as the century proceeded and paying a deputy to take on the role became increasingly common practice. The Minutes of the London Society for Prosecuting Felons recorded with satisfaction in March 1799 that Mr Churton, an Oxford Street hosier, had obtained a Tyburn ticket, and when shopkeeper Thomas Lodge prosecuted Alice Guy in 1807, her counsel extracted an admission that Lodge had specifically enquired whether he would be entitled to one.[29]

The Shoplifting Act was now law, but few English statutes remain inviolate: case law clarifies, interprets and adapts intention over time. In eighteenth-century England an informal process was observed whereby disputes over law could be referred from criminal trials to the twelve common law judges for arbitration and legal ruling.[30] Langbein has noted a tendency in their rulings towards limiting the scope of capital punishment and certainly a gradual tightening of the Act can be observed as the century progressed.[31] Summarised in a 1755 Justice's manual thus: 'Every person that shall, by night or by day, in any shop, warehouse, coach-house or stable, privately and feloniously steal any goods, wares or merchandizes, to the value of 5s, although it be not broken open, nor any person be therein, shall be guilty of felony without benefit of clergy', few of its key elements would escape challenge in court.[32]

Early cases suggest that the Act was initially treated expansively by the courts as a catch-all for shop theft. Thomas Knight was indicted for 'privately stealing' under the Act in 1721. Having 'broke open the shop with an augre, which he had left in the shop, and which the prosecutor produced in court', Knight pleaded in vain that this was not shoplifting and was declared guilty.[33] And in the same year it eventually fell to the jury to amend the charge against John Cauthrey for stealing from his master's shop, the transcript stating that

27 JHC, vol. 14, p. 463.
28 5 Anne, c. 6 (1706).
29 LMA, CLA/074/03/012, Rough Minute Book, 15 March 1799; OBP, January 1807, Alice Guy (t18070114-39).
30 Langbein, The Origins of Adversary Criminal Trial, pp. 212–13.
31 Langbein, The Origins of Adversary Criminal Trial, p. 302.
32 Richard Burn, The Justice of the Peace, and Parish Officer, 2 vols (London, 1755), vol. 2, p. 105.
33 OBP, January 1721, Thomas Knight (t17210113-9).

'The jury considering the matter, and judging it not to come within the statute of shop-lifting (he being the prosecutor's servant) found him guilty.'[34] However, subsequent case law steadily determined the scope and reach of the Act.

The trial of Thomas Mills at the Old Bailey in 1755, when he was accused of stealing 15 shillings from John Clark's shop, established that money did not constitute 'goods, wares or merchandise' under the Act.[35] In 1777 at Carlisle assizes, the clause regarding 'breaking open' was called into question in the case of Ann Gregg. In entering Mary Furness's shop to steal, she had put her hand into the shop and unbolted the half-door. Unlatching was pronounced to be a form of forced entry, exempt from the Act.[36] In the trial of James Godfrey at the Old Bailey in 1783 for stealing woollen cloth from the warehouse of factor Edward Shepherd, the judge once again denied that the Act applied, confirming a judge's opinion from a 1751 case that the word 'warehouse' in the statute did not mean a mere repository for goods, but a place where traders keep their goods for sale, in the nature of shops.[37] The following year, in the trial of William Stone, charged with stealing a watch from the shop of John Alcock in St Martins Lane, it emerged that the watch taken from the display case had been there for mending and not for sale. This again was held to exclude use of the Act, with Stone merely found guilty of larceny.[38]

Of all the words in the Act, however, the interpretation of 'privately' was most frequently contested in court, defence counsel repeatedly pressing judges on the fateful term. When Mary Talbot and Sarah Davis were spotted stealing a length of lace from haberdasher Henry Pearson, two further cards of his lace were retrieved from their clothing that they had taken unobserved. The judge ruled that the sighting of the initial act was sufficient to exclude the charge of private stealing for the whole theft.[39] In the trial of David English a year later, the shopwoman said she had seen him 'feeling in his pocket' before she missed her lace. The judge made the fine distinction to the jury that if such fumbling was after the theft had been accomplished it was a felony under the Act, but if it was part of the act of stealing itself, merely larceny.[40] And even less predictable issues arose with regard to the Act. When

---

34 *OBP*, May 1721, John Cauthrey (t17210525-28).

35 Thomas Leach, *Cases in Crown Law, Determined by the Twelve Judges; By the Court of King's Bench; and by Commissioners of Oyer and Terminer, and General Gaol Delivery* (London, 1792), p. 43; *OBP*, January 1755, Thomas Mills (t17550116-2).

36 TNA, PRO ASSI 43/9, Assizes, Northern Circuit, Miscellaneous Books 1, Notebook containing precedents and analyses of points of law 1750–1800, fols 197–9. See also p. 83 above.

37 Leach, *Cases in Crown Law*, pp. 235–6; *OBP*, December 1783, James Godfrey (t17831210-20).

38 Leach, *Cases in Crown Law*, p. 274; *OBP*, July 1784, William Stone (t17840707-65).

39 *OBP*, February 1784, Mary Talbot, Sarah Davis (t17840225-18).

40 *OBP*, June 1785, David English (t17850629-65).

James Dollanson, working with two accomplices, was caught red-handed attempting to steal some stockings that shopkeeper James Shannon had tied by a cord to his door-frame, he was fortunate to escape conviction. The court reporter recorded, 'had the string broke, or been separated but an inch, it would have been a felony; this was a felony began but not completed, they were all three acquitted'. The concern of the court at this statutory failing was sufficient for Shannon to be recommended an improved device:

> place a small weight of lead, with an upright pin, about an inch long on the top, upon the end of a shelf; let a loop at the end of the string be put over the upright pin, which will disengage itself as the lead falls, which fall may either disturb a bell, or fall upon any thing that will alarm'.[41]

Legal rulings on the Act gradually refined and defined its scope, but it retained its broad intention.

Co-operating with magistrates to boost the efficacy of the law

In spite of these occasional challenges, The Shoplifting Act appeared to be serving its purpose. By mid-century, when Henry Fielding took over the Bow Street magistracy, there is little indication that London retailers were openly dissatisfied with the capital's criminal justice provision. However, alarmed by his perception of an increasing crime rate, Fielding actively set about incentivising and facilitating public participation in crime prevention, and retailers were one of his target groups. Chiding victims for their apparent reluctance to prosecute, Henry, and later his brother John, conducted a concerted campaign to mobilise shopkeepers to combat crime more effectively on their premises.[42] Through the *Covent-Garden Journal*, and later the *Public Advertiser* and *Gazetteer*, they encouraged increased communication between all who were party to criminal attack. In January 1755 John Fielding placed an advertisement in the press:

> Whereas many thieves and robbers daily escape justice for want of immediate pursuit, it is therefore recommended to all persons who shall henceforth be robbed on the highway, or in the street, or whose shops or houses should be broke open, that they give immediate notice thereof, together with as accurate a description of the offenders as possible, to JOHN FIELDING, Esq; at his house in Bow Street, Covent-Garden. By which means, joined to an advertisement, containing an account of the things lost (which is

---

41 *OBP*, January 1768, Mary Anthony, Ann Claxton, James Dollanson (t17680114-24).
42 Fielding, *An Enquiry*, pp. 106–9.

also taken in there) thieves and robbers will seldom escape; as most of the principal pawnbrokers take in this paper, and by the intelligence they get from it, assist daily in discovering and apprehending rogues.[43]

For good measure, on the same page, Fielding had submitted a news item puffing the success of his strategy:

It is remarkable that by the spirit that has lately been infused among the Peace Officers and by the bravery of Mr Fielding's people, that within a month this town has been freed from numbers of pickpockets, from no less than twenty pilfering shoplifters, one gang of housebreakers, two very extraordinary horsestealers, and two different gangs of street-robbers.

Three years earlier Fielding had, in fact, persuaded sixty-two London pawnbrokers to publicly declare that they would peruse the *Public Advertiser* daily, 'and if any lost or stolen goods shall be advertised ... we will, to our utmost, endeavour to secure the property for the owner, and to bring the offender to justice'.[44] This courting of shopkeepers, providing the suggested means and support for them to tackle offenders, quickly bore fruit. Advertising for stolen goods became commonplace, the number of references to this in court tripling between the 1743–54 and 1765–74 London samples. John Greenfield, a Fleet Street linen draper, testified in 1765 that when he lost some handkerchiefs he 'went to Mr. Fielding, for his advice: he advised me to advertise; I did, and printed some hand-bills, and sent them to the pawnbrokers'; a second linen draper in Holborn, targeted by the same thieves the following day, also 'went directly to Sir John Fielding, upon missing the two dozen, and had them advertised'.[45] Recruiting pawnbrokers to the cause also fostered retailers' engagement. Mercer William Shrigley told the court that on losing 63 yards of silk from his shop he 'sent the cryer to crye it; which had no effect. The next day I advertised it, and Mr. Coney, the pawnbroker in Holborn, brought me eight yards of it. He ... gave me instructions to go to Sir John Fielding's to get a list of the brokers.'[46] Bow Street became a byword for justice even among retailers in villages outside London. When Hanwell watchmaker Richard Howard lost some silver-plated shoe buckles from his shop, he testified, 'I caused a hue and cry to be made about the country ... I was coming to London, to acquaint Sir John Fielding of it'.[47]

Fielding's drive for collaboration in tackling crime was unrelenting, with repeated advice to shopkeepers and those likely to come into contact with

---

43 *Public Advertiser*, 20 January 1755, p. 1.
44 *Public Advertiser*, 2 December 1752, p. 1.
45 OBP, February 1765, Mary Carroll, John Carroll and Mary Carroll (t17650227-23).
46 OBP, February 1772, Hannah Messiter (t17720219-57).
47 OBP, April 1766, John Upgood (t17660409-28).

shoplifters. Pawnbrokers were optimistically asked to shut their shops at 9 p.m. each evening to give them time to examine advertisements for stolen goods before those responsible called at their shops to convert them.[48] Shopkeepers were enjoined to fit bells to their shop doors; to beware of 'shoplifters' breaking shop windows; and in 1761, as we have already seen, recommended to combine to form a trade protection society.[49] When offenders were caught, retailers were invited to attend examinations at Bow Street and identify any stolen goods recovered.[50] In 1773, all householders were encouraged to fix handbills with the names and residence of local constables to the back of their street door, as this 'may be found useful in cases of robbery, shoplifting, disturbances and fires'.[51] Descriptions were circulated of those still to be captured. For instance, readers of the *Public Advertiser* were informed that 'the said sattin was stolen by a woman shoplifter, who appeared to be about 30 years of age, of the middle size, a little pitted with the small-pox, her hair powdered, rather long visaged, has the Irish dialect, and was neatly dressed'.[52] And this effort was not confined to London. John Fielding's General Preventative Plan, devised in 1772, sought to broadcast such warnings, disseminate information and engage traders nationally.[53] Fielding's energetic campaign was supported by an annual stipend of £400, paid from public funds.[54] It is also probable that he was able to place his adverts free or at favourable rates; the *Gazetteer* is known to have paid him £50 per annum from 1775, an acknowledgement of his role in increasing their circulation.[55] No succeeding magistrate worked with shopkeepers quite so constructively, or took on a facilitating role with such enthusiasm until, perhaps, Patrick Colquhoun at the turn of the century. Retailers did co-operate, and tested out many of his suggestions, but it was a struggle to fully engage them in crime prevention.[56] If preventative measures protected their stock more cheaply and effectively than prosecution, self-interest was liable to trump public-spiritedness.

Shopkeepers who did resort to law, however, became increasingly adept at interpreting and manipulating the process to their advantage. In concert with

---

48 See, for example, *Public Advertiser*, 9 October 1758, p. 3.
49 *Public Advertiser*, 26 January 1757, p. 2; 9 February 1760, p. 3. See also ch. 5, p. 135.
50 *Public Advertiser*, 5 March 1764, p. 3; 6 March 1764, p. 3.
51 *Public Advertiser*, 23 December 1773, p. 4.
52 *Public Advertiser*, 6 December 1780, p. 3.
53 Styles, 'Sir John Fielding and the Problem of Criminal Investigation', pp. 129, 138. See also pp. 71–2 above.
54 Leon Radzinowicz, *A History of English Criminal Law and its Administration from 1750*, vol. 3 (London, 1956), p. 34.
55 Robert Haig, *The Gazetteer 1735–1797: A Study in the Eighteenth-Century English Newspaper* (Carbondale, 1960), p. 64.
56 References to advertising are rarer in the later London samples, although this may be due to increases in advertising tax. See Styles, 'Print and Policing', p. 70.

those who legally advised them, including officials responsible for drawing up indictments, they worked to increase prosecution success by developing hedging strategies. At the Cumberland assizes in the 1770s and 1780s it was routine to indict any high-value shop theft under both the Shoplifting Act and a later 1713 Theft from a House Act which had removed benefit of clergy from thefts from a house exceeding 40 shillings.[57] This proved expedient in the case of Ann Gregg, noted earlier for setting a precedent on forced entry. As the value of the theft exceeded 40 shillings and the shop was also Furness's dwelling-house, Gregg was convicted of the alternative charge. The option of using this substitute Act was further strengthened in 1785 when a judge's ruling on a case heard at the Surrey assizes determined that the 1713 Act applied to theft from a shop contained within the curtilage of a house, even where there was no internal communication between the shop and the house.[58] A trial at the Old Bailey in 1792 does suggest that some shopkeepers may have been pressured by magistrates or court officers to use the Theft from a House Act to obtain a capital conviction against a shoplifter for whom it was not possible to sustain a charge of private stealing. Linen draper John Scoffeld apparently had good cause to be hostile to shoplifters, testifying that 'the prisoner at the bar came into the shop rather hastily; and took up this property ... I had that day week lost about £20 worth'. Yet his plea to the court at the end of the trial, 'I petition you to tell the jury to find the value of the things under 40s', implies that the indictment was not of his own volition.[59] However, this reluctance was not necessarily universal. Linen draper Joseph Craig, the aggressive prosecutor we encountered in the last chapter, only suffered losses exceeding 40 shillings in one of the sixteen cases he pursued, and one where the theft had been clearly observed by his shopman. Craig chose to prosecute it as theft from a house.[60]

Such apparent will to inflict the death penalty prompted much hostile accusation from defence counsel in court. Representing two shoplifters in 1785, Garrow demanded of the shopman, 'Recollect and tell us, whether the next morning after the loss of these goods, you did not say you had observed these things taken, but you was advised not to say so, that it might be a capital offence?'; and in another case in 1792 the seasoned defender Knapp insinuated a draper's assistant had been coached by his master to the same end: 'He perhaps has been giving you a little instructions?'[61] However, given the contrasting

---

57   12 Anne, c. 7 (1713), an Act primarily directed at theft by servants; TNA, PRO ASSI 41/7–8, Assizes, Northern and North-Eastern Circuits, Crown and Civil Minute Books.
58   Leach, *Cases in Crown Law*, pp. 287–8 (Case of Gibson, Mutton and Wiggs).
59   *OBP*, December 1792, Barnaby Yates (t17921215-113).
60   *OBP*, July 1807, Judith Lawler (t18070701-8).
61   *OBP*, June 1785, Ann Sheldon, Mary Williams (t17850629-43); September 1794, Ann Morton (t17940917-92).

instances of retailers demanding leniency, there is little reason to believe that the range of retailers' sympathies differed markedly from that in the general population. From mid-century many individuals were starting to militate for capital law reform, reflecting a growing public disenchantment with the death penalty for minor non-violent crime. Concern for potential victims was also prevalent in the poorer communities that shopkeepers served, and would not wish to alienate.[62] So, some retailers' apparent support for capital punishment may simply have been a pragmatic manoeuvre. Well aware of the vagaries of eighteenth-century law, few retailers would be ignorant of the frequency with which juries avoided death sentences by awarding partial verdicts, or judges by recommending pardon. They were accordingly prepared to 'play the system' to seek a preferred outcome. Nowhere is this better demonstrated than in the 1773 trial of milliner Sarah Tonge, in which journeyman William Gunston's testimony clearly implied that he had seen her steal his employer's lace.[63] This was Gunston's second witness appearance in court. Thirteen years earlier, when shopman to a Ludgate Hill haberdasher, he had given evidence in a shoplifting case brought as larceny.[64] Accused now on the stand of threatening to see the defendant hanged, Gunston demurred, explaining:

> No. I have said, that as being an old offender in the trade, I was afraid if lenity was shewn to her, and that if the affair was only laid for transportation, she would get at large; I said, if it is laid capital, she may get off for transportation; that she may get out of the kingdom. For I cast one in this court once, and she obtained a pardon, and a week after she came to the door and abused me.

Gunston merely wished to see Sarah Tonge transported, so had factored into his calculation the virtual certainty of her charge or sentence being commuted, when making the decision to prosecute under capital law.

Government funding for transportation, introduced legislatively in 1718, had increased the effectiveness and consequent favouring of this as a punishment by the courts for felony offences.[65] Statistics show that it was used indiscriminately as a punishment for both shoplifting and grand larceny, and was also the most common outcome for those whose death sentence was commuted. Over 90% of those convicted at the Old Bailey of grand larceny in the earlier two samples were transported and even 69% of those in 1785–89, a period when the loss of the American colonies temporarily obstructed such deportations. Transportation was a satisfactory outcome for

---

62   See p. 91 above.
63   *OBP*, April 1773, Sarah Tonge (t17730421-2).
64   *OBP*, January 1760, Elizabeth Turner (t17600116-15).
65   4 Geo I, c. 11 (1718).

retail prosecutions, efficiently removing the problem while avoiding any moral or social opprobrium attached to taking a life. It would seem there was strong reason for shopkeepers to report they had seen a theft to invoke the lesser charge. And there is some evidence of retailers pressing for this. Linen draper John Percival was surprised to find his case indicted under the Shoplifting Act in 1788, stating in court, 'I told the clerk of the indictments that it was not privately, and I desired him not to lay it capital'.[66]

Capital law reform and the repeal of the Shoplifting Act

In 1771, Mary Jones was one of the last shoplifters to be executed for the crime.[67] Working the shops of Ludgate Hill with an accomplice, her theft had been no more audacious than others committed that year, but she had been unable to restrain herself in abusing the court: 'G-d b--st you all together', reported one paper; 'Blast you all, you old fogrums', recorded another.[68] Such aggressive and 'troublesome' female behaviour had consequences. Palk, in her study of the gendered treatment of late-eighteenth-century shoplifters, identified it as a key factor negating an otherwise more favourable outcome for women within the judicial system.[69] The *General Evening Post*, reporting on her execution, also subscribed to this view:

> Mary Jones ... one of the unhappy convicts executed on Wednesday at Tyburn, was about twenty-six years of age, red-haired, and remarkably handsome. Had not her indecent behaviour to the Judge and Jury on her trial prevented it, she probably might have been respited.[70]

This already rare instance of capital punishment under the Shoplifting Act provoked a response in the same paper a few days later. A letter to the editor, signed 'Humanity', demanded 'upon what principle of reason or equity we can justify a punishment so much out of all proportion to the crime', and concluded, 'I profess I can read the account of one savage feasting upon another with a far less degree of horror than I can read the account of what happens in a civilized country – a poor unhappy woman "ordered for execution, for stealing twelve yards of thread-lace"'.[71]

---

66 *OBP*, February 1788, Ann Wheeler, Elizabeth Barnsley (t17880227-54).
67 *OBP*, September 1771, Mary Jones, Ann Styles (t17710911-32).
68 *Bingley's Journal*, 7–14 September 1771, p. 4; *The Craftsman or Say's Weekly Journal*, 21 September 1771, p. 2.
69 Palk, *Gender, Crime and Judicial Discretion*, pp. 52–3, 65.
70 *The General Evening Post*, 17–19 October 1771, p. 1.
71 *The General Evening Post*, 22–24 October 1771, p. 4.

The letter's author was expressing views that were gaining increasing purchase by the 1770s, echoing the incipient criticism of leading jurists. They reflected the humanitarian disquiet of a growing middling stratum of society at the unrestrained use of capital punishment. Whether, as Randall McGowen has argued, such protest was founded on a genuine sympathy and fellow feeling, or as Vic Gatrell has countered, a more measured social conformity, the cult of sensibility and evangelical piety provide an impetus to the late-eighteenth-century reform movement.[72]

By 1777, when Sir William Meredith invoked her case in an impassioned speech to Parliament on capital law reform, Mary Jones had achieved emblematic status with blame for her plight turned decisively from her own failings to that of City retailers:

> The woman's husband was pressed, their goods seized for some debts of his, and she, with two small children, turned into the streets a-begging. 'Tis a circumstance not to be forgotten, that she was very young, (under nineteen) and most remarkably handsome. She went to a linen-draper's shop, took some coarse linen off the counter, and slipped it under her cloak; the shopman saw her, and she laid it down: for this she was hanged. ... it seems, there had been a good deal of shop-lifting about Ludgate; an example was thought necessary, and this woman was hanged for the comfort and satisfaction of some shopkeepers in Ludgate-Street.[73]

Such rhetoric had resonances of an earlier and largely discarded vilification of retailers.[74] As we have seen, there is no evidence that the majority of shopkeepers felt satisfaction at the hanging of those they indicted. In fact with their predominantly middling backgrounds many of them moved in the same communities as the reformers. Holborn haberdasher Major Blundell, discussed in the previous chapter, was a strong evangelical Christian and congregant at the Bedford Row Chapel, closely associated with the Clapham Sect. In his study of the role of evangelicalism in criminal law reform, Richard Follett suggests that followers would have accorded weight to the fact, authoritatively stated by Sir William Blackstone in his *Commentaries on the Laws of England* of 1769, that the Bible advocated restitution rather than death as the appropriate community punishment for property crimes.[75]

72 McGowen, 'A Powerful Sympathy', pp. 312–34; Gatrell, *The Hanging Tree*, pp. 225–41; Randall McGowen, 'Revisiting the Hanging Tree: Gatrell on Emotion and History', *British Journal of Criminology* 40/1 (2000), 1–13.
73 *The Parliamentary Register or History of the Proceedings and Debates of the House of Commons* (31 October 1776–6 June 1777), 13 May 1777, p. 178.
74 Cox, 'Beggary of the Nation', pp. 26–51.
75 Follett, *Evangelicalism*, p. 82; Sir William Blackstone, *Commentaries on the Laws of England*, 3rd edn, vol. 4 (Oxford, 1769), p. 237.

Blundell's apparent propensity to recharge his staff for commercial losses and his absence of shoplifting prosecutions may even have been an expression of such a principle.

Beyond humanitarian concern, more compelling critiques of the utility of capital laws were appearing in print. The Italian jurist Beccaria's *On Crimes and Punishments* had been published in England in 1767 and his arguments echoed by Sir William Blackstone in his influential *Commentaries* of 1769, and by William Eden in his *Principles of Penal Law* of 1771.[76] They proposed that it was certainty of punishment rather than severity that had the greater deterrent effect. This resonated with some parliamentarians as crime rates soared to new heights following the American War, although a proposed commission to consider reform in 1787 gained insufficient support. Sceptics of the current system held that criminals such as shoplifters had no fear of the death sentence since they well knew how frequently it was commuted and how seldom it was put into effect. It was argued that punishments should be proportional to the crime, that the law should specify lesser but mandatory penalties for minor offences. This was an anathema to traditionalists who believed the discretion allowed to judges and juries in applying the law to individual cases was an integral principle of English common law.

While public debate on capital punishment continued, the practical reach of the Shoplifting Act steadily retracted. As illustrated in chapter 2 (Chart 2), cases brought under the Act became a diminishing percentage of all shoplifting prosecutions at the Old Bailey. And even in those cases there was an apparently increasing reluctance of juries to convict capitally. Palk's analysis of shoplifting verdicts at the Old Bailey during sample periods between 1780 and 1823, drawn from Home Office Criminal Registers, reveals the proportion of death sentences declined from 29% in 1780–82 to 8% in 1803–08.[77]

But it was not until the early nineteenth century that Sir Samuel Romilly, an MP with a legal background and long-standing commitment to law reform, commenced a sustained Parliamentary campaign to remit the death penalty for a number of non-violent offences. After an initial success with pickpocketing legislation in 1808, Romilly turned his attention to shoplifting, introducing a Bill to restore benefit of clergy to three Acts that dealt respectively with theft from a shop, theft from a dwelling-house and theft from a vessel on a navigable river. In a speech to Parliament on 9 February 1810, later published as *Observations on the Criminal Law of England*, he laid out his criticisms of the capital nature of these laws.[78] They were, he pointed out, now rarely

---

76 Cesare Beccaria, *An Essay on Crimes and Punishments* (London, 1767); Blackstone, *Commentaries*; William Eden, *Principles of Penal Law* (London, 1771).

77 Palk, *Gender, Crime and Judicial Discretion*, p. 45, Table 2.

78 Sir Samuel Romilly, *Observations on the Criminal Law of England as it Relates to Capital Punishments and on the Mode in which it is Administered* (London, 1810).

enforced as originally intended and the reason for this was a change 'in the manners and character of the nation, which are now so repugnant to the spirit of these laws, that it has become impossible to carry them into execution'.[79] He censured the judicial discretion applied in sentencing as introducing an unacceptable level of subjectivity and uncertainty to the law. He suggested such law had no deterrent effect as offenders were predisposed to gamble upon receiving a light penalty. Certainty of detection and punishment was the only true deterrent and while accepting this as unattainable, he set out his ideal: 'by a vigilant police, by rational rules of evidence, by clear laws, and by punishments proportioned to the guilt of the offender, to approach as nearly to that certainty as human imperfection will admit'.[80] He acknowledged that placing discretion in the power of the judiciary was preferable to its resting, as often in current practice, in the hands of reluctant prosecutors, witnesses and juries. However, as judges gave no explanation for their discretionary judgments, these lost any useful exemplary purpose in deterring others.

Romilly then proceeded to defuse opposing arguments by an extended critique of the most influential proponent of the status quo, William Paley, whose *Principles of Moral and Political Philosophy*, first published in 1785, contained a robust defence of the existing system.[81] Paley held that the terror of capital punishment was necessary to deter crime in society and that the degree of severity of punishments should reflect differences in the difficulty of prevention. Thus, shoplifting, which was difficult to prevent, demanded a harsher punishment than theft from a house. Granting sentencing discretion to judges enabled the deterrent power of capital punishment to prevail for all such offences, while ensuring that only the most heinous examples of type received the ultimate penalty. Perhaps significantly, given the limited opposition to the 1808 Bill, the one crime that Paley excluded from his general tenet was pickpocketing.[82]

Reaction to Romilly's proposal was mixed. A correspondent to *The Times*, 'Anti-Draco', concurred that reform of the Shoplifting Act was overdue while confirming that it had come to have a largely symbolic significance for most prosecutors:

> This Act has come under the consideration of the Judges as often as any in the whole code, and has received many constructions; yet the common practice has always been (in indictments upon it) to put in a count for larceny at common law, and trust to *that*, at the trial; by which means the statute becomes waste-paper. And why? Because the punishment is

---

79   Romilly, *Observations*, p. 5.
80   Romilly, *Observations*, p. 21.
81   William Paley, *The Principles of Moral and Political Philosophy* (London, 1785), pp. 526–53.
82   Paley, *Principles*, pp. 527, 529, 532–4.

too great for the offence; and prosecutors are very tender in pressing for a conviction upon it.[83]

But in the Commons many MPs, including the Solicitor-General, were quick to praise Paley and voice alarm at the prospect of reform. Even so, the Bill achieved a third reading on 3 May 1810 and passed to the Lords, where at its second reading on 30 May it had a more damaging reception. Lord Ellenborough led the opposition, stating defensively that 'Much had been said about humanity, and no one was more disposed than himself to the exercise of clemency; still there was not the slightest ground for the insinuations that had been cast upon the present administration of the law.'[84] Turning to the specific issue of the Shoplifting Act, he feared for the effect of the Bill:

> In this metropolis, where the retail trade had become so great and so beneficial to the ends of commerce, and from whence such a considerable portion of the taxes was raised, it was the duty of the legislature to protect such property from being plundered. Indeed were the terror of death, which now, as the law stood, threatened the depredator, to be removed, it was his opinion, the consequence would be that shops would be liable to unavoidable losses from depredations, and, in many instances, bankruptcy and ruin must be the lot of honest and laborious tradesmen.[85]

But particulars aside, the core of Ellenborough's argument was that this was the thin end of the wedge; to concede that the death penalty was too severe in this case was to openly invite wholesale reform to a judicial system in which he was invested, and that he believed had long served the public in good stead. He informed the House that he had consulted the other judges who were of a like opinion. Lord Holland, who had introduced the Bill, hastened to assure him that there was 'no intention to alter the common law, but only to alter the effect of a statute', and that the penalty in its current form appeared to be more a deterrent to prosecutors than criminals.[86] He invoked Dr Johnson and Patrick Colquhoun as two establishment figures who had expressed similar views.[87] Unmoved by this, the Lords rejected the Bill by a majority of two-thirds.

Romilly reintroduced the Bill in 1811, where it was once again passed by the Commons and then defeated in the Lords. Recognising that the opposition was greater to repeal of the statutes covering theft from a dwelling-house and boat, Romilly restricted his efforts to steering a discrete Shoplifting Bill

---

83 *The Times*, 16 February 1810, p. 4.
84 Hansard, HL (series 1), vol. 17, col. 195 (30 May 1810).
85 Hansard, HL (series 1), vol. 17, col. 196 (30 May 1810).
86 Hansard, HL (series 1), vol. 17, col. 198 (30 May 1810).
87 See Colquhoun, *A Treatise on the Police*, pp. 6, 313–14.

through Parliament on three further occasions in 1813, 1816 and 1818, each attempt suffering a similar fate. Debates in the Lords had become polarised and entrenched, with supporters claiming milder punishments would bring more to justice and opponents reasserting that terror was more efficacious in that it deterred the initial commission of the crime. In spite of this, at Romilly's death in November 1819, the strength of feeling in the country and among Parliamentary supporters was mounting. The Common Council of the City of London presented a petition for law reform to Parliament on 25 January 1819, though once again its wording perhaps implied the diminishing significance of the Shoplifting Act to City traders:

> That upwards of two hundred crimes very different in their degrees of enormity are equally subject to the punishment of death, which is enacted not only for the most atrocious offences, for burglary, for rape, for murder, and for treason, but for many offences unattended with any cruelty or violence, for various minor crimes, and even for stealing privately to the amount of five shillings in a shop.[88]

It prompted seventy-six similar petitions from towns and cities around England, and within weeks Parliament had been persuaded to set up the Select Committee on Criminal Laws to examine the issue of capital punishment.[89] Led by Sir James Mackintosh, another leading reformer, the Committee took evidence from sixty-one individuals sympathetic to reform and on 8 July 1819 published a predictably favourable report. To deflect criticism that they had not consulted or taken evidence from any of the current judges, the Committee disingenuously explained they had done so out of consideration for their situation as 'It appeared unbecoming and inconvenient that those whose office it is to execute the criminal law should be called on to give an opinion whether it ought to be altered.' They stated that for the 'most accurate and satisfactory evidence' of the effect of the law they had principally relied 'On this class of persons, where the crimes are most frequent, and where long and extensive experience allows little room for error and none for misrepresentation, or in other words, on the traders of the cities of London and Westminster.'[90] This testimony was to be bolstered by that of clerks, magistrates and officers of the criminal courts.

Over a four-month period the Committee heard repeated evidence from individual traders and merchants of their personal experience of refusing to

---

88   Hansard, HC (series 1), vol. 39, col. 82 (25 January 1819).
89   Radzinowicz, *A History of English Criminal Law*, vol. 1 (London, 1948), pp. 527–8; Follett, *Evangelicalism*, p. 150.
90   *Report from the Select Committee on Criminal Laws*, 1819, pp. 8–9.

prosecute cases of forgery, fraud, burglary, and staff theft.[91] Some witnesses stated that the risk of capital punishment similarly deterred shopkeepers from prosecuting shoplifting, but no actual instances were produced. Perhaps to the Committee's chagrin, it appeared that shoplifting was a crime on which the fear of this penalty had less impact than most. Asked if capital laws discouraged prosecution in almost all instances, Thomas Shelton, Clerk of the Old Bailey replied, 'No, not generally', and proceeded to explain that prosecutors regularly undervalued shoplifted goods. Probing further, the Committee asked him if he had come across shoplifting prosecutors forfeiting their recognisances rather than appear, or wilfully withdrawing a material witness: 'No', responded Shelton.[92] A series of witnesses involved in the administration of the law confirmed the frequency of shoplifting charges being reduced to larceny. William Evans, barrister and Vice-chancellor of the County Palatine of Lancaster, gave evidence that since 1783 few shoplifting cases had been heard at the assizes as Lancashire magistrates had 'been very much in the habit of exercising the discretion of not committing for a capital offence, but only committing for larceny', adding 'it was very generally the custom to commit to the quarter sessions, as for mere larcenies'.[93] Sir Archibald Macdonald, a former Old Bailey judge, similarly qualified his answer, when asked if there was reluctance to convict for shoplifting: 'Yes; there is very great reluctance in convicting of that offence; that is, circumstances are laid hold of to avoid a capital conviction.'[94] Francis Hobler, Clerk to the Lord Mayor, and Samuel Yardley, Chief Clerk to the Magistrates at Worship Street also testified that prosecutors invariably sought to reduce charges to larceny in shoplifting cases.[95]

Some witnesses went further, hinting that perhaps the retailers' reluctance arose from a more wholesale disenchantment with judicial remedy. Bookseller Josiah Condor warned,

> as far as my experience extends, the public opinion is entirely in favour of a melioration of the criminal laws; at the same time the Committee must be aware, that there are so many considerations besides that of the capital punishment, to deter persons from prosecuting, that it is rendered more difficult to come at cases of the precise nature, which might be given in evidence.[96]

---

91 *Report from the Select Committee on Criminal Laws*, 1819: see, for example, Josiah Condor, p. 89; John Gaun, pp. 91–2; Stephen Curtis, pp. 96–7; Ebenezer Johnson, p. 100; Frederick Thornhill, p. 106.
92 *Report from the Select Committee on Criminal Laws*, 1819, pp. 22, 26.
93 *Report from the Select Committee on Criminal Laws*, 1819, p. 28.
94 *Report from the Select Committee on Criminal Laws*, 1819, p. 50.
95 *Report from the Select Committee on Criminal Laws*, 1819, pp. 83, 85.
96 *Report from the Select Committee on Criminal Laws*, 1819, p. 89.

Alderman Matthew Wood agreed that if obliged to prosecute, retailers would only do so as larceny, but had observed of several that 'they scarcely ever would prosecute if they could help it'.[97] John Gaun, a merchant and sometime juror, contributed similar thoughts: 'I have known several instances in which the middle class, and more particularly retail shopkeepers, have entirely foregone prosecuting for small offences (shoplifting especially), chusing rather that the offenders should be turned off with disgrace and obloquy'.[98] This last comment perhaps illuminates the behaviour of the shopkeeper in the Minories whose 'new and effectual method of exposing a shoplifter' was reported in the *Star* in November 1791: 'He detected a female who had often been a pretended customer, and, instead of prosecuting her, insisted upon her accompanying him bare-headed to every shop in the street.'[99]

The report heralded the beginning of the end of the Lords' resistance to shoplifting reform. Capitalising on its favourable reception, Mackintosh introduced a Bill for the repeal of the Shoplifting Act in the Commons in May 1820. It reached the Lords, perhaps by design, in July when the twelve judges were absent on their assize circuits. However, the Lord Chancellor objected that,

> while it appeared a harsh thing to condemn a man to death for stealing privately in a shop to the amount of five shillings, the present bill did not provide sufficiently against the loss of property to an amount which, though it could not distress some, might effectually ruin many shop-keepers.[100]

He moved for an amendment establishing a higher-value threshold of £15 at which shoplifting would remain a capital offence and the Bill became law in this form as the Stealing in Shops etc. Act, 1820.[101] It took a further three years for opposition to sufficiently dissipate to sanction the repeal of this Act. Shoplifting finally ceased to be a capital offence in 1823 with transportation or imprisonment thereafter specified as the maximum punishment for the crime.[102]

This chapter has shed light on retailers' experience of the criminal justice system. An account of the law on shoplifting is, conventionally, a narrative of the introduction of capital legislation in the 1690s, its questionable effectiveness as a deterrent throughout the eighteenth century and ultimate repeal under the pressure of a liberal reforming agenda in the 1820s. However, from

97   *Report from the Select Committee on Criminal Laws*, 1819, p. 86.
98   *Report from the Select Committee on Criminal Laws*, 1819, p. 92.
99   *The Star*, 26 November 1791, p. 3.
100 Hansard, HL (series 2), vol. 2, col. 493 (17 July 1820).
101 1 Geo IV, c. 117 (1820).
102 4 Geo IV, c. 53 (1823), 'An Act for extending Benefit of Clergy to several Larcenies therein mentioned', later consolidated in The Larceny Act, 7 & 8 Geo IV, c. 29 (1827).

the retailers' perspective their relationship with the law was not uniquely governed by the Shoplifting Act. Over the course of the century they became adept at interpreting the flexibility available to them within a range of felony laws on theft and exploiting this to achieve their desired outcome. There were certainly periods of considerable engagement with the legislative establishment, including London retailers' instrumentality in bringing the Shoplifting Act into being, and later co-operation with the Fielding brothers' agenda. But the Act itself gradually diminished in importance. In respect of shoplifting, there is limited indication that the criminal law reform movement of the late eighteenth and early nineteenth centuries was viewed as commercially significant by the retail sector. Evidence presented to the Select Committee on Criminal Laws in 1819 revealed that traders were chiefly troubled by the harshness of capital punishment for forgery, fraud and staff theft. Larceny laws already provided them with an effective accommodation for shoplifting.

7

Public Attitudes to the Crime

Perusing their morning newspaper on 4 June 1764, the largely middling readership of the *Public Advertiser* would have spotted a strange juxtaposition of items among the regular death notices:

> *Marie-Magdelaine Sohier, Widow, died lately at Conde in Flanders, in the 105th year of her age; she had never had a day's illness.*
>
> *On Thursday last died in Hurst, in the County of Berks, in the 95th year of her age, Mrs Terrick, the mother of the Lord Bishop of London.*
>
> *On Friday died at his house in Good-man's Fields, in the 71st year of his age, Joshua Forrester, sen. Esq; an eminent silk merchant.*
>
> *On Friday night died in Newgate, Dinah Dowling, a noted shoplifter and pickpocket, who was a felon convict, and was to have gone off with the Transports on Saturday morning.*[1]

Although accustomed to columns presenting an almost random jumble of news, this may have caused them to pause. How appropriate was it for the death in Newgate of Dinah Dowling, a shoplifter, to be reported in the same company as that of the mother of a Lord Bishop or an eminent merchant? This surprising conjunction draws us to reflect on seeming disparities in eighteenth-century public attitudes to the offence. Property crime was conventionally viewed with alarm, particularly 'crime waves' following war, and 1764 had witnessed a predictable spike in offences in the aftermath of the Seven Years War.[2] A press item the following year greeted the trial of several ringleaders of 'dangerous gangs', indiscriminately listing these as comprising

---

1 *Public Advertiser*, 4 June 1764, p. 3.
2 Beattie, *Crime and the Courts*, pp. 218–22.

housebreakers, shoplifters, street-robbers and pickpockets.[3] In such a climate, inclusion of the Dowling entry may have been intended to convey public reassurance. It has been suggested that published reports of sentencing and punishment were often so designed, with rumour that some might be fabricated to this end.[4] And it is true that no official record of Dowling's conviction can be found today. Yet this cannot detract from the fact that the death announcement of a 'noted' shoplifter was judged a newsworthy adjunct to that of the great and the good, or at least as holding the same curiosity for the public as the longevity of a 104-year-old Flanders woman.

This ambiguity can be seen as one expression of a more fundamental transition taking place at this time in the public perception of offenders. The publishing of the notice was coincident with a period when, historians have contended, an older concept of crime in terms of a moral discourse of sin and possible redemption was giving way to a new secular, sociological construct of a criminal type.[5] While recognising that the traditional view of crime as a moral failing persisted in some printed sources throughout the century, Andrea McKenzie has identified a progressive reluctance to recognise criminals as 'everyman'. From mid-century the better sort were embracing a new notion of offenders as a set of individuals whose low origin congenitally predisposed them to crime.[6] With the respectable reading public beginning to comfortably distance themselves from a perceived criminal class, we can observe shoplifters becoming the focus of a prurient and even entertaining interest. But as we shall discover, this idyll was abruptly dispelled by the very public arrest and trial of Jane Austen's wealthy aunt for shoplifting in 1800.

This chapter examines public attitudes to shoplifting within the framework of this wider transition in perception of crime. It explores the mentalities that underpinned contemporary attitudes to the crime and the extent to which these were shared by high and low, by both potential victims and the offenders themselves, and concludes by reflecting on the degree to which public consciousness of the crime altered between the preceding century and that

---

3   *Lloyd's Evening Post*, 13–16 September 1765, p. 271.
4   Peter King, 'Newspaper Reporting and Attitudes to Crime and Justice in Late-Eighteenth-and Early-Nineteenth-Century London', *Continuity and Change* 22/1 (2007), 73–112 (pp. 95–6); Robert Shoemaker, 'Print Culture and the Creation of Public Knowledge about Crime in Eighteenth-Century London', in *Urban Crime Prevention, Surveillance and Restorative Justice: Effects of Social Technologies*, ed. P. Knepper, J. Doak and J. Shapland (Boca Raton, 2009), pp. 1–21 (pp. 7–8).
5   Nicholas Rogers, 'Confronting the Crime Wave: The Debate over Social Reform and Regulation, 1749–1753', in *Stilling the Grumbling Hive: The Response to Social and Economic Problems in England, 1689–1750*, ed. L. Davison, T. Hitchcock, T. Kiern and R. Shoemaker (Stroud, 1992), pp. 77–98 (p. 93); Devereaux, 'From Sessions to Newspaper?', pp. 12–13.
6   Andrea McKenzie, *Tyburn's Martyrs: Execution in England, 1675–1775* (London, 2007), pp. 88–90.

which followed. This is an ambitious undertaking as references to shoplifting remain limited outside court documents and newspapers. However, the growth in digital collections of eighteenth-century texts and images in recent years has brought a wealth of new and accessible resources to researchers. To determine what the eighteenth-century public thought of this one specific criminal transgression we call on a wide range of printed sources: trial transcripts, depositions, newspapers, pamphlets, periodicals, manuals, plays, novels and images.

While an examination of literary and textual material is vital to understanding how this particular crime was represented and experienced, the use of literature in historical study requires caution. It cannot be simply treated as a window on the past. As Ian Bell states, 'literature is always a construction, not just a revelation'. We must accept that it will routinely privilege the extraordinary and striking, and necessarily tend to promote the personal, didactic and political views of the author.[7] We have also to be aware that, as with court records, the literature produced by each age can inherit certain rhetorical conventions that may not reflect contemporary societal beliefs and attitudes.[8] And there are other factors that will bear on the relationship between text, perception and reality. Authors may craft their works to appeal to a particular readership. Those reading novels in the eighteenth century have been typified as having predominantly urban concerns, tastes and attitudes.[9] Although literacy rates were high in this period, and newspapers were routinely recirculated, the rising cost of printed literature functioned to restrict readers from lower ranks. For, whereas chapbook accounts of crime in the previous century might be priced at a few pence, Defoe's crime novels of the 1720s retailed at 5–6 shillings.[10] Furthermore, we cannot be sure how any literature read was interpreted. Reading is an unstable occupation. The reception and interpretation of each specific text will depend upon the character, attitudes, reading ability and expectations of the individual reader.[11] And, as we saw at the start of this chapter, how the information is presented on the printed page, its inclusion or separation from other material, can also affect perception.[12] Yet,

7   Ian A. Bell, *Literature and Crime in Augustan England* (London, 1991), pp. 21–2.
8   Garthine Walker, '"Demons in Female Form": Representations of Women and Gender in Murder Pamphlets of the Late Sixteenth and Early Seventeenth Centuries', in *Writing and the English Renaissance*, ed. W. Zunder and S. Trill (London, 1996), pp. 124–37 (p. 137).
9   J. Paul Hunter, *Before Novels: The Cultural Contexts of Eighteenth-Century English Fiction* (New York, 1990), p. 76.
10   John Feather, 'The Power of Print: Word and Image in Eighteenth-Century England', in *Culture and Society in Britain, 1660–1800*, ed. J. Black (Manchester, 1997), pp. 51–68 (p. 57); Lincoln B. Faller, *Crime and Defoe: A New Kind of Writing* (Cambridge, 1993), p. 74.
11   Roger Chartier, 'Texts, Printing, Readings', in *The New Cultural History*, ed. L. Hunt (London, 1989), pp. 154–75 (pp. 155–6).
12   James Raven, 'New Reading Histories, Print Culture and the Identification of Change: the Case of Eighteenth-Century England', *Social History* 23/3 (1998), 268–87 (p. 280).

in spite of these caveats, print culture is still one of the best sources available
to us for interpreting mentalities, if predominantly of the literate classes.

Fear and anxiety

We might begin by asking whether the public were as anxious about shoplifting
as they were about other property crime. Historians, in diagnosing a rise
in the level of public fear in this period, have persistently implicated crime
writing.[13] This genre had a long history as crime captivated the reading public
and those who enjoyed such tales aurally through recital and ballads. Coney-
catching chapbooks, warning of the tricks and wiles of thieves, first appeared
in the sixteenth century. These were soon joined by broadside accounts of
key executions, ballad sheets and pamphlets on sensational murders and,
from the mid seventeenth century, trial accounts and biographies of notorious
criminals.[14] The 1670s significantly saw the arrival of the serial *Proceedings* of
the Old Bailey, and the *Ordinary of Newgate's Accounts* of the final confessions of executed criminals. Twenty years on, the lapse of the Licensing Act
in ending press censorship precipitated a surge in the periodical press and
the launching of the first daily newspapers. By 1750 seven million newspaper
copies were printed annually, devoting regular column inches to crime.[15] We
might expect to find references to shoplifting there and indeed accounts of
the crime would have been only too familiar to the extensive London and
provincial newspaper-reading public. It featured regularly in the recurrent
press reports of those detained, those tried and sentenced at the Old Bailey,
assize or quarter sessions courts, and occasionally among the commentary on
those hanged. Readers would also spot the term in advertisements requesting
information on shop goods lost or found, on thieves sought, or promoting
the sale of publications such as the *Proceedings* of the Old Bailey. And from
time to time press columns would contain warnings or suggested schemes for
dealing with offenders.

The portrayal of crime in the press will to an extent both reflect and
influence public opinion. But did the apparent ubiquity of shoplifting inspire
fear? The early-modern canon of crime severity habitually assigned it a lowly
position. A 1726 pamphlet graded each crime on the slippery slope to the
gallows:

13   For instance, Beattie, *Policing and Punishment*, p. 22; Robert Shoemaker, 'Fear of Crime
in Eighteenth-Century London', in *Understanding Emotions in Early Europe*, ed. Michael
Champion and Andrew Lynch (Turnhout, 2015), pp. 233–49 (pp. 234–5).
14   Faller, *Crime and Defoe*, p. 4; http://ballads.bodleian.ox.ac.uk/collections.html.
15   Feather, 'The Power of Print', pp. 52–3.

So in this Academy of the Devil, his scholars are entered first pickpockets, or divers, then shoplifters, filers, and several of the lowest rate thieves, till, as they improve, they commence graduates; such as foot-pads, street-robbers, house-breakers, highwaymen, and murtherers, and so to the gallows, which is the last gradation of their preferment.[16]

Certainly, press coverage of shoplifting was relatively benign. Offenders were typically described as 'dexterous' or 'proficient' when other criminals might have the epithets 'cruel' or 'desperate' attached. Court cases attest that only a small minority of shoplifting cases involved any form of physical aggression, and that was invariably employed in an attempt to escape capture by shop staff. More rarely still were such incidents reported in the press. And even if shoplifters might occasionally retaliate, it was significant that almost uniquely among the crimes listed in the passage above, the ordinary public did not have to fear that they might personally become a victim.

The absence of public risk undoubtedly encouraged a degree of complacency, accounting for the brevity of most newspaper mentions and a general lack of interest in the lives of shoplifters, a finding consistent with the scholarship that has ascribed fear to a more limited set of violent personal and property crimes.[17] There was a public demand in the early eighteenth century for more substantial collections of criminal biographies, notably Captain Alexander Smith's *The History of the Lives of the Most Notorious Highway-men, Foot-pads, House-breakers, Shop-lifts and Cheats*. But in spite of his title, Smith's volumes contained few histories of shoplifters. Typically, only four were included among the 135 lives in his most extensive 1719 edition.[18] The same bias was apparent in newspaper reporting. A quantitative study of a provincial paper *The Kentish Post*, published from 1717 to 1768, found that around 30% of all reportage was on crime, but two-thirds of this was on violent crime.[19] And a similar analysis of three national papers between 1787 and 1821 concluded that it was murder, robbery and burglary that dominated column inches on crime. They comprised 76% of reports of unsolved crimes, while shoplifting only accounted for 1%.[20]

There were other indications of a lack of anxiety. Crime literature fell traditionally into two categories, one designed to alert the public to criminals' tricks and deceptions, the other to draw a moral lesson from

16   *A Brief Historical Account of the Lives of Six Notorious Street Robbers Executed at Kingston* (London, 1726), p. 5.
17   Beattie, *Policing and Punishment*, p. 20; Shoemaker, 'Fear of Crime', pp. 233–8.
18   Alexander Smith, *A Compleat History of the Lives and Robberies of the Most Notorious Highway-men, Foot-pads, Shop-lifts and Cheats*, 3 vols (London, 1719).
19   Esther Snell, 'Discourses of Criminality in the Eighteenth-Century Press: the Presentation of Crime in *The Kentish Post*, 1717–1768', *Continuity and Change* 22/1 (2007), 13–47 (pp. 21–2).
20   King, 'Newspaper Reporting', pp. 88 (Table 6), 90.

criminals' lives and ultimate fate. The first of these devoted limited space to the traits of shoplifting. Certainly, 'canting' dictionaries claimed that shoplifters were known to each other as a 'bloss', 'bob' or 'hoister', which served to reinforce readers' belief in their belonging to a distinct criminal subculture.[21] And manuals such as *Thieving Detected* and *The New Cheats of London Exposed*, which were reprinted throughout the century, also initially contained cautionary advice on the modus operandi of shoplifters. But as these warnings for retailers were presumably of less concern to the general public, they were noticeably often omitted from later versions.[22] In fact, in keeping with such apparent insouciance, shoplifting was often found as a trope, woven into the entertainments of the period. In Henry Fielding's play, *The Author's Farce*, a bookseller seeking to recruit a replacement for his translator, currently in Newgate for shoplifting, tells of his having 'gotten the trick of translating out of the shops as well as out of the languages'.[23] An earlier play compares the state of the heroine after her mother discovers she has a secret suitor to 'a baited shop-lifter just out of the hands of the mob'.[24] If we accept that shoplifting was unthreatening to the middling and elite reading public, did they nevertheless see it as sinful? We next consider the role of religion and morality in attitudes to the crime.

Sinfulness and greed

Until mid-century, crime writing customarily adhered to the prevailing understanding of crime as a personal moral lapse. Irrespective of social background, moral weakness could cause any individual to succumb to a life of gambling, drink or other excess, precipitating a descent into petty and ultimately more serious crime.[25] A similar ethic permeated many early novels. By the 1720s Defoe had extended his prolific writing output into crime fiction, perhaps encouraged by the huge popular sales of true crime accounts. On the title page of his 1722 novel, *The Fortunes and Misfortunes of the Famous Moll Flanders*, we are told how she,

> was born in NEWGATE, and during a life of continu'd variety for threescore years, besides her childhood, was twelve year a whore, five times

---

21 Bell, *Literature and Crime*, p. 63.
22 *Thieving Detected: Being a True and Particular Description of the Various Methods and Artifices used by Thieves and Sharpers to Take in and Deceive the Public* (London, 1777), pp. 48–53; King, *The New Cheats of London Exposed*, pp. 86–9.
23 Henry Fielding, *The Author's Farce: and the Pleasures of the Town* (London, 1730), p. 22.
24 Mary Davys, *The Northern Heiress: or, the Humours of York* (London, 1716), p. 40.
25 McKenzie, *Tyburn's Martyrs*, pp. 59–66.

a wife (whereof once to her own brother) twelve year a thief, eight year a transported felon in Virginia, at last grew rich, liv'd honest, and died a penitent.[26]

We shall discuss shortly the association of sex and shoplifting, but his depiction of crime in this novel was clearly influenced by the crime biography genre. Indeed, Maximillian Novak ascribes to Defoe an article in the *Weekly Journal* of 16 September 1721, in which the author states that Alexander Smith was his 'master in biography ... the inventor of this manner of writing, I only the improver'.[27] Literary critics identify the genre as having two classic presentations, the picaresque account where the exploits of the criminal rogue are designed primarily to entertain, and the cautionary moral tale, intended to instruct.[28] In *Moll Flanders*, Defoe combines elements of both without remaining true to either. Much of Moll's thieving is shoplifting and, authentically, she comes to this later in life at a time of dire financial need. But Defoe does not assign to poverty more than a triggering effect. Having stolen enough to relieve her distress, Moll contemplates abandoning crime, but admits,

> my fate was otherwise determin'd; the busie Devil that so industriously drew me in, had too fast hold of me to let me go back; but as poverty brought me into the mire, so avarice kept me in, till there was no going back.[29]

Moll is subject to greed, the curse of the age, and more fundamentally, to the influence of the devil. Shoplifting is a crime decipherable in both social and providential terms.

This association of shoplifting with greed was clearly a preoccupation of Defoe, and we can conjecture that he was influenced in this by wider social opinion. Scholars have remarked on the frequency of digressive episodes in eighteenth-century novels and that Defoe, by emphasising Moll Flanders' life of 'variety' on its title page, signalled his intention to follow this tradition.[30] In the preface, Defoe emphasises that his novel is 'A work from every part of which something may be learned, and some just and religious inference ... drawn, by which the reader will have something of instruction, if he pleases

---

26 Defoe, *Moll Flanders*, p. 35.

27 *Weekly Journal or Saturday's Post*, 16 September 1721, p. 1; Maximillian E. Novak, *Realism, Myth, and History in Defoe's Fiction* (London, 1983), pp. 129–30.

28 Lincoln B. Faller, *Turned to Account: The Forms and Function of Criminal Biography in Late Seventeenth- and Early Eighteenth-Century England* (Cambridge, 1987), pp. 2–4.

29 Defoe, *Moll Flanders*, p. 268.

30 Hunter, *Before Novels*, p. 23; Kate Loveman, '"A Life of Continu'd Variety": Crime, Readers and the Structure of Defoe's *Moll Flanders*', *Eighteenth-Century Fiction* 21/1 (2013), 1–32 (p. 5).

to make use of it.'[31] So the novel afforded Defoe extensive licence to promote his personal convictions. Certainly his habitual proselytising and didacticism is as evident in the novel as in his later trade manual, *The Complete English Tradesman*, and covers very similar ground. Moll is never slow to draw attention to the deficiencies of retailers that facilitate her thieving.[32] And the chapter in the manual, 'Of Extravagant and Expensive Living, another step to a Tradesman's disaster', reprises the lesson of Moll's second marriage. Wed to a linen draper with aspirations to be a '*Gentleman-Tradesman*', she relates how her husband 'having liv'd like quality indeed, as to expence', is soon bankrupt.[33] Defoe was not unique in his concern at excess. His belief that avarice induced shoplifting derived from a growing unease in early-eighteenth-century society at the impact of the greater availability of consumer goods on all ranks of society. This same disquiet persisted mid-century, and in 1750 Henry Fielding railed at the mischief caused by the 'vast torrent of luxury which of late years hath poured itself into this nation', raising the aspirations and increasing the idleness of the poor, with the result that 'the more simple and poor-spirited betake themselves to a state of starving and beggary, while those of more art and courage become thieves, sharpers and robbers'.[34]

Not all agreed. Even among contemporaries there were those who sensed a double standard was being applied to rich and poor in this debate, some specifically engaging shoplifting in their discourse. An early journal, the *Athenian Gazette or Casuistical Mercury*, achieved enormous popularity during the 1690s in answering questions of the readership on ethical issues.[35] Quizzed in one issue on the morality of debt payment, the *Mercury*'s editorial bemoans:

> it seems a hardship in our laws, that a poor shop-lift shou'd be hanged for ... pilfering a few goods, not perhaps five pound; nay not perhaps twenty shilling value; and yet one that takes one hundred, two hundred, or a thousand pounds worth, after having rioted away one part of it, shou'd with impunity carry off the other in the *Mint* or *Fryares*.[36]

We can also perceive this downplaying of shoplifting as an indicator of greed in the work of Laurence Sterne. The character Parson Yorick in his most celebrated work, *Tristram Shandy*, is acknowledged to be based on Sterne

---

31 Defoe, *Moll Flanders*, p. 40.
32 Defoe, *Moll Flanders*, pp. 274, 282.
33 Defoe, *The Complete English Tradesman*, p. 109; *Moll Flanders*, pp. 104–6.
34 Fielding, *An Enquiry*, pp. 3–4.
35 Helen Berry, *Gender, Society and Print Culture in Late-Stuart England: the Cultural World of the Athenian Mercury* (Aldershot, 2003), pp. 18–22.
36 *The Athenian Oracle: Being an Entire Collection of All the Valuable Questions and Answers in the Old Athenian Mercuries*, vol. 3 (London, 1716), p. 66.

himself. When Yorick wishes to express his aversion to gravity, which he appears to equate with a solemnity disguising false authority, he compares the deception of 'bubbling' with shoplifting as the opposing ends of a spectrum:

> Sometimes, in his wild way of talking, he would say, That gravity was an errant scoundrel; ... and that, he verily believed, more honest, well-meaning people were bubbled out of their goods and money by it in one twelve-month, than by pocket-picking and shop-lifting in seven.[37]

Moreover the latter's role as a counterpoint to higher crime was a theme of *The Beggar's Opera*, staged to huge acclaim in 1728. In the second act of the play we find two women from the anti-hero Macheath's disorderly entourage recounting their shoplifting exploits.[38] The work, a comic reimagining of the trickery and venality of highwayman Jack Sheppard and thief-catcher Jonathan Wild, was also a satire on Robert Walpole's government.

Defoe is perhaps truer to the conventions of crime literature when he has Moll Flanders attribute her criminal intent to the promptings of the devil. Caught in his snare, Moll is 'touch'd ... to the very soul' on contemplating her victims, but has still 'cast off all remorse and repentance'.[39] Her confessional account, abounding with such symbolic religious references, is seemingly in the tradition of spiritual autobiographies. Yet Moll's constant self-justifications and backsliding, even when she finally repents in Newgate, also subvert the genre. In conventional moral biographies criminals fully acknowledged their sinfulness and the justice of their punishment. Lincoln Faller suggests that Defoe was intent on making his readership reflect individually on Moll's actions within the compass of their own more complex moral understanding.[40] In spite of its growing commercialism, eighteenth-century society was still fundamentally religious, creating a constant tension. Sermons and tracts inspired by the Reformation of Manners movement emphasised that Sabbath-breaking was the first step toward criminality, the trope of the 'slippery slope'. Clergyman Samuel Walker, asserting that 'when a man bears testimony against himself, his testimony must be true', wrote how 'several notorious offenders' had confessed to him that 'From Sabbath-breakers they commenc'd house-breakers, tiplers, debauchees, shop-lifters, thieves, and robbers.'[41] And conventional religious morality imbued attitudes towards shoplifters in court. Accused of stealing silk ribbon worth 5 shillings

---

37 Laurence Sterne, *The Life and Opinions of Tristram Shandy, Gentleman* (1760; London, 2003), p. 25.
38 John Gay, *The Beggar's Opera*, Act 2, Scene 4 (London, 1728).
39 Defoe, *Moll Flanders*, pp. 272–3.
40 Faller, *Crime and Defoe*, pp. 66, 128.
41 Samuel Walker, *Reformation of Manners Promoted by Argument in Several Essays* (London, 1711), pp. 306–7.

from a Fleet Street haberdasher, servant Mary Martin sought support from her long-term employer who, it emerged, was also her common-law husband. 'You cannot expect protection from God's providence if you live in such an unlawful manner', Judge Eyre lectured:

> this is as much forbid in the word of God as robbery or murder: how can you expect prosperity in living in this way? The best thing you can do is to go and marry her the moment the trial is over. It is very melancholy to see people no way thoughtful in distinguishing virtue from vice; you cannot expect the jury will give credit to one word you say.[42]

Found guilty on a lesser charge, Martin was sentenced to be whipped.

Shame, guilt and restorative justice

Such ethical codes were not only the province of those in authority. They also influenced the attitudes and mentalities of the poor, as we observe from testimony in the *Proceedings*. Although transgressing its rules, shoplifters were part of the hegemonic society. Socially constructed ethical and moral values, and perceived social cost, have been identified by modern criminology to be a stronger determinant of a shoplifter's individual decision to steal than any immediate situational morality.[43] We might speculate that such dominant codes of belief prompted the behaviour of the shoplifter George Hill. A bookseller's apprentice described how he observed him walking back and forth before his master's shop, periodically examining the books on the stall: 'he would take them up and put them under his coat, and lay them down again, he kept on for two hours'.[44] A similar mental conflict may explain Mary Buckley's hesitation: 'In looking over the muslin she shuffled up her petticoats and conveyed a piece under them. She seem'd presently after to be in a great deal of confusion, then put her hand to her pocket and shuffled the piece down again, so got off the stool and took it up and laid it on the counter again.'[45] That the shopkeeper remarked on her 'confusion' in his testimony was not accidental. Derived from religious and popular beliefs of earlier centuries, the conviction that qualities such as virtue and honesty could be reliably established from an individual's physiognomy and behaviour was deep-seated. Conversely composure,

---

42 *OBP*, April 1766, Mary Martin (t17660409-52).
43 Eduardo Ferreira and Helena Carvalho, 'Inhibiting Factors in a Hypothetical Shoplifting Situation: A Contribution to Crime Prevention', *Issues of Business and Law*, 1 (2009), 101–14 (pp. 101, 105).
44 *OBP*, September 1806, George Hill (t18060917-94).
45 *OBP*, July 1751, Mary Buckley (t17510703-12).

chronicled to have been exhibited by divinely inspired Christian martyrs, was seen as a convincing indicator of innocence, a word itself value-laden with both legal and religious significance.[46] Shoplifters frequently claimed they were 'as innocent as the child unborn', a reference to the doctrine of original sin.[47]

While we cannot be sure how receptive the poor were to formal moral and religious teachings, and these certainly may have been rejected by many in their daily life, it is evident that ingrained religious mores routinely informed offenders' behaviour. Defendants, who were not legally allowed to give evidence under oath, ostensibly to protect the guilty from risk of perjuring themselves, sought other performative demonstrations of their essential virtue. Falling on their knees and begging for mercy, a simulacrum of prayer or receiving sacrament, was an almost instinctive response for many shoplifters upon being caught. John Hunt's shopman deposed that when Ann Austin, was brought back to his master's shop with the stolen goods, she cried, 'Good God, what have I got, a cloak! and seemed affected with the charge; she did not deny it, but made a great noise; she went down on her knees two or three times and asked Mr. Hunt forgiveness.'[48] Similarly, a witness reported how shoplifter Sarah Pembridge had begged a haberdasher's wife to let her go before her husband returned to the shop. She 'offered to go down upon her knees', he related.[49] Nor was such an emotive act of penitence the prerogative of female offenders. John Beale, indicted in 1788 for stealing a ring from jeweller John Sarbutt, denied guilt until a constable was sent for and 'then he owned it, and went down on his knees three or four times and begged for mercy'.[50] This behaviour also simulated the formal act of obeisance that offenders were required to make, blessing 'the King and all the honourable Court', if they were offered pardons or acquitted.[51] Predictably over time such begging became closely associated with guilt rather than virtue. By 1805, when a witness to the capture of three shoplifters testified, 'they all three fell down on their knees, and begged that I would not be so base and cruel to swear falsely against them', one of the group was anxious to deny it, countering, 'I never went on my knees; if that young gentleman can look me in the face and say that, there he is, he never said so before the Justice'.[52]

---

46 Andrea McKenzie, 'God's Tribunal: Guilt, Innocence and Execution in England 1675–1775', *Cultural and Social History* 3/2 (2006), 121–44 (pp. 122, 138–9).
47 For example, *OBP*, January 1754, Anne Jones (t17540116-36); December 1763, James Noony (t17631207-11).
48 *OBP*, September 1773, Ann Austin (t17730908-47).
49 *OBP*, May 1771, Sarah Pembridge (t17710515-4).
50 *OBP*, September 1788, John Beale (t17880910-95).
51 Andrea McKenzie, 'From True Confessions to True Reporting? The Decline and Fall of the Ordinary's *Account*', *London Journal* 30/1 (2005), 55–70 (p. 58); Beattie, *Policing and Punishment*, p. 289.
52 *OBP*, December 1805, Mary Wilson, Mary Morgan, Elizabeth Walker (t18051204-3).

Redemptive rituals also infected verbal exchanges. In the immediate aftermath of a crime, occasional or opportunist thieves frequently exhibited signs of shock or remorse. Faced abruptly with their transgression they sought to distance it from their 'true' moral nature, through self-reproach and confession. Passing by an untended silversmith's shop in 1767, street hawker Sarah Dalton could not resist the opportunity to grab a handful of jewellery from a cabinet. When pursued and brought back to the shop, she readily echoed the shopkeeper's accusation: 'I am a wicked wretch, and I have done it'. Though at her trial a few days later, having reflected, she denied the charge.[53] Ann Russel, caught stealing handkerchiefs from a Holborn haber-dasher declared 'she wanted to be out of the world'.[54] Signs of remorse and repentance could also work on the sympathies of the victims, particularly if the offender was not from a class where susceptibility to crime was presumed endemic.[55] William Corbyn, son of a London merchant taylor and one-time East India Company army cadet, sent a request for silversmith William Spaldin to visit him in the Liverpool gaol where he had been committed on a charge of stealing silver buckles from Spaldin's shop. He complied, and later reported to the magistrate that Corbyn had fully admitted his crime and shown remorse. Although Corbyn was also accused of thefts from two other shops, and had shown a high level of skill and deception in accomplishing these, Spaldin ungrudgingly told him that 'he would shew him for his part all the mercy and lenity in his power as he had been so open in his confession'.[56]

Court transcripts and depositions provide further evidence of mentality. In contrast to pleas of moral responsibility, some shoplifters sought to neutralise their guilt, to blame their moral weakness on the effects of alcohol, or more rarely, mental disability. In 5% of Old Bailey trials in the sample, defendants or witnesses suggested their judgement had been impaired to a greater or lesser degree by alcohol. Pleas ranged from ignorance of the theft ('I drank with them too freely, I do not know how I came into the shop, I do not recollect any thing at all till I was in the Compter') to the exculpatory ('I am a very poor woman, have three children, and was in liquor: I never did such a thing before').[57] As we noted earlier, 'tipling' was a familiarly cited step on the presumed descent to criminality. Dana Rabin has lucidly discussed how early modern thinkers were torn between their observation that alcohol could produce aberrant but fleeting misbehaviour, and their conviction that, where the poor were concerned, drunkenness nevertheless required stern

---

53   OBP, July 1767, Sarah Dalton (t17670715-45).
54   OBP, December 1751, Ann Russel (t17511204-10).
55   Peter Linebaugh, *The London Hanged: Crime and Civil Society in the Eighteenth Century* (London, 1991), pp. 428–30.
56   TNA, PL 27/5, Lancaster, Crown Court, 12 August 1780, William Corbyn.
57   OBP, May 1805, Ann Macgrath (t18050529-7); July 1751, Sarah Newby (t17510703-6).

punishment to prevent an inevitable slide into more dangerous misdeeds.[58] Law commentators had no such conflict. William Blackstone advised, 'as to artificial, voluntarily contracted madness, by *drunkenness* or intoxication, which, depriving men of their reason, puts them in a temporary phrenzy; the law looks upon this as an aggravation of the offence, rather than as an excuse for any criminal misbehaviour'.[59] However, the fact that judges often asked for corroboration from prosecutors or witnesses of a defendant's claim of drunkenness implies that it was a factor they were disposed to take into account, or at least give the appearance of doing so. Rabin suggests that the eighteenth-century courtroom became a site for displaying sensibility and that 'judges and jurors may have accepted some sentimental pleas because they affirmed their own superior sense of self and sensibility'.[60] And in spite of this, there is little indication from the sample that such consideration resulted in any significant diminution in sentencing. Outside the courtroom, communities familiar with the disinhibiting effect of alcohol may have been more forgiving of the consequent moral lapses of its members. When John Brooks stole a table from a shop window there was consternation, but neighbours and friends rallied round. His prosecutor admitted, 'I really thought he was in liquor'; a neighbour declared, 'He never used to get drunk; nor I never heard him accused of any thing in the world.' And his apprentice master added, 'I was the most surpriz'd to hear this, he was so sober a man, I thought he would not have done this fact. While he was an apprentice he belong'd to a religious society ... but when he gets a little liquor he is like a mad-man.'[61]

If neighbours could treat shoplifting in the light of a moral lapse, we should complete this account of the religious and moral thinking that underpinned attitudes to shoplifting by asking how common was the practice of community-administered justice? Print culture, which predominantly represented London habits, customs and interests, can help us less here.[62] In the smaller and more close-knit settlements of northern England, the tradition of the community dealing informally with miscreants within their ranks may have been more customary, conceivably even accounting in part for the fewer cases of shoplifting reaching the assize courts. Such a tendency is suggested by Richard Oyes intervention in the theft of lawn from Whitehaven mercer and draper John Wilson in 1786. Oyes was a wealthy local property owner and Overseer of the Poor for the town. Perhaps in consequence of the intelligence this role brought him, he came to hear that a local woman, Ann Robinson,

---

58 Dana Rabin, 'Drunkenness and Responsibility for Crime in the Eighteenth Century', *Journal of British Studies* 44/3 (2005), 457–77 (pp. 459–66).
59 Blackstone, *Commentaries*, pp. 24–5.
60 Rabin, 'Drunkenness and Responsibility', p. 469.
61 *OBP*, July 1747, John Brooks (t17470715-21).
62 Feather, 'The Power of Print', p. 57.

had been offering lawn for sale and immediately went to her house to enquire its provenance. Distrusting her explanation, he personally followed the trail of the cloth to one of the women to whom Robinson admitted she had sold the lawn, and summoned Wilson's shopman and two apprentices to identify it. As the evidence mounted, Robinson capitulated and admitted her guilt, at which Oyes despatched her to her house in company with Wilson's shopman to retrieve the last of the lawn before she was eventually taken into custody.[63] There are other indications that the legacy of an older, paternalistic form of justice persisted into the eighteenth century. In September 1778, a brief item appeared in the daily news:

> A very genteel young female shoplifter was detected on Monday last pilfering some muslin at a tradesman's shop in Holborn. Her father living but a short way off, being sent for, took hold of her right hand, and thrust it in to the fire. The girl screamed hideously, and promised never to be again guilty of the like offence.[64]

This episode has the ring of a popular cautionary tale, but also calls to mind the statutory sentence of branding on the thumb, which had not yet entirely fallen out of use for shoplifting. The notion of restorative justice remained in both the popular and judicial imagination, for at this period some criminals were still being condemned to punishment at the scene of their crime.[65] A *Scheme for Punishing Felonies*, attributed to the writer Bonell Thornton, satirically advocated 'That every pick-pocket and shop-lifter have their hands chopt off in open court; which shall afterwards be smoke-dried, and nailed upon the inside of the prison-gate.'[66] And such thinking was not merely an imaginative construct. Shoplifter Eleanor Gravenor, sentenced to death in 1712 for stealing calico, was reported as saying she 'would contentedly yield to have her right hand cut off, which had done so much mischief, and pick up a poor livelihood in gathering of rags with her left hand, which ever was honest, and therefore should not suffer with the other'.[67]

63 TNA, ASSI 45/35/3/159, Criminal Depositions and Case Papers, 15 August 1786, Ann Robinson.
64 *Public Advertiser*, 30 September 1778, p. 3.
65 Matthew White, '"For the Safety of the City": The Geography and Social Politics of Public Execution after the Gordon Riots', in *The Gordon Riots: Politics, Culture and Insurrection in Late Eighteenth-Century Britain*, ed. I. Haywood and J. Seed (Cambridge 2012), pp. 204–25 (pp. 208–9).
66 *The Repository: a Select Collection of Fugitive Pieces of Wit and Humour, in Prose and Verse*, vol. 3 (London, 1777), p. 214.
67 OBP, *Ordinary's Account*, 31 October 1712 (OA17121031).

Female sexuality

Moral censure of criminality was applied universally, but women attracted particular opprobrium. Female thieves were burdened by an earlier tradition of popular literature which routinely attributed their behaviour to deviant sexuality.[68] A published life of Moll Hawkins, executed in 1703, related that 'adultery and fornication was her common recreation, as well as shop-lifting'.[69] Shoplifters operated on public streets and, as Robert Shoemaker has observed of early modern London, 'printed discussions of women in public places in this period rarely venture far from sex: women are portrayed as either virtuous or as whores'.[70] While he has later contended that a more sympathetic understanding of female criminality was starting to take root as verbatim recording in the early-eighteenth-century *Proceedings* and *Ordinary's Accounts* gave women their own voice, the impact of this was limited.[71] Representations of female shoplifters were obstinately conflated with those of prostitutes and freely sexualised. The early-century satirical writer, Edward Ward, invariably linked the two in his works. In *The London-Spy*, the female recipients of a stream of insults are a 'durty salt-ass'd-brood of night-walkers and shop-liftes'; his political work *Hudibras Redivivus* itemises 'Jilts, shoplifts, files and brimstone b---es'; and in his *Nuptial Dialogues*, the cheated husband accuses:

> What wanton sorc'ress have I wedded?
> What beggar hugg'd? What strumpet bedded?
> Some shoplift, full of tricks and wiles
> Perhaps bred up in sweet *St. Giles*;[72]

St Giles was popularly associated with prostitution. Writing a few years later, Daniel Defoe gave Moll Flanders, the most celebrated shoplifter in literature, a name which would convey resonances of theft and prostitution to his readership.[73] And this novel came within a long tradition of salacious moral tales that singularly associated the two offences. The opening page of *The Remarkable Life* [...] *of Charlotte Crutchey* summarised:

68   Robert Shoemaker 'Print and the Female Voice: Representations of Women's Crime in London, 1690–1735', *Gender and History* 22/1 (2010), 75–91 (pp. 77–80).
69   Smith, *A Compleat History*, vol. 1, p. 146.
70   Shoemaker, 'Gendered Spaces', p. 148.
71   Shoemaker, 'Print and the Female Voice', pp. 80–7.
72   Edward Ward, *The London-Spy Compleat, in Eighteen Parts*, part VII (London, 1700), p. 4; *Hudibras Redivivus, or a Burlesque Poem on the Various Humours of Town and Country*, 2 vols (London, 1707), vol. 2, part V, p. 16; *Nuptial Dialogues and Debates*, 2 vols (London, 1710), vol. 2, pp. 175–6.
73   David Blewett, 'Introduction', in Defoe, *Moll Flanders*, pp. 1–24 (pp. 3–5).

How she was decoyed away from a boarding school at Kensington, and debauched by Mr Smith, of the same place, when she was fourteen years of age; her being cast for death for shoplifting, pardoned, and afterwards twice transported.

Likewise her marrying abroad, her coming back to England, and keeping a bawdy-house in the Strand; her standing twice in the pillory at Charing-Cross, and is now converted by the Rev. Mr. Romain, and become a sincere Christian in the 70th year of his age, and now living in Bloomsbury.[74]

A similar tale of Betty Ireland, forced into prostitution in her teens and later arrested for shoplifting, was being advertised for sale in 1741, and remained in print throughout the century.[75]

We may question why this particular association should persist. Certainly both prostitution and shoplifting could be forms of makeshift. Testifying against three shoplifters in 1768, a shopman recalled, 'I asked them, they being so young, why they should take to such a way of life; Lewis made answer, how do you think we can live, but by whoring and thieving'.[76] But case evidence from London courts reveals a far closer statistical conjunction of prostitution and pickpocketing: theft from clients was commonplace. The connection is perhaps less scientific and more intuitive, the frequent reference to the body in shoplifting cases as a harbour for stolen goods encouraging a free licence to sexual allusion.

The artist John Collet was a master of innuendo, so it is unsurprising to find such content in his satirical print, *Shop-Lifter Detected*, first published in 1778 (Plate 7 shows a later copy from 1787). The only known representation of a shoplifter in the period, we cannot fail to notice that this print is redolent with sexual imagery. In retrieving their employer's stolen lace and ribbons, the two shopmen have been given licence to molest the well-dressed shoplifter, which they are apparently exploiting with relish. The constable's truncheon to the right of the picture and the placing of the shoplifter's hands further signpost this subtext. The scene readily recalls Moll Flanders' complaint, on being detained for shoplifting, that 'Some of the servants likewise us'd me saucily, and had much ado to keep their hands off of me.'[77]

Admittedly, the print has had other interpretations. Collet specialised in prints of characters transgressing stereotypes, frequently women indulging in thrill-seeking activities traditionally associated with men. Patricia Crown, in her essay on Collet's prints 'Sporting with Clothes', promotes such a

74 *The Remarkable Life and Transactions of Charlotte Crutchey, a Banker's Daughter, in Lombard Street* (London, 1775), p. 1.
75 *The Secret History of Betty Ireland* (London, 1765), p. 2; *London Evening Post*, 24–26 February 1741, p. 4.
76 OBP, September 1768, Anne Darlin, Elizabeth Lewis, Anne Price (t17680907-8).
77 Defoe, *Moll Flanders*, p. 312.

Plate 7   *Shop-Lifter Detected: from an original picture painted by Mr. John Collett,*
1787

meaning. She suggests that 'the exchange of smiles and glances prompts us to regard her pilfering as initiating a game of skill, in which chances are taken and sometimes lost, with no very heavy punishment for losing'.[78] We are invited to see the picture as a representation of excitement-seeking behaviour, a motivation commonly admitted by modern offenders.[79] However, it is doubtful that this was Collet's primary intention. The two riding prints issued by his publishers, Robert Sayer and J. Bennet, immediately before and after *Shop-Lifter Detected*, entitled *The Favourite Footman, or Miss Well Mounted*, and *Miss too Much for him, or John not Master of Sixteen Stone* are both as sexually suggestive as their titles imply.[80]

Of course, eighteenth-century society was far from puritanical and people of all ranks sought pleasure in erotic or bawdy entertainments.[81] It is instructive that the *Morning Chronicle* in its brief reporting of one of the longest and most controversial mid-century shoplifting trials, that of the businesswoman Sarah Tonge, picked out a sexual exchange as the highlight for its middling and elite readership:

> Mrs Tonge, who kept a milliner's shop in Fleet-Street, was tried upon two indictments for shoplifting. The first was for privately stealing a piece of lace in the shop of Mr. Joseph Green in Cheapside. Upon the shopman's charging her with stealing the lace, she offered him twenty guineas to let her go, but he still persisting in sending for a constable, she threw her arms round him, told him she was not married, and that if he would drop the matter, she would give him an hundred pounds, and he should have free access to her bedchamber whenever he pleased; but as the case did not properly come within the letter of the act, respecting a secret and private stealing, she was, after two long trials, acquitted of that part of both the indictments, and received sentence of transportation.[82]

Predictably such attitudes to female sexuality extended into the courtroom itself. Risqué testimony was uttered to discredit witnesses or gratuitously, to the delight and titillation of spectators. Shopkeeper Ann Crouch described how she had stripped and searched Mary Morris before finding her stolen lace

---

78 Patricia Crown, 'Sporting with Clothes: John Collet's Prints in the 1770s', *Eighteenth-Century Life* 26/1 (2002), 119–35 (p. 120).
79 Katz, *Seductions of Crime*, pp. 59–60.
80 David Alexander, 'Prints after John Collet: Their Publishing History and a Chronological Checklist', *Eighteenth-Century Life* 26/1 (2002), 136–46 (pp. 145–6).
81 Roy Porter, *English Society in the Eighteenth Century* (London, 1991), pp. 259–62; Roy Porter, *Enlightenment: Britain and the Creation of the Modern World* (London, 2000), pp. 271–5; White, *London in the Eighteenth Century*, p. 311.
82 *Morning Chronicle and London Advertiser*, 27 April 1773, p. 3.

in the shoplifter's 'private parts'.[83] Elizabeth Metcalf alleged in her defence that after entering his shop to buy a ribbon, the haberdasher's apprentice:

> put his hand down my bossom, and up my coats; I asked what that was for, he said he thought I had something about me that did not belong to me; I said if I had, it was proper a woman should search me, he said he should think it no sin to rip me open, and let my puddings out.[84]

Many shopkeepers were scrupulous, or perhaps simply prudent, in insisting that female shoplifters only be searched by female relatives, assistants or neighbours. However, others appear to have no qualms in allowing male staff or law officers to do the same. This may have sometimes been for practical reasons but more commonly because they felt the shoplifters' behaviour placed them beyond the proprieties and consideration customarily afforded women.

Elite entertainment

As the century progressed, the moral framing of shoplifting in print culture lessened. Simon Devereaux has demonstrated that the prevailing perception of law-breaking as a moral lapse was increasingly challenged by press reports and publications, such as the Newgate Calendars, that implied criminality was both congenital and a condition invariably linked to the poor.[85] This new understanding allowed the wealthy to cognitively disassociate themselves from any stigma attached to shoplifting. As an aberration of the poor and criminally degenerate, the concept of shoplifting among their own ranks ostensibly became a source of diversion. Frances Burney, born into a professional family, had a keen interest in the mores of her contemporaries. While always concerned to retain the social approval of family and friends, even to the extent on occasion of being persuaded not to publish, her work was informed by her personal experience.[86] Burney's fiction explores the implications of individuals' relationships in an increasingly commercial society.[87] Her third novel, *Camilla*, published in 1796, has been described by Julia Epstein as both a complex psychological work and a critique of social ideology.[88] In a key episode, the genteel heroine Camilla is shopping with a somewhat dubious

83   *OBP*, January 1779, Mary Morris (t17790113-27).
84   *OBP*, May 1753, Elizabeth Metcalf (t17530502-13).
85   Devereaux, 'From Sessions to Newspaper?, pp. 12–18.
86   Hunter, *Before Novels*, pp. 193–4, 294; Lynch, 'Counter Publics', p. 214.
87   Deidre Shauna Lynch, *The Economy of Character: Novels, Market Culture, and the Business of Inner Meaning* (Chicago, 1998), p. 169.
88   Julia Epstein, *The Iron Pen: Frances Burney and the Politics of Women's Writing* (Bristol, 1989), p. 125.

companion, Mrs Mittin, in Southampton High Street when they are mistaken for shoplifters. Mrs Mittin, we learn, intends to sample the consumer delights of this fashionable spa town in a manner that avoids pecuniary commitment:

> While she entered almost every shop, with inquiries of what was worth seeing, she attended to no answer nor information, but having examined and admired all the goods within sight or reach, walked off, to obtain, by similar means, a similar privilege further on; boasting to Camilla, that, by this clever device they might see all that was smartest, without the expence of buying any thing.[89]

From the frequent grumblings of trade manuals and press, this appears to be classic eighteenth-century shopping behaviour.[90] Yet, rather unexpectedly, Burney portrays the Southampton shopkeepers as disturbed by the couple's meanderings:

> Some supposed they were only seeking to attract notice; others thought they were deranged in mind; and others, again, imagined they were shoplifters, and hastened back to their counters, to examine what was missing of their goods.[91]

Pursuing the two women, the shopkeepers come across Camilla's suitor and in response to his query, reveal to him their suspicions. His reaction instructs us on the social placing of shoplifting in the consciousness of higher society:

> The curiosity of Edgar would have been converted into ridicule, had he been less uneasy at seeing with whom Camilla was thus associated; Mrs Mittin might certainly be a worthy woman, and, if so, must merit every kindness that could be shewn to her; but her air and manner so strongly displayed the low bred society to which she had been accustomed, that he foresaw nothing but improper acquaintance, or demeaning adventures, that could ensue from such a connection at a public place.[92]

While Burney attaches no blame to her heroine for this incident, she ensures her readers observe that Camilla is meanwhile becoming culpably involved in another form of acquiring goods 'without the expence of buying'. Her erstwhile companion Mrs Mittin, a former milliner's assistant, makes her living by parasitically attaching herself to members of the fashionable

---

89   Frances Burney, *Camilla or A Picture of Youth* (1796; Oxford, 1972), p. 607.
90   For example Defoe, *The Complete English Tradesman*, p. 85; *Spectator*, 454, 11 August 1712, p. 2.
91   Burney, *Camilla*, p. 608.
92   Burney, *Camilla*, pp. 610–11.

elite and offering them various forms of practical assistance; we are told that 'to please was her incessant desire'.[93] Mrs Mittin solicitously anticipates the heroine's sartorial needs as a spa resort visitor and, misinformed as to her wealth, orders high-fashion clothes and trimmings for Camilla from suppliers happy to offer credit on the basis of her apparent status. Burney may have intended Mrs Mittin's name to echo 'mittimus', the legal term for a prison warrant, as Camilla's father is ultimately committed to gaol for his daughter's debts.

The parallels between shoplifting and credit debt to tradesman had not escaped all. A letter signed 'Philanthropus' printed in *The Weekly Miscellany* in 1738 purports to describe the shocking but edifying effect of observing Old Bailey trials. He declares:

> What is most dreadful to us in our *waking* moments is apt to rise up to view, with double terror, when asleep. To the horror of such crimes it is owing that I am sometimes a shoplifter in my dream; which has such an effect upon me that I am not easy 'till all my tradesmen are discharg'd; and fancy that whilst their goods are unpaid for in my possession, I am but little inferior to the character I assumed in my sleep.[94]

But there are signs that the later-century elite were less conscience-ridden. Deidre Shauna Lynch has even suggested that women who by 'waiting too long to pay, turned shopping into theft' may have been doing so intentionally to fortify the boundaries of social class'.[95] In an apparent parody of the recently published Lord Chesterfield's *Letters*, written to his son, 'Letters from a Lady of Fashion, lately deceased, to her daughter', printed in the *Morning Chronicle* in January 1775, offers financial advice to a society wife with limited means of her own.[96] Have less concern about tradesmen, the mother advises: 'The shortest way is not to pay them at all; and this is adopted by most people of fashion. Nothing upon earth is so mean and vulgar as to pay our debts.' There are shrewder ways to get by, the mother instructs her daughter: Lady E_ C_ who 'has not above five hundred a year', relies on making money at cards and through 'shoplifting makes shift to appear tolerably decent in the world. Methinks I see you start at the last article; but you were ever of a strange narrow way of thinking.'[97]

It is perhaps unsurprising to find shoplifting adopted as a high-society metaphor. 'Sunday being a day resembling spring, it invited the multitude

---

93 Burney, *Camilla*, p. 688.
94 *The Weekly Miscellany*, 4 November 1738, p. 1.
95 Lynch, 'Counter Publics', p. 223.
96 Philip Dormer Stanhope, *Letters written by the late Right Honourable Philip Dormer Stanhope, Earl of Chesterfield, to his son, Philip Stanhope, Esq*, 4 vols (London 1774).
97 *Morning Chronicle*, 21 January 1775, pp. 1–2.

Plate 8   *The Muff*, 1787

into Hyde Park', commenced a light-hearted fashion piece in the press in December 1789, continuing:

> The Mercer had hopes, for elegant ladies were dressed in silks and satins; and it must be confessed, the silk dress adds much to the beauty of the wearer: – a beautiful woman, elegantly dressed, is as a fine picture, richly framed and glazed. The Russia fur tippet, which supports the syllabub handkerchief, has a grand appearance, and was worn in general; but the disproportionable bear-skin muff, should, on so mild a day, have been carried by the servant. Many of them were so large as to rob the wearer of her height, as well as her delicacy. It was asked by some wags, *en passant*, if these were the muffs they call Shoplifters.[98]

Apparently so, for in October 1791 the same newspaper tells us, 'The Promenade was elegant for the season, and if fashion can reconcile the town

98   *Public Advertiser*, 10 December 1789, p. 3.

to enormous muffs – then muffs as large as bears must be called handsome. Miss Pumpkin carried one, big enough for her to sleep in. The Shoplifter of last season was a baby to it'[99] (Plate 8). By 1796, a Tattersall sale advertisement on behalf of a 'Gentleman' in Leicestershire for his horse, 'Shoplifter, a grey gelding, seven years old, got by Botany Bay', demonstrated that the county set had no embarrassment at adopting criminal signifiers for their studs.[100]

Growing to adulthood in these years, the clergyman's daughter Jane Austen honed her literary skills by writing short plays and stories as entertainments for her family and friends. Now known as her *Juvenilia*, they reveal a nascent fascination with crime. One of the works, *The Beautifull Cassandra*, 'a novel in twelve chapters' written around 1788, was dedicated to her older sister, suggesting she would take her namesake's role in good part. The heroine, a Bond Street milliner's daughter, exhibits a decidedly free-handed attitude to acquisition. She commences an eventful day by 'chancing to fall in love with an elegant Bonnet her Mother had just completed, bespoke by the Countess of —, she placed it on her gentle Head and walked from her Mother's shop'. Two chapters on from this incipient act of shoplifting, we learn that Cassandra has 'proceeded to a Pastry-cook's, where she devoured six ices, refused to pay for them', before taking a hackney coach ride to Hampstead for which she is unable to pay the fare. The story concludes at home, where 'Cassandra smiled & whispered to herself, "This is a day well spent."'[101] Jillian Heydt-Stevenson sees in the *Juvenilia* Austen expressing a generalised critique of society's constraints:

> She laughs at all of it: the advice from conduct books, philosophical tracts, sermons, and medical manuals; at the idea that women's sexuality should be closely guarded; that private pleasures should be controlled; that gender should dictate behavior; and that any conceivable appetite – sexual, criminal, alimentary, and liquid – should be governed.[102]

Theft does indeed figure frequently in the works, albeit with little consequence. Sophia in *Love and Friendship* steals a banknote, as does Eliza in *Henry and Eliza*. And Jane Austen was not unfamiliar with contemporary symbols of criminal justice.[103] In the latter work, the 'Dutchess' maintains a 'Newgate ... erected for the reception of her own private Prisoners'.[104]

99   *Public Advertiser*, 26 October 1791, p. 3.
100 *Morning Post*, 15 April 1796, p. 4.
101 Jane Austen, *Minor Works*, ed. R. W. Chapman (Oxford, 1954), pp. 45–7.
102 Jillian Heydt-Stevenson, '"Pleasure is now, and ought to be, your business": Stealing Sexuality in Jane Austen's Juvenilia', in *Historicizing Romantic Sexuality*, ed. R. C. Sha (http://www.rc.umd.edu/praxis/sexuality/heydt/heydt.html, accessed 19 April 2018).
103 Austen, *Minor Works*, pp. 34, 96.
104 Austen, *Minor Works*, p. 36.

However, a shocking family event in 1799 may have generated an aversion in Austen to developing similar themes in her more famous later works.

While staying in Bath, her aunt Jane Leigh-Perrot was accused of shoplifting a card of white lace from a milliner's shop. Considerably wealthier than Jane's family, and with numerous friends in county society, Leigh-Perrot's arrest was almost unprecedented, as was her seven-month detention in Ilchester Gaol awaiting the spring assizes. The subsequent trial at Taunton in March 1800 lasted seven hours, culminating in Jane Leigh-Perrot producing fourteen character witnesses including leading landowners, clergy and Members of Parliament for her home county of Berkshire, and several respected Bath tradesmen. The *Morning Post* correspondent, returning his copy to London twenty-four hours later by 'special express', reported that the judge having summed up the evidence 'with that candour and humanity that he is ever known to exercise', the jury promptly found her 'not guilty'.[105] Appearing in the *Post* under the heading 'The Interesting Trial of Mrs Jane Lee Perrot', the trial was covered in length by eleven other London papers and also by the provincial press. Within a fortnight a pamphlet account of the proceedings was being advertised for sale for 1 shilling.[106]

Although acceptance and acknowledgement that the better-off shoplifted only gradually found open expression over the next twenty years, this trial was clearly a watershed. By 1819 a witness before the parliamentary Select Committee on Criminal Laws, had little hesitation in confirming that many shoplifters 'are not persons who are regular traders in thieving, but are persons in better circumstances, particularly the women'.[107] And Richard Arthur Austen-Leigh, the Austen family biographer, has drawn attention to the fact that Jane Leigh-Perrot's counsel later felt able to express doubts as to her innocence. In a letter of 1832 Joseph Jekyll wrote of ladies who 'mistake other people's property for their own. It was the blunder of my client, Mrs Leigh Perrot, in former days, and I am told is still frequently committed.'[108] Leigh-Perrot, by contrast in her correspondence, virulently attacked the dishonest conduct of her accusers.[109] This accords with a tendency, identified by Tammy Whitlock, for early-nineteenth-century opinion to transfer blame for middle-class shoplifting from the offenders to their retailer victims.[110] Thomas

---

105   *Morning Post and Gazetteer*, 31 March 1800, pp. 1–2.
106   *The Sun*, 9 April 1800, p. 1.
107   *Report from the Select Committee on Criminal Laws*, 1819, p. 27.
108   Richard Arthur Austen-Leigh, 'Captain Francis William Austen and some others', *Notes and Queries* 192/22 (1 November 1947), 474–5.
109   Adela Pinch, 'Stealing Happiness: Shoplifting in Early Nineteenth-Century England', in *Border Fetishisms: Material Objects in Unstable Spaces*, ed. P. Spyers (London, 1998), pp. 122–49 (pp. 131–2).
110   Tammy Whitlock, *Crime, Gender and Consumer Culture in Nineteenth-Century England* (Aldershot, 2005), pp. 129, 145–6.

de Quincey's tale, *The Household Wreck*, written in 1838, was predicated on a shopkeeper falsely accusing a suburban housewife of shoplifting.[111] Distrust of retailers had been prevalent a century earlier. *Moll Flanders* contains an episode where a mercer mistakenly and unjustly detains Moll for stealing from his shop while the true culprit goes free.[112] Defoe even felt it necessary to devote a key passage of *The Complete English Tradesman* to refuting any persuasion that tradesmen were less honest than other men.[113] But economic and social developments in the new century were creating a climate which refocused and polarised the public attitudes of the previous century.

Mass production of consumer goods, the development of ever-larger shops and department stores, and the ascendancy of the middle-class female leisure shopper constrained by their idealised Victorian domestic role, all combined to produce fresh criminal concerns about shoplifting. No longer able to deny that individuals of all classes shoplifted, and unable to reconcile this with narratives of need or of a criminal type, society developed new explanations. The genteel wife, the moral guardian of the private domestic sphere was said to have been 'demoralised' by retailers' evermore insistent marketing, providing temptations that drove them even to steal.[114] A syndrome termed kleptomania, developed in the early nineteenth century and defined as an obsessive impulse to steal irrespective of economic need, provided an acceptable explanation for the otherwise apparently irrational theft by wealthy female shoppers.[115] As shoplifting became increasingly medicalised for this social group, women were represented as victims rather than perpetrators, driven by forces beyond their control.[116] Eighteenth-century critiques of the impact of the new availability of consumer goods, Fielding's 'torrent of luxury', endorsed as we saw earlier by Defoe, made way to reconfigured anxieties over the corrupting effects of the glittering decor and enticing merchandise of the Victorian department store.[117] Émile Zola's 1883 novel *The Ladies' Paradise* (*Au Bonheur des Dames*), set in a Parisian department store, dramatises the spirit of the age. A customer, the countess Madame de Boves, is detained by a shop-walker for stealing 12 metres of Alençon lace. We learn that:

> Ravaged by a furious, irresistible urge, Madame de Boves had been stealing like this for a year. The attacks had been getting worse, increasing until they

111   Pinch, 'Stealing Happiness', pp. 133–5.
112   Defoe, *Moll Flanders*, pp. 311–17.
113   Defoe, 'Of Honesty in Dealing; and Of Telling Unavoidable Trading Lyes', in *The Complete English Tradesman*, pp. 226–40.
114   Tammy Whitlock, *Crime, Gender and Consumer Culture*, p. 152.
115   Pinch, 'Stealing Happiness', p. 124; Elaine S. Abelson, *When Ladies Go A-Thieving: Middle-Class Shoplifters in the Victorian Department Store* (Oxford, 1989), pp. 182–3.
116   Abelson, *When Ladies Go A-Thieving*, pp. 7–8.
117   Abelson, *When Ladies Go A-Thieving*, ch. 2, pp. 42–62.

had become a sensual pleasure necessary to her existence, sweeping away all the reasonings of prudence and giving her an enjoyment which was all the more keen because she was risking, under the very eyes of the crowd, her name, her pride, and her husband's important position.[118]

The store deals with the matter privately, displaying the same discretion and deference to class common in the previous century, but the psychologising of shoplifting is a characteristic of the later age. And 'kleptomania' served to excuse other explanations. Elaine Abelson has conjectured that rather than succumbing to irresistible temptation, middle-class women may have been motivated by a desire to undermine or circumvent patriarchal control. Having to account for all expenditure to their husbands, they might steal items that would be otherwise unacceptable. There is also the suggestion that where social standing depended upon a certain level of conspicuous consumption, social pressures might put a strain on economic means.[119] Yet Victorian retailers' efforts to develop more effective non-judicial means of protecting their businesses, collaborating to form national trade protection associations and distributing warning information on offenders through circulars and trade journals, implicitly suggests they were subscribing to the 'mania' myth.[120] For ultimately the ascribing of shoplifting to the psychological vulnerability of women offered nineteenth-century society a welcome means of diverting censure from the less violable targets of authoritarian family structures and the free expansion of consumer capitalism.[121]

In examining public attitudes to shoplifting this final substantive chapter has explored some cultural facets of the crime. It reveals that while shoplifting may have prompted less alarm or reader interest than other crimes in the period, it still attracted significant moral censure. This was propagated in polemic on plebeian greed and degeneracy, such violation of socially configured standards of behaviour often internalised by offenders who responded with ritualised expressions of their essential virtue. The crime was also routinely sexualised for female offenders, a moral discrediting encouraged by the use of the body for concealing goods. And while changing attitudes to criminal nature initially enabled the elite to easily distance themselves from the crime, this became increasingly untenable as the nineteenth century dawned.

---

118 Émile Zola, *The Ladies' Paradise* (*Au Bonheur des Dames*) (1883; Oxford, 2008), p. 422.
119 Abelson, *When Ladies Go A-Thieving*, pp. 165–8.
120 Finn, *The Character of Credit*, pp. 289–90; Whitlock, *Crime, Gender and Consumer Culture*, p. 6.
121 Abelson, *When Ladies Go A-Thieving*, p. 12.

Conclusion

With the passing of the Shoplifting Act in 1699, the crime of shoplifting acquired a new prominence. Heightened alarm at retail losses and a pervading belief in the deterrent effect of harsher laws had converged to make shoplifting a capital offence, a notorious status that it retained for the next 120 years. The focus of this book has been how retailers and the wider population experienced and responded to customer theft within the cultural and economic context of the period. It has analysed the crime's social characteristics, its impact on commerce and its potential influence on the development of contemporary criminal justice and material culture, exhibiting the emblematic nature of the offence. The preceding chapters have examined in some detail the demography of those charged with shoplifting, their tactics and shopkeepers' countermeasures, the nature and significance of what was stolen, and the economic effect of the crime on the retail sector. At the same time the book has followed the changes in retailers' relationship to the law on shoplifting and concurrent shifts in public attitudes, arguing that in both of these there was a notable transformation in outlook and perception over time.

Shoplifting became an accustomed expedient for some of the most economically vulnerable in society, attracting both men and women. The nation's multiplying stores were increasingly available and the routine of shopping offered a plausible pretext for customers constrained to steal. Theft from neighbourhood shops and those with busy passing trade furnished some of the poorest, largely urban populace with a source of intermittent subsidy. Analysis of the occupational circumstances and times of theft of those prosecuted indicates that shoplifting was only a full-time occupation for a minority of these thieves, for most it was a casual and opportunist means to supplement low incomes or tide them over patches of unemployment. Few shoplifters from higher classes reached court, certainly in part due to retailers' demonstrable reluctance to suspect or detain such customers. But while we cannot know the degree to which this disguised the scale of middling theft, there is no evidence to suggest it was substantial in this period.

Shoplifting was undoubtedly more extensive than court appearances suggest. Retailers complained of losses from undetected theft and they faced significant disincentives to prosecution. Travelling distance and infrequency of sessions deterred northern shopkeepers, and even in London the costs to business involved in attending court were sufficiently oppressive to persuade many retailers to countenance a degree of loss. Shopkeepers informally recouped these where possible through illegal compounding, or simply imposed a de facto exclusion of offenders from their premises. Certain trades faced greater risk. While shoplifters stole food, jewellery and household goods, their primary targets were textiles, clothing and haberdashery. These were the goods most marketable in the period, those which were in greatest demand in working communities and for which disposal routes were most readily available. As a consequence thieves sought out specialist shops, drapers, mercers and clothes shops. In the north, the slower introduction and regional distribution of such stores contributed to the lower number of cases, and pattern of prosecutions. It was London, where England's most fashionable shops were located, that became the epicentre of the crime. Yet a plotting of prosecutions over time reveals that its finest outlets were not the most common victims. Shoplifters, the majority of whom were amateur, favoured smaller, local shops. These stores were familiar, had fewer staff to detect theft, and a clientele among whom their dress and manner would not appear conspicuous. As the century progressed, recorded incidents were increasingly located to the north and east of London's conurbation, rather than the elite shopping streets at its centre.

We learn from the testimony of shop staff that shoplifters commonly planned and reconnoitred shops to identify the best prospects. Whether intending to steal by snatching the goods and running or taking them more surreptitiously having engaged and distracted staff, an item's accessibility and portability was of the essence. They developed performance skills and a range of diversionary tactics to remove spoils undetected from counters, windows and external displays. Clothing was customised to conceal and remove their pickings from the shop. Retailers responded pragmatically to this threat by developing forms of 'situational prevention' that would deter shoplifters by increasing the likelihood of detection and capture. Those who had the means glazed windows, secured counters, improved lighting, fitted mirrors and glass panels, and increased staff complements, all of which served to limit their risk. In consequence, older styles of retailing, open shops and those sometimes left unattended, were particularly vulnerable while larger modish stores became less so. However, even small shopkeepers testified to implementing innovative means of safeguarding their stock by the strategic display of goods and staff protocols.

The textiles and clothing stolen were predominantly those of everyday wear in working communities. Certain items did reflect the growing adoption of popular style, but shoplifters also serviced more traditional needs and relatively few seized the opportunity shops offered to acquire the high-end fashions or decorative goods being purchased by the elite. Shoplifters facilitated, but did not manifestly accelerate the spread of consumer goods to the lower classes. Their astute thieving was closely integrated with other routine means of daily survival in working communities: pawning, sale of goods in second-hand markets, or borrowing from neighbours. Shoplifters stole items that had maximum exchange value – the same cheaper linens and cottons, handkerchiefs and stockings that had a regular market among their peers. The economic insecurity of plebeian life was not conducive to forming an affective attachment to goods and this is exhibited in the little they apparently stole to keep or for their own adornment. Any possessions were investments to be converted at times of hardship. The intermittent proceeds of shoplifting were a survival strategy, enabling them to feed their families, perhaps subsidise their daily business, and maintain their standing and ties in the community.

Shoplifting losses took their toll on retailers. Although not as critical to business solvency as credit failure, they eroded profit margins, particularly of the smaller retailers that were most vulnerable to the threat. Maintaining liquidity with limited stock and low turnover was precarious, and extra impositions, such as that of the short-lived Shop Tax, exacerbated the situation. Trade protection and prosecution societies offered a form of self-insurance, but their contribution was primarily through mutual support and guidance, complementing the informal assistance shopkeepers regularly afforded each other in policing the sector. Nevertheless, there was little discernible correlation between financial risk and prosecution rates. The book contends that a more reliable indicator of a propensity to seek legal redress was a retailer's attitude and business temperament, a tendency to combativeness in this respect often being nurtured in succeeding generations through the apprenticeship system.

Retailers' vantage point changed as the century progressed. As shoplifting began to escalate their preliminary response was to turn to the traditional corrective of statutory law. City of London traders, influenced by current thinking on crime, lobbied successfully for harsher penalties. The resultant Shoplifting Act, however, proved a limited and ineffective tool. The continued increase in shoplifting incidents demonstrated the futility of its deterrent impact; the Act's restricted definition, a series of rulings on legal precedent, and the propensity of judges and juries to reduce its effect mitigated its capital penalty. So, over time, retailers devised more constructive ways of managing the hazard of shoplifting. With the success or survival of their business paramount, shopkeepers' prevention strategy became increasingly 'risk-based' rather than 'crime-based'. They invested in situational prevention and co-operated with judicial initiatives where this might help recover goods, advertising losses, liaising with pawnbrokers and reporting incursions to magistrates at Bow Street. But their pragmatism extended still further. We observe retailers manipulating legal charges to achieve desired outcomes, in particular transportation, the most functional means to remove the threat. As this was a punishment awarded indiscriminately to those found guilty of shoplifting or grand larceny, the utility of the Shoplifting Act diminished further; retailers did not need to court public disapproval as the humanitarian campaign for capital law reform became more vociferous. When the Act came again to the forefront of public attention, spearheading Samuel Romilly's crusade to commute the death penalty, shopkeepers felt little compulsion to fight for its survival. By the start of the nineteenth century there had been a transformation in retailers' commercial equanimity and competency in combating the crime.

This change in retailers' outlook was not achieved in a vacuum. It reflected current attitudes to crime and capital punishment. Shoplifting may have become, as a form of makeshift, part of the fabric of neighbourhood communities, but it was never accorded full ethical licence. Although crime was traditionally viewed as a moral lapse to which any individual was subject, it was the poor who were conventionally seen as more predisposed to embark on this 'slippery slope'. The general public, and even shoplifters themselves, reacted to the crime within a moral universe that encompassed ideas of shame, guilt and restorative justice, and one where women were treated with particular opprobrium. An observable consequence of this was that retailers were not obliged to rely solely on mutual aid. They could count on the regular help and participation of their customers to thwart any observed misdemeanour, and those in the street to eagerly track and detain offenders. The understanding of shoplifting as a crime of the poor became more entrenched as the century progressed, and public thinking began to embrace the concept of offending as restricted to a congenital criminal class. Within this context, contemporary literature repeatedly portrayed the possibility of middling or elite shoplifting as a humorous trope. Thus the arrest and trial of Jane Leigh-Perrot for the crime at the close of the century was a rude awakening for retailers and their elite clients alike. While deferential treatment persisted, retailers were forced to confront the reality of shoplifting by their wealthier patrons. By the 1820s, as the Shoplifting Act faced repeal, the retail climate was inexorably changing and the sector was obliged to adjust to a class-wide, if increasingly medicalised, nineteenth-century concept of the crime.

Bibliography

Manuscript primary sources

London Metropolitan Archives, City of London (LMA)

CLA/005/01/004–015, Guildhall Justice Room, City of London collection, Minute Books 1775–81

CLA/074/03/012, Clubs and Societies collection, Proceedings of Society for Prosecuting Felons etc. Rough Minute Book, April 1795–April 1800

CLC/B/025/MS10033, MS10033A, Major Blundell collection, Deeds of property, Ledger, and Business papers

CLC/477/MS09939/037, William Mawhood collection, Diary, 15 November 1783–23 July 1784

CLC/477/MS09940, William Mawhood collection, Cash account and note book

COL/CC/GPC/05/003, Corporation of London collection, Miscellaneous Papers and Rough Minutes in Relation to the Court of Requests

MJ/SR/3453, 3455, 3457–3458, 3460, 3462, 3464, 3466, Middlesex Sessions of the Peace, Court in Session collection, Session Rolls 1785

MJ/SR/3712, 3714, 3716–3717, 3719, 3721–3722, 3724, 3726, 3728–3729, 3731, Middlesex Sessions of the Peace, Court in Session collection, Session Rolls 1805

OB/SP/1773/12/006, 1786/05/037, 1787/01/039, 1788/09/071–072, 1788/10/012, 1789/04/048, Gaol Delivery Sessions at the Old Bailey post-1754 collection, Session Papers, Statements and Informations

The National Archives (TNA)

ASSI 41/1–14, Assizes, Northern and North-Eastern Circuits, Crown and Civil Minute Books

ASSI 43/9, Assizes, Northern Circuit, Miscellaneous Books 1, Notebook containing precedents and analyses of points of law 1750–1800

ASSI 45/15/4–45/62, Assizes, Northern and North-Eastern Circuits, Criminal Depositions and Case Papers

C105/30, Chancery, Master Lynch's Exhibits, Willan v. Clement, Valuation of lace and millinery, Strand, Westminster

HO 26/1–13, Home Office, Criminal Registers, Middlesex
PL 27/2–10, Palatinate of Lancaster, Crown Court, Depositions
PRO 30/8/280 and 30/8/281, William Pitt, 1st Earl of Chatham, Papers, 2nd
    series, papers relating to Revenue and Finance

Tyne and Wear Archives, Newcastle
QS.NC/74–77, 79–84, 87/2, 89–100, Newcastle Borough Quarter Sessions,
    Sessions Papers 1767–1785

West Yorkshire Archive Service, Wakefield (WYAS)
QS1/125–132, West Riding of Yorkshire Quarter Session Rolls 1786–1792

Published primary sources

British Library
*The Great Grievance of Traders and Shopkeepers, by the Notorious Practice
    of Stealing their Goods out of their Shops and Warehouses, by Persons
    commonly called Shoplifters; Humbly Represented to the Consideration
    of the Honourable House of Commons* (1699)

Guildhall Library, City of London
Broadside 7.143 (Case of the Retail Shopkeeper – March 8 1788)

Parliamentary Papers
Hansard, House of Commons (series 1), vol. 39 (1819)
Hansard, House of Lords (series 1), vol. 17 (1810)
Hansard, House of Lords (series 2), vol. 2 (1820)
Journal of the House of Commons, vol. 12 (1697–1699)
Journal of the House of Commons, vol. 14 (1702–1705)
Journal of the House of Commons, vol. 25 (1745–1750)
Journal of the House of Lords, vol. 16 (1696–1701)
*The Parliamentary Register or History of the Proceedings and Debates of the
    House of Commons* (31 October 1776–6 June 1777)
Report from the Select Committee on Criminal Laws (1819)

Newspapers and periodicals
Bingley's Journal
The Craftsman or Say's Weekly Journal
The Gazetteer and New Daily Advertiser
General Advertiser

The General Evening Post
Lancaster Gazette
Lloyd's Evening Post
London Evening Post
London Gazette
Morning Chronicle and London Advertiser
Morning Post and Gazetteer
Newcastle Courant
Notes and Queries
The Oracle and Daily Advertiser
Public Advertiser
Sheffield Register
Spectator
St James's Chronicle
The Star
The Sun
The Times
Weekly Journal or Saturday's Post
The Weekly Miscellany
The World

Contemporary books and articles

The Athenian Oracle: Being an Entire Collection of All the Valuable Questions and Answers in the Old Athenian Mercuries, vol. 3 (London, 1716)

A Brief Historical Account of the Lives of Six Notorious Street Robbers Executed at Kingston (London, 1726)

A List of Members of the Guardians; or Society for the Protection of Trade against Swindlers and Sharpers (London, 1799)

The Lives of the Most Remarkable Criminals, who have been Condemn'd and Executed, 3 vols (London, 1735)

The Remarkable Life and Transactions of Charlotte Crutchey, a Banker's Daughter, in Lombard Street (London, 1775)

The Repository: a Select Collection of Fugitive Pieces of Wit and Humour, in Prose and Verse, vol. 3 (London, 1777)

The Secret History of Betty Ireland (London, 1765)

Thieving Detected: Being a True and Particular Description of the Various Methods and Artifices used by Thieves and Sharpers to Take in and Deceive the Public (London, 1777)

Aretino, Pietro, *The Wandering Whore continued* (London, 1660)

Austen, Jane, *Minor Works*, ed. R. W. Chapman (Oxford, 1954)

Beccaria, Cesare, *An Essay on Crimes and Punishments* (London, 1767)

Blackstone, Sir William, *Commentaries on the Laws of England*, 3rd edn, vol. 4 (Oxford, 1769)

Burney, Frances, *Camilla or A Picture of Youth* (1796; Oxford, 1972)

———, *The Witlings and the Woman-Hater*, ed. Peter Sabor and Geoffrey Sill (Peterborough, Ontario, 2005)

Burn, Richard, *The Justice of the Peace, and Parish Officer*, 2 vols (London, 1755)

Campbell, R., *The London Tradesman* (London, 1747)

Collyer, Joseph, *The Parent's and Guardian's Directory and the Youth's Guide in a Choice of a Profession or Trade* (London, 1761)

Colquhoun, Patrick, *A Treatise on Indigence* (London, 1806)

———, *A Treatise on the Police of the Metropolis* (London, 1796)

Davys, Mary, *The Northern Heiress: or, the Humours of York* (London, 1716)

Defoe, Daniel, *The Complete English Tradesman*, 3rd edn, vol. 1 (London, 1727–32)

———, *The Fortunes and Misfortunes of the Famous Moll Flanders &c.* [London, 1722] (London, 1989)

Eden, Sir Frederick Morton, *The State of the Poor: or an History of the Labouring Classes in England*, 3 vols (London, 1797)

Eden, William, *Principles of Penal Law* (London, 1771)

Fielding, Henry, *The Author's Farce: and the Pleasures of the Town* (London, 1730)

———, *An Enquiry into the Causes of the Late Increase of Robbers &c with some Proposals for Remedying this Growing Evil* (London, 1751)

Fielding, John, *Extracts from Such of the Penal Laws as Particularly Relate to the Peace and Good Order of this Metropolis* (London, 1761)

Gales & Martin, *A Directory of Sheffield* (Sheffield, 1787)

Gay, John, *The Beggar's Opera* (London, 1728)

Grose, Francis, *A Classical Dictionary of the Vulgar Tongue* (London, 1788)

Head, Richard, *The Canting Academy, or, The Devils Cabinet Opened* (London, 1673)

King, Richard, *The New Cheats of London Exposed; or the Frauds and Tricks of the Town Laid Open to Both Sexes* (London, 1780)

Lackington, J., *To the Booksellers of London and Westminster* (London, 1788)

———, *Memoirs of the First Forty-Five Years of the Life of James Lackington, the present Bookseller in Chiswell Street, Moorfields, London* (London, 1791)

Leach, Thomas, *Cases in Crown Law, Determined by the Twelve Judges; By the Court of King's Bench; and by Commissioners of Oyer and Terminer, and General Gaol Delivery* (London, 1792)

Mawhood, William, *The Mawhood Diary: Selections from the Diary*

Notebook of William Mawhood, Woollen-Draper of London, for the Years 1764–1790, ed. E. E. Reynolds (London, 1956)

Owen, Robert, *The Life of Robert Owen, Written by Himself* (London, 1857)

Paley, William, *The Principles of Moral and Political Philosophy* (London, 1785)

Perceval, Spencer, *The Duties and Powers of Public Officers and Private Persons with Respect to Violations of the Public Peace* (London, 1792)

Romilly, Sir Samuel, *Observations on the Criminal Law of England as it Relates to Capital Punishments and on the Mode in which it is Administered* (London, 1810)

Smith, Alexander, *A Compleat History of the Lives and Robberies of the Most Notorious Highway-men, Foot-pads, Shop-lifts and Cheats*, 3 vols (London, 1719)

Stanhope, Philip Dormer, *Letters written by the late Right Honourable Philip Dormer Stanhope, Earl of Chesterfield, to his son, Philip Stanhope, Esq*, 4 vols (London, 1774)

Sterne, Laurence, *The Life and Opinions of Tristram Shandy, Gentleman* (1760; London, 2003)

Townley, James, *High Life below Stairs: a Farce of Two Acts* (London, 1759)

Vaizey, D. (ed.), *The Diary of Thomas Turner 1754–1765* (Oxford, 1984)

von la Roche, Sophie, *'Sophie in London' 1786: Being the Diary of Sophie v la Roche*, trans. Clare Williams (London, 1933)

Walker, Samuel, *Reformation of Manners Promoted by Argument in Several Essays* (London 1711)

Ward, Edward, *Hudibras Redivivus, or a Burlesque Poem on the Various Humours of Town and Country*, 2 vols (London, 1707)

——, *The London-Spy Compleat, in Eighteen Parts* (London, 1700)

——, *Nuptial Dialogues and Debates*, 2 vols (London, 1710)

Zola, Émile, *The Ladies' Paradise (Au Bonheur des Dames)* (1883; Oxford, 2008)

Published secondary sources

Abelson, Elaine S., *When Ladies Go A-Thieving: Middle-Class Shoplifters in the Victorian Department Store* (Oxford, 1989)

Alexander, David, 'Prints after John Collet: Their Publishing History and a Chronological Checklist', *Eighteenth-Century Life* 26/1 (2002), 136–46

Allen, Robert C., 'Why the Industrial Revolution was British: Commerce, Induced Invention and the Scientific Revolution', *Economic History Review* 64/2 (2011), 357–84

Allen, R. C. and J. L. Weisdorf, 'Was there an "Industrious Revolution" before the Industrial Revolution? An Empirical Exercise for England, c. 1300–1830', *Economic History Review* 64/3 (2011), 715–29

Austen-Leigh, Richard Arthur, 'Captain Francis William Austen and some others', *Notes and Queries* 192/22 (1 November 1947), 474–5

Beattie, J. M., *Crime and the Courts in England, 1660–1800* (Princeton, 1986)

———, 'The Criminality of Women in Eighteenth-Century England', *Journal of Social History* 8/4 (1975), 80–116

———, *The First English Detectives: The Bow Street Runners and the Policing of London, 1750–1840* (Oxford, 2014)

———, 'London Crime and the Making of the "Bloody Code", 1689–1718', in *Stilling the Grumbling Hive: The Response to Social and Economic Problems in England, 1689–1750*, ed. L. Davison, T. Hitchcock, T. Keirn and R. Shoemaker (Stroud, 1992), pp. 49–76

———, 'London Juries in the 1690s', in *Twelve Good Men and True: The Criminal Trial Jury in England, 1220–1800*, ed. J. S. Cockburn and T. A. Green, (Princeton, 1988), pp. 214–53

———, *Policing and Punishment in London, 1660–1750: Urban Crime and the Limits of Terror* (Oxford, 2001)

Bell, Ian A., *Literature and Crime in Augustan England* (London, 1991)

Bennett, Ann, *Shops, Shambles and the Street Market: Retailing in Georgian Hull, 1770 to 1810* (Wetherby, 2005)

Bennett, Robert J., 'Supporting Trust: Credit Assessment and Debt Recovery through Trade Protection Societies in Britain and Ireland, 1776–1992', *Journal of Historical Geography* 38/2 (2012), 123–42

Berg, Maxine, 'Consumption in Eighteenth- and Early Nineteenth-Century Britain', in *The Cambridge Economic History of Modern Britain*, vol. 1: *Industrialisation, 1700–1860*, ed. R. Floud and P. Johnson (Cambridge, 2004), pp. 357–87

———, *Luxury and Pleasure in Eighteenth-Century Britain* (Oxford, 2005)

Berry, Helen, *Gender, Society and Print Culture in Late-Stuart England: the Cultural World of the Athenian Mercury* (Aldershot, 2003)

———, 'Polite Consumption: Shopping in Eighteenth-Century England', *Transactions of the Royal Historical Society*, 6th series, 12 (2002), 375–94

———, 'Prudent Luxury: The Metropolitan Tastes of Judith Baker, Durham Gentlewoman', in *Women and Urban Life in Eighteenth-Century England: 'on the Town'*, ed. R. Sweet and P. Lane (Aldershot, 2003), pp. 131–56

Blewett, David, 'Introduction', in Daniel Defoe, *The Fortunes and Misfortunes of the Famous Moll Flanders &c.* (London, 1989), pp. 1–24

Brantingham, Patricia L. and Brantingham, Paul J., 'Notes on the Geometry of Crime', in *Environmental Criminology*, ed. P. L. Brantingham, and P. J. Brantingham (London, 1981), pp. 27–54

Buck, Anne, *Dress in Eighteenth-Century England* (London, 1979)

Burman, Barbara and Seth Denbo, *Pockets of History: the Secret Life of an Everyday Object* (Bath, 2007)

Callahan, Kathy, 'On the Receiving End: Women and Stolen Goods in London 1783–1815', *London Journal* 37/2 (2012), 106–21

Campbell, Colin, 'Understanding Traditional and Modern Patterns of Consumption in Eighteenth-Century England: a Character-Action Approach', in *Consumption and the World of Goods*, ed. J. Brewer and R. Porter (London, 1993), pp. 40–57

Chalklin, Christopher, *The Rise of the English Town, 1650–1850* (Cambridge 2001)

Chartier, Roger, 'Texts, Printing, Readings', in *The New Cultural History*, ed. L. Hunt (London, 1989), pp. 154–75

Cox, Dena, Anthony D. Cox and George P. Moschis, 'When Consumer Behaviour Goes Bad: An Investigation of Adolescent Shoplifting', *Journal of Consumer Research* 17/2 (1990), 149–59

Cox, Nancy, '"Beggary of the Nation": Moral, Economic and Political Attitudes to the Retail Sector in the Early Modern Period', in *A Nation of Shopkeepers: Five Centuries of British Retailing, 1550–2000*, ed. J. Benson and L. Ugolini (London, 2003), pp. 26–51

———, *The Complete Tradesman: A Study of Retailing, 1550–1820* (Aldershot, 2000)

Cox, Nancy and Claire Walsh, '"Their Shops are Dens, the Buyer is their Prey": Shop Design and Sales Techniques', in N. Cox, *The Complete Tradesman: A Study of Retailing, 1550–1820* (Aldershot, 2000), pp. 76–115

Crown, Patricia, 'Sporting with Clothes: John Collet's Prints in the 1770s', *Eighteenth-Century Life* 26/1 (2002), 119–35

Dabhoiwala, Faramerz, 'Summary Justice in Early Modern London', *English Historical Review* 121/492 (2006), 796–822

Dabney, Dean A., Richard C. Hollinger and Laura Dugan, 'Who Actually Steals? A Study of Covertly Observed Shoplifters', *Justice Quarterly* 21/4 (2004), 693–728

Davis, Dorothy, *A History of Shopping* (London, 1966)

Devereaux, Simon, 'From Sessions to Newspaper? Criminal Trial Reporting, the Nature of Crime, and the London Press, 1770–1800', *London Journal* 32/1 (2007), 1–27

de Vries, Jan, *The Industrious Revolution: Consumer Behaviour and the Household Economy, 1650 to the Present* (Cambridge, 2008)

Earle, Peter, *The Making of the English Middle Class: Business, Society and Family Life in London, 1660–1730* (London, 1989)

Emsley, Clive, *Crime and Society in England 1750–1900* (London, 1987)

Emsley, Clive, Tim Hitchcock and Robert Shoemaker, 'The Proceedings – The Value of the Proceedings as a Historical Source', *OBP* (https://www.oldbaileyonline.org/static/Value.jsp, accessed 19 April 2018)

Epstein, Julia, *The Iron Pen: Frances Burney and the Politics of Women's Writing* (Bristol, 1989)

Erickson, Amy Louise, 'Married Women's Occupations in Eighteenth-Century London', *Continuity and Change* 23/2 (2008), 267–307

Faller, Lincoln B., *Crime and Defoe: A New Kind of Writing* (Cambridge, 1993)

——, *Turned to Account: The Forms and Functions of Criminal Biography in Late Seventeenth- and Early Eighteenth-Century England* (Cambridge, 1987)

Farrington, David P., 'Measuring, Explaining and Preventing Shoplifting: A Review of British Research', *Security Journal*, 12 (1999), 9–27

Feather, John, 'The Power of Print: Word and Image in Eighteenth-Century England', in *Culture and Society in Britain, 1660–1800*, ed. J. Black (Manchester, 1997), pp. 51–68

Felson, Marcus, 'Preventing Retail Theft: An Application of Environmental Criminology', *Security Journal*, 7 (1996), 71–5

Ferreira, Eduardo and Helena Carvalho, 'Inhibiting Factors in a Hypothetical Shoplifting Situation: A Contribution to Crime Prevention', *Issues of Business and Law*, 1 (2009), 101–14

Finn, Margot C., *The Character of Credit: Personal Debt in English Culture, 1740–1914* (Cambridge, 2003)

Follett, Richard R., *Evangelicalism, Penal Theory and the Politics of Criminal Law Reform, 1808–30* (Basingstoke, 2001)

Freeman, Lisa A., *Character's Theater: Genre and Identity on the Eighteenth-Century English Stage* (Philadelphia, 2002)

Gatrell, V. A. C., *The Hanging Tree: Execution and the English People, 1770–1868* (Oxford, 1994)

Glennie, P. D. and N. J. Thrift, 'Consumers, Identities, and Consumption Spaces in Early-Modern England', *Environment and Planning A* 28/1 (1996), 25–45

Gray, Drew, *Crime, Policing and Punishment in England, 1660–1914* (London, 2016)

——, *Crime, Prosecution and Social Relations: The Summary Courts of the City of London in the Late Eighteenth Century* (Basingstoke, 2009)

Haig, Robert, *The Gazetteer 1735–1797: A Study in the Eighteenth-Century English Newspaper* (Carbondale, 1960)

Harris, Andrew T., *Policing the City: Crime and Legal Authority in London 1780–1840* (Columbus, 2004)

Heller, Benjamin, 'The 'Mene Peuple' and the Polite Spectator: The Individual in the Crowd at Eighteenth-Century London Fairs', *Past and Present*, 208 (2010), 131–57

Henry, Stuart, *The Hidden Economy: The Context and Control of Borderline Crime* (London, 1978)

Heydt-Stevenson, Jillian, '"Pleasure is now, and ought to be, your business": Stealing Sexuality in Jane Austen's Juvenilia', in *Historicizing Romantic Sexuality*, ed. R. C. Sha (http://www.rc.umd.edu/praxis/sexuality/heydt/heydt.html, accessed 19 April 2018)

Hitchcock, Tim and Robert Shoemaker, *London Lives: Poverty, Crime and the Making of the Modern City, 1690–1800* (Cambridge, 2015)

Hoppit, Julian, *Risk and Failure in English Business, 1700–1800* (Cambridge, 1987)

———, 'The Use and Abuse of Credit in Eighteenth-Century England', in *Business Life and Public Policy: Essays in honour of D. C. Coleman*, ed. N. McKendrick and R. B. Outhwaite (Cambridge, 1986), pp. 64–78

Horrell, Sara, 'Consumption, 1700–1870', *The Cambridge Economic History of Modern Britain*, vol. 1: *1700–1870*, ed. R. Floud, J. Humphries and P. Johnson (Cambridge 2014), pp. 237–63

Horrell, Sara, Jane Humphries and Ken Sneath, 'Consumption Conundrums Unravelled', *Economic History Review* 68/3 (2015), 830–57

———, 'Cupidity and Crime: Consumption as Revealed by Insights from the Old Bailey Records of Thefts in the Eighteenth and Nineteenth Centuries', in *Large Databases in Economic History: Research Methods and Case Studies*, ed. M. Casson and N. Hashimzade (Abingdon, 2013), pp. 246–67

Humphries, Jane, 'Household Economy', in *The Cambridge Economic History of Modern Britain*, vol. 1: *Industrialisation, 1700–1860*, ed. R. Floud and P. Johnson (Cambridge, 2004), pp. 238–67

Hunt, Margaret R., *The Middling Sort: Commerce, Gender and the Family, 1680–1780* (London, 1996)

Hunter, J. Paul, *Before Novels: The Cultural Contexts of Eighteenth-Century English Fiction* (New York, 1990)

Katz, Jack, *Seductions of Crime: Moral and Sensual Attractions in Doing Evil* (New York, 1988)

King, Peter, *Crime, Justice and Judicial Discretion in England, 1740–1820* (Oxford, 2000)

———, *Crime and Law in England, 1750–1840: Remaking Justice from the Margins* (Cambridge, 2006)

———, 'Female Offenders, Work and Life-Cycle Change in Late-Eighteenth-Century London', *Continuity and Change* 11/1 (1996), 61–90

———, 'Newspaper Reporting and Attitudes to Crime and Justice in Late-Eighteenth- and Early-Nineteenth-Century London', *Continuity and Change* 22/1 (2007), 73–112

King, Stephen and Geoffrey Timmins, *Making Sense of the Industrial Revolution: English Economy and Society 1700–1850* (Manchester, 2001)

Klemke, Lloyd W., *The Sociology of Shoplifting: Boosters and Snitches Today* (Westport, 1992)

Kowaleski-Wallace, Elizabeth, *Consuming Subjects: Women, Shopping and Business in the Eighteenth Century* (New York, 1997)

Lambert, Miles, '"Cast-off Wearing Apparell": The Consumption and Distribution of Second-hand Clothing in Northern England during the Long Eighteenth Century', *Textile History* 35/1 (2004), 1–26

Landers, John, *Death and the Metropolis: Studies in the Demographic History of London, 1670–1830* (Cambridge, 1993)

Langbein, John H., *The Origins of Adversary Criminal Trial* (Oxford, 2003)

Lemire, Beverly, *The Business of Everyday Life: Gender, Practice and Social Politics in England, c. 1600–1900* (Manchester, 2005)

———, *Dress, Culture and Commerce: The English Clothing Trade before the Factory, 1660–1800* (Basingstoke, 1997)

———, *Fashion's Favourite: The Cotton Trade and the Consumer in Britain, 1660–1800* (Oxford, 1991)

———, 'Peddling Fashion: Salesmen, Pawnbrokers, Taylors, Thieves and the Second-hand Clothes Trade in England, c. 1700–1800', *Textile History* 22/1 (1991), 67–82

———, 'Plebeian Commercial Circuits and Everyday Material Exchange in England, c. 1600–1900', in *Buyers and Sellers: Retail Circuits and Practices in Medieval and Early Modern Europe*, ed. B. Blondé, P. Stabel, J. Stobart and I. Van Damme (Turnhout, 2006), pp. 245–66

———, 'Second-hand Beaux and "Red-armed Belles": Conflict and the Creation of Fashions in England c.1660–1800', *Continuity and Change* 15/3 (2000), 391–417

———, 'The Theft of Clothes and Popular Consumerism in Early Modern England', *Journal of Social History* 24/2 (1990), 255–76

Linebaugh, Peter, *The London Hanged: Crime and Civil Society in the Eighteenth Century* (London, 1991)

Loveman, Kate, '"A Life of Continu'd Variety": Crime, Readers and the Structure of Defoe's *Moll Flanders*', *Eighteenth-Century Fiction* 21/1 (2013), 1–32

Lynch, Deidre Shauna, 'Counter Publics: Shopping and Women's Sociability', in *Romantic Sociability: Social Networks and Literary Culture in Britain, 1770–1840*, ed. G. Russell and C. Tuite (Cambridge, 2002), pp. 211–36

———, *The Economy of Character: Novels, Market Culture, and the Business of Inner Meaning* (Chicago, 1998)

McGowen, Randall, 'A Powerful Sympathy: Terror, the Prison and Humanitarian Reform in Early Nineteenth-Century Britain', *Journal of British Studies* 25/3 (1986), 312–34

———, 'Revisiting the Hanging Tree: Gatrell on Emotion and History', *British Journal of Criminology* 40/1 (2000), 1–13

MacKay, Lynn, 'Why they Stole: Women in the Old Bailey, 1779–1789', *Journal of Social History* 32/3 (1999), 623–39

McKendrick, Neil, 'The Consumer Revolution of Eighteenth-century England', in *The Birth of a Consumer Society: The Commercialization of Eighteenth-Century England*, ed. N. McKendrick, J. Brewer and J. H. Plumb (London, 1982), pp. 9–33

McKenzie, Andrea, 'God's Tribunal: Guilt, Innocence and Execution in England 1675–1775', *Cultural and Social History* 3/2 (2006), 121–44

———, 'From True Confessions to True Reporting? The Decline and Fall of the Ordinary's *Account*', *London Journal* 30/1 (2005), 55–70

———, *Tyburn's Martyrs: Execution in England, 1675–1775* (London, 2007)

Morrison, Kathryn A., *English Shops and Shopping: an Architectural History* (New Haven and London, 2003)

Mui, Hoh-cheung and Lorna H. Mui, *Shops and Shopkeeping in Eighteenth-Century England* (London, 1989)

Muldrew, Craig, *The Economy of Obligation: The Culture of Credit and Social Relations in Early Modern England* (London, 1998)

Mullins, Paul R. and Nigel Jefferies, 'The Banality of Gilding: Innocuous Materiality and Transatlantic Consumption in the Gilded Age', *International Journal of Historical Archaeology* 16/4 (2012), 745–60

Neale, Matt, 'Making Crime Pay in Late Eighteenth-Century Bristol: Stolen Goods, the Informal Economy and the Negotiation of Risk', *Continuity and Change* 26/3 (2011), 439–59

Novak, Maximillian E., *Realism, Myth, and History in Defoe's Fiction* (London, 1983)

Palk, Deirdre, *Gender, Crime and Judicial Discretion, 1780–1830* (Woodbridge, 2006)

———, 'Private Crime in Public and Private Places: Pickpockets and Shoplifters in London, 1780–1823', in *The Streets of London: From the Great Fire to the Great Stink*, ed. T. Hitchcock and H. Shore (London, 2003), pp. 135–50, 233–5

Philips, David, 'Good Men to Associate and Bad Men to Conspire: Associations for the Prosecution of Felons in England 1760–1860', in *Policing and Prosecution in Britain, 1750–1850*, ed. D. Hay and F. Snyder (Oxford, 1989), pp. 113–70

Pinch, Adela, 'Stealing Happiness: Shoplifting in Early Nineteenth-Century England', in *Border Fetishisms: Material Objects in Unstable Spaces*, ed. P. Spyers (London, 1998), pp. 122–49

Pincus, Steve, *1688: The First Modern Revolution* (Yale, 2009)

Porter, Roy, *English Society in the Eighteenth Century* (London, 1991)

———, *Enlightenment: Britain and the Creation of the Modern World* (London, 2000)

Rabin, Dana, 'Drunkenness and Responsibility for Crime in the Eighteenth Century', *Journal of British Studies* 44/3 (2005), 457–77

Radzinowicz, Leon, *A History of English Criminal Law and its Administration from 1750*, vol. 1 (London, 1948), vol. 3 (London 1956)

Raven, James, 'New Reading Histories, Print Culture and the Identification of Change: the Case of Eighteenth-Century England', *Social History* 23/3 (1998), 268–87

Rees, Sian, *The Floating Brothel: The Extraordinary True Story of an Eighteenth-Century Ship and its Cargo of Female Convicts* (London, 2001)

Reynolds, Elaine, *Before the Bobbies: The Night Watch and Police Reform in Metropolitan London, 1720–1830* (Basingstoke, 1998)

Riello, Giorgio, *Cotton: The Fabric that Made the Modern World* (Cambridge, 2013)

———, *A Foot in the Past: Consumers, Producers and Footwear in the Long Eighteenth Century* (Oxford, 2006)

Rogers, Nicholas, 'Confronting the Crime Wave: The Debate over Social Reform and Regulation, 1749–1753', in *Stilling the Grumbling Hive: The Response to Social and Economic Problems in England, 1689–1750*, ed. L. Davison, T. Hitchcock, T. Keirn and R. Shoemaker (Stroud, 1992), pp. 77–98

Schneider, Jacqueline L., 'The Link between Shoplifting and Burglary: the Booster Burglar', *British Journal of Criminology*, 45 (2005), 395–401

Schwarz, Leonard D., *London in the Age of Industrialisation: Entrepreneurs, Labour Force and Living Conditions 1700–1850* (Cambridge, 1992)

Shammas, Carole, *The Pre-Industrial Consumer in England and America* (Oxford, 1990)

Shapland, Joanna, 'Preventing Retail Sector Crime', in *Building a Safer Society: Strategic Approaches to Crime Prevention*, ed. M. Tonry and D. P. Farrington (London, 1995), pp. 263–342

Shoemaker, Robert B., 'Fear of Crime in Eighteenth-Century London', in *Understanding Emotions in Early Europe*, ed. Michael Champion and Andrew Lynch (Turnhout, 2015), pp. 233–49

———, 'Gendered Spaces: Patterns of Mobility and Perceptions of London's Geography, 1660–1750', in *Imagining Early Modern London: Perceptions and Portrayals of the City from Stow to Strype, 1598–1720*, ed. J. F. Merritt (Cambridge, 2001), pp. 144–65

———, *The London Mob: Violence and Disorder in the Eighteenth Century* (London, 2004)

———, 'The Old Bailey Proceedings and the Representation of Crime and Criminal Justice in Eighteenth-Century London', *Journal of British Studies* 47/3 (2008), 559–80

———, 'Print Culture and the Creation of Public Knowledge about Crime in Eighteenth-Century London', in *Urban Crime Prevention, Surveillance and Restorative Justice: Effects of Social Technologies*, ed. P. Knepper, J. Doak and J. Shapland (Boca Raton, 2009), pp. 1–21

————, 'Print and the Female Voice: Representations of Women's Crime in London, 1690–1735', *Gender and History* 22/1 (2010), 75–91

————, 'Worrying about Crime: Experience, Moral Panics and Public Opinion in London, 1660–1800', *Past and Present* 234/1 (2017), 71–100

Shore, Heather, *Artful Dodgers: Youth and Crime in Early Nineteenth-Century London* (London, 1999)

————, 'Crime, Criminal Networks and the Survival Strategies of the Poor in Early Eighteenth-Century London', in *The Poor in England 1700–1850: An Economy of Makeshifts*, ed. S. King and A. Tomkins (Manchester, 2003), pp. 137–65

Snell, Esther, 'Discourses of Criminality in the Eighteenth-Century Press: the Presentation of Crime in *The Kentish Post*, 1717–1768', *Continuity and Change* 22/1 (2007), 13–47

Stobart, Jon, 'Leisure and Shopping in the Small Towns of Georgian England', *Journal of Urban History* 31/4 (2005), 479–503

————, 'Shopping Streets as Social Space: Leisure, Consumerism and Improvement in an Eighteenth-Century County Town', *Urban History* 25/1 (1998), 3–21

————, *Spend, Spend, Spend: A History of Shopping* (Stroud, 2008)

————, 'Status, Gender and Life Cycle in the Consumption Practices of the English Elite. The Case of Mary Leigh, 1736–1806', *Social History* 40/1 (2015), 82–103

Stobart, Jon and Andrew Hann, 'Retailing Revolution in the Eighteenth Century? Evidence from North-West England', *Business History* 46/2 (2004), 171–94

Stobart, Jon, Andrew Hann and Victoria Morgan, *Spaces of Consumption: Leisure and Shopping in the English Town, c. 1680–1830* (London 2007)

Styles, John, 'Clothing the North: The Supply of Non-Elite Clothing in the Eighteenth-Century North of England', *Textile History* 25/2 (1994), 139–66

————, *The Dress of the People: Everyday Fashion in Eighteenth-Century England* (New Haven, 2007)

————, 'Fashion and Innovation in Early-Modern Europe', in *Fashioning the Early Modern: Creativity and Innovation in Europe, 1500–1800*, ed. Evelyn Welch (Oxford, 2017), pp. 33–55

————, 'Lodging at the Old Bailey: Lodgings and their Furnishing in Eighteenth-Century London', in *Gender, Taste, and Material Culture in Britain and North America, 1700–1830*, ed. J. Styles and A. Vickery (New Haven, 2006), pp. 61–80

————, 'Manufacturing, Consumption and Design in Eighteenth-Century England', in *Consumption and the World of Goods*, ed. J. Brewer and R. Porter (London, 1993), pp. 527–54

————, 'Print and Policing: Crime Advertising in Eighteenth-Century

Provincial England', in *Policing and Prosecution in Britain, 1750–1850*, ed.
D. Hay and F. Snyder (Oxford, 1989), pp. 55–112

———, 'Sir John Fielding and the Problem of Criminal Investigation in
Eighteenth-Century England', *Transactions of the Royal Historical
Society*, 5th series, 33 (1983), 127–49

Tomkins, Alannah, *The Experience of Urban Poverty, 1723–82: Parish,
Charity and Credit* (Manchester 2006)

Toplis, Alison, 'The Illicit Trade in Clothing, Worcestershire and
Herefordshire, 1800–1850', *Journal of Historical Research in Marketing*
2/3 (2010), 314–26

Voth, Hans-Joachim, 'Living Standards and the Urban Environment', in *The
Cambridge Economic History of Modern Britain*, vol. 1: *Industrialisation,
1700–1860*, ed. R. Floud and P. Johnson (Cambridge, 2004), pp. 268–94

Waddell, Brodie, 'The Politics of Economic Distress in the Aftermath of
the Glorious Revolution, 1689–1702', *English Historical Review* 130/543
(2015), 318–51

Walker, Garthine, *Crime, Gender and Social Order in Early Modern England*
(Cambridge 2003)

———, '"Demons in Female Form": Representations of Women and
Gender in Murder Pamphlets of the Late Sixteenth and Early Seventeenth
Centuries', in *Writing and the English Renaissance*, ed. W. Zunder and
S. Trill (London, 1996), pp. 124–37

———, 'Women, Theft and the World of Stolen Goods', in *Women, Crime
and the Courts in Early Modern England*, ed. J. Kermode and G. Walker
(London, 1994), pp. 81–105

Walsh, Claire, 'Shop Design and the Display of Goods in Eighteenth-Century
London', *Journal of Design History* 8/3 (1995), 157–76

———, 'Shopping at First Hand? Mistresses, Servants and Shopping for the
Household in Early-Modern England', in *Buying for the Home: Shopping
for the Domestic from the Seventeenth Century to the Present*, ed. D. E.
Hussey and M. Ponsonby (Aldershot, 2008), pp. 13–26

———, 'Shops, Shopping, and the Art of Decision Making in Eighteenth-
Century England', in *Gender, Taste, and Material Culture in Britain and
North America, 1700–1830*, ed. J. Styles and A. Vickery (New Haven,
2006), pp. 151–77

———, 'Social Meaning and Social Space in the Shopping Galleries of
Early Modern London', in *A Nation of Shopkeepers: Five Centuries of
British Retailing, 1550–2000*, ed. J. Benson and L. Ugolini (London, 2003),
pp. 52–79

Weatherill, Lorna, *Consumer Behaviour and Material Culture in Britain,
1660–1760* (London, 1996)

———, 'The Meaning of Consumer Behaviour in Late Seventeenth- and

Early Eighteenth-Century England', in *Consumption and the World of Goods*, ed. J. Brewer and R. Porter (London, 1993), pp. 206–27

White, Jerry, *London in the Eighteenth Century: A Great and Monstrous Thing* (London, 2012)

White, Matthew, '"For the Safety of the City": The Geography and Social Politics of Public Execution after the Gordon Riots', in *The Gordon Riots: Politics, Culture and Insurrection in Late Eighteenth-Century Britain*, ed. I. Haywood and J. Seed (Cambridge 2012), pp. 204–25

Whitlock, Tammy, *Crime, Gender and Consumer Culture in Nineteenth-Century England* (Aldershot, 2005)

Online resources

17th and 18th Century Burney Collection Newspapers
  https://www.gale.com/uk/c/17th-and-18th-century-burney-newspapers
  -collection
British Library Newspapers
  https://www.gale.com/uk/c/british-library-newspapers-part-i
  https://www.gale.com/uk/c/british-library-newspapers-part-ii
Ancestry
  http://www.ancestry.co.uk
Broadside Ballads Online
  http://ballads.bodleian.ox.ac.uk/collections.html
Early English Books Online
  http://eebo.chadwyck.com
Eighteenth-Century Collections Online
  https://www.gale.com/uk/c/eighteenth-century-collections-online-part-i
  https://www.gale.com/uk/c/eighteenth-century-collections-online-part-ii
Historical Calendar
  http://www.arc.id.au/Calendar.html
History of Parliament
  http://www.historyofparliamentonline.org
The London Gazette
  https://www.thegazette.co.uk/all-notices
London Lives 1690–1800
  http://www.londonlives.org
Old Bailey Proceedings Online
  http://www.oldbaileyonline.org.uk
The Times Digital Archive, 1785–2012
  https://www.gale.com/c/the-times-digital-archive

Index

Page numbers are followed by a suffix to indicate charts (c), illustrations and maps (illus) and tables (tab). References to material in footnotes are indicated by the suffix n and the note number (e.g. 57n35).

communities
  and attitudes to crime 122, 124
  and informal justice 178–9
commutation of charges 4, 144–5, 146, 156, 159
compensation for legal costs 44
compounding 44–5, 92, 133, 140, 149
confession narrative 174–5
confessions 46–7, 57, 59, 177
consumerism 7, 8, 9, 123–4
  and demand 2, 94–5
  theft, motivated by 104–6, 110, 190–1
consumption 3, 8, 9, 94
conviction 2, 159, 162–3
corporal punishment 34, 145
cost of living 16–17
cotton 3, 29, 99–100, 99tab, 106, 124
counters 70tab, 71tab, 84, 85illus
court records 10–12, 12n36, 18, 39–40, 59n80
  City Justice Rooms 40
  for quarter sessions 39–40
  sampling 11–12, 12n36, 18
  See also Newgate Criminal Registers; Northern Circuit assizes; Old Bailey
courts
  Bow Street magistracy 152–3
  magistrates 40
  quarter sessions 38–40
  See also Northern Circuit assizes; Old Bailey
Covent-Garden Journal (newspaper) 152
Cox, Nancy 6
Craig, Joseph 141
credit
  for businesses 127–9, 136, 143
  for customers 127, 132–4, 142, 186
  and non-payment 132, 186
crime
  as congenital disorder 10, 167, 184
  as entertainment 171, 184–91
  fear of 169–71
  in fiction 184–91
  histories of 4–6
  illicit thrill of 30–1, 181, 190–1
  methods 65–75
  as moral failing 167, 171–5, 175–6
  opportunist 56–7, 65
  organised 15, 27–30, 166–7
  planning of 62–5

press portrayal of 169–71
property 37–8
public attitudes to 5, 9–10, 14, 122, 166–91
  and social class 30–3, 184–91
  unreported 35, 40–6
  waves 2, 38, 159, 166
  and women 180–4
crime prevention 6, 82–93, 152–4, 191
  by customers 13–14, 89–90
  and display of goods 83–6
  labelling/marking of goods 86–7
  and lighting 84
  by members of public 13–14, 71–2, 89–92
  police service 92–3, 138
  by retailers 82–93, 134–8
  and shop security 83–4
  and shop staff 87–8
  surveillance 87–8
  trade protection societies 7, 13, 134–8
  traps 84–5, 152
  vigilantism 88
criminology 13, 35, 56, 122, 175
cross-examination 46
crowds 60
Crown, Patricia 181–3
customers
  credit 127, 132–4, 142, 186
  and crime prevention 13–14, 89–90
  status of 75, 132–3

Davies, Reverend David 103
days of week offences committed 63–4, 64c
de Quincey, Thomas, *The Household Wreck* 189–90
de Vries, Jan 9, 94
death penalty. *See* capital punishment
defence counsel 29, 41, 46, 155–6
Defoe, Daniel
  The Complete English Tradesman 127–8, 132, 173, 190
  Moll Flanders 120–1, 171–3, 180, 181, 190
demography 13
  age 17–18, 18–19, 19tab, 20–2, 21tab
  gender 17, 18, 18tab, 19tab, 21tab, 65tab, 146
  occupations 22, 22tab, 23tab, 24tab
deprivation 5, 16–17, 30

PEOPLE, MARKETS, GOODS:
ECONOMIES AND SOCIETIES IN HISTORY

ISSN: 2051-7467